AF323463

The Emergence of African American Literacy Traditions

The Emergence of African American Literacy Traditions

Family and Community Efforts in the Nineteenth Century

Phyllis M. Belt-Beyan

Foreword by
Ronald Lewis

Westport, Connecticut
London

Library of Congress Cataloging-in-Publication Data

Belt-Beyan, Phyllis M.
The emergence of African American literacy traditions : family and community efforts in the nineteenth century / Phyllis M. Belt-Beyan ; foreword by Ronald Lewis.
p. cm.
Includes bibliographical references and index.
ISBN 0-89789-799-4 (alk. paper)
1. African Americans—Education—History—19th century. 2. Literacy—United States—History—19th century. 3. African Americans—Books and reading—History—19th century. 4. African Americans—Social conditions—19th century. I. Title.
LC2741.B45 2004
371.829'96073'09034—dc22 2004053791

British Library Cataloguing in Publication Data is available.

Library of Congress Catalog Card Number: 2004053791
ISBN: 0-89789-799-4

First published in 2004

Praeger Publishers, 88 Post Road West, Westport, CT 06881
An imprint of Greenwood Publishing Group, Inc.
www.praeger.com

Printed in the United States of America

The paper used in this book complies with the Permanent Paper Standard issued by the National Information Standards Organization (Z39.48–1984).

10 9 8 7 6 5 4 3 2 1

To my late parents,
Jerome R. Belt and Patricia M. Belt

Contents

Foreword *by Ronald Lewis* ix

Acknowledgments xiii

1. Emergent African American Literacy Traditions: Theoretical and Conceptual Frameworks 1

2. Family 41

3. Visible and Invisible Institutions 91

4. Community 115

5. Conclusions 153

References 183

Index 199

Foreword

In a discussion about Edward P. Jones's Pulitzer Prize–winning novel about American slavery, *The Known World*, a dubious reader asked whether it was historically possible that there could have been a black schoolteacher in Virginia who taught slaves to read and write when it was against the law. In *The Emergence of African American Literacy Traditions: Family and Community Efforts in the Nineteenth Century*, Phyllis Belt-Beyan shows how, against sometimes staggering odds, literacy took form and developed in the African American community. Although not widespread in the South, African American literacy was not uncommon and was highly prized by the black community. The "peculiar institution" was governed by slave laws, but on a daily basis masters were a law unto themselves, and some of them chose to teach selected slaves how to read, write, and cipher. History has recorded some of the most famous individual examples, but it is not generally known that slaves were employed as accountants, vendors, clerks, ministers, and in nearly all of the skilled crafts where reading, writing, and arithmetic were vital skills. Some slave owners who fathered children with slave women sent them to the North where they were freed and educated. Others, like the most famous former slave, Frederick Douglass, became literate only because of their dogged determination and the knowledge that to be literate was to be nearly free. As might be expected, literacy was much more extensive among the free black populations in both the North and South.

Most of the scholarship on African American literacy in the nineteenth century focuses on a few prominent individuals, but this book expands the definition of the "black community" by examining the evolution of African American literacy traditions across all classes within the community. Dr. Belt-Beyan demonstrates that if we extend our definition of literacy to include records, diaries, letters, gospel and folk songs, speeches, autobiographies, biographies, journals, and other narrative forms, literacy was instrumental in the formation of the African American community.

Superbly researched in quantitative and qualitative sources, this book makes three definitive statements. First, it departs from other studies of African Americans in the nineteenth century that dismiss the importance of the African American family and community as too weak for such an important function as literacy development. The author demonstrates that, in fact, literacy acquisition was an internal function that was passed along to the next generation and grew geometrically over time and geography. Second, this intergenerational transfer of knowledge transformed the thought, discourse, and actions of African Americans by providing the means to articulate their own desires and goals both individually and collectively. In other words, African American literacy did not replicate European American literacy traditions, but rather evolved into a force of its own, one worthy of study in its own right. Third, this book provides an important contribution to our understanding of the process by which literacy traditions were institutionalized within the black community. If family-taught literacy gave voice to the thoughts of individuals, then institutional vehicles expressed collective goals. African American churches, benevolent societies, newspapers, literary societies, arts, and formal and informal schools all supported, and depended upon, the development of literacy. Community literacy, in turn, gave rise to national and international African American literacy traditions as they expressed the collective hopes and aspirations of human beings whose place in the world was defined by their race.

The author argues that African American family and community was the most important force in the development of African American literacy. Intellectual desires and the urgency of protecting the family and community in a hostile, racist world marked out the social dynamic within which these traditions grew. Like social institutions, literacy traditions were institutionalized by and for African Americans in order to articulate the aspirations of a people moving from slavery to segregation in the nineteenth century when freedom was still a dream. The progress of this historical course has been charted in many forms and media, but in this welcome addition to the literature, Dr. Belt-Beyan provides a new and penetrating analysis of the role literacy played in the formation of this rich cultural history.

Ronald L. Lewis
Joyce and Stuart Robbins Chair in History
West Virginia University

Acknowledgments

I extend gratitude to my former Kent State University doctoral dissertation advisors, College of Education Distinguished Professors Dr. Nancy D. Padak and Dr. Richard Vacca, Emeritus. They are unique for their admirable abilities to balance their own contributions to literacy education and research with commitment to their students. I especially appreciate the time they invested in the development of my scholarly pursuits. I respect their exemplary support, knowledge, and professional advice.

I am thankful for the scholarly expertise and support of historian Dr. Ronald L. Lewis of West Virginia University's history department, distinguished professor and Joyce and Stuart Endowment chair in history. His career as an author and researcher in the areas of labor history, African American history, and Appalachian history demonstrates excellence. His generous assistance helped make this work evolve as a multidisciplinary approach to the study of family and community literacy.

I express a special thank you to my former master's degree advisor and professor, Dr. Marilyn Fairbanks of West Virginia University, now Emeritus after a productive career of teaching, research, and service. She encouraged my interests in literacy research many years ago and she is not forgotten.

I am indebted to my late parents, Jerome R. Belt and Patricia M. Belt. They were my first teachers and advisors. Their love of literature, drawing, watercolor painting, reading, writing, storytelling, and music passed on to my children and me. They kept me safe from the realities of growing up an African American child in the sixties. They taught me when to take a stand and fight for what is right. They fought to tear down barriers to my learning and lived just long enough to watch me do things they were unable to do themselves. For this and much more they live forever.

I owe much to my brothers Jerome R. Belt, Michael E. Belt, and Jonathan D. Belt, along with my sisters Leslie L. Belt and Linda Renee Belt-Pursley. They are, and will be always, my first and best friends.

Finally, I thank my husband, historian and professor Dr. Amos J. Beyan of Western Michigan University. He gave unconditional love and support to my endeavors. He read and edited my drafts, listened to my concerns, and gave of his time and expertise. I thank our sons, Kolubah Amos Beyan (Kolby) and Stephen Quoi Quoi Beyan for being so loving, patient, and supportive over the too many summers, holidays, and weekends that they were to share my love for them with my commitment to literacy research and teaching.

Chapter 1

Emergent African American Literacy Traditions

Theoretical and Conceptual Frameworks

African American families and communities have significant literacy traditions (Durkin, 1974–1975; Heath, 1983; Taylor & Dorsey-Gaines, 1988). This book examines the makings of these at their nineteenth century developmental stages. Although manifestations of the traditions were evident much earlier, this was indeed a critical moment. For it was to be a formative age; generations of enslaved and free persons constructed foundations of their Africanized, American institutions—despite myriad challenging social and economic circumstances inimical to those efforts (Blassingame, 1972; Cone, 1971; Genovese, 1976; Gutman, 1977; Levine, 1979; Raboteau, 1980; Stuckey, 1987).

Since patterns of literacy behaviors, as with all seemingly individual human behaviors, tend to thrive best through collective efforts, this study might have housed many a cavernous chamber, walls lined with vast numbers of shelves, full to overflowing. The focus here, however, is limited to the evolving relationships among African American literacy events, uses, attitudes, interests, perceptions, and motivations that originated within their community and family ways of life before, during, and immediately following the American Civil War.

With emphasis on the dynamic nature of literacy, family, and community development, the persistence of the traditions is also considered. The work examines family and community lives of the many who were to leave America, recreating their social and cultural institutions, including family, community, church, and education elsewhere on the North American mainland and especially abroad. This work, therefore, moves to specifically examine the continuation of the preceding relationships among the people who, during this period, immigrated to the coast of West Africa. Many recall this was to come about when the 1816 formation of the American Colonization Society (ACS) in Richmond, Virginia, followed by a decisive 1817 meeting of the organization held in Washington, D.C., led to the "voluntary repatriation" of approximately 18,000 freeborn and newly emancipated African Americans. The ACS-sponsored immigrants sailed from America to the western coast of the African continent in search of homeland. Beginning in 1820, they were to settle in what became the Republic of Liberia (Beyan, 1991). The departure of these African Americans from their place of birth is marked by the gradual arrival of thousands more soon-to-be European Americans to the same land, seeking the same rights and privileges denied the former group for over 200 years.

Within these contexts, the work examines trends in familial and organized group behaviors and events that constituted and determined the nature of African American evolving literacy traditions, and the social and historical mechanisms that reinforced these, together with their embedded theoretical, conceptual, and chronological frameworks. This attempt toward a multidimensional explanation of developing African American family–community literacy traditions at historical, social, and cultural distances raised many questions that threatened to make too many demands on this work.

The study contends, however, with three simple, yet nonetheless, compelling questions about these literate Americans: (1) What were the family and community literacy motivations, functions, perceptions, interests, and attitudes that determined their traditions; (2) In what concrete ways did the family and community support literacy development; and (3) What was the formative nature of their family and community literacy traditions?

Inquiry related to nineteenth-century African American literacy behaviors and events as nascent family–community traditions is indeed fragile. Images that appear in major works are essentially atheoretical and predicated on narrow definitions of literacy; this renders them not only educationally irrelevant but dysfunctional to literacy development explanations.

Worst yet, what remain are at least two static, ingenuous images of the nineteenth century African Americans as readers and writers. Either approach highlights mere literacy acquisition (particularly individual literacy attainment pursuits) or organized efforts to foster reading and writing skills, presumably external to and beyond African American direct control. Notably, with few exceptions, major works about nineteenth century African American life and society not only ignore literacy developments initiated within their own spheres of influence, but, again, also ignore current theories regarding the developmental-stage nature of literacy as a linguistic thinking process.

For example, one image of the literate African American is borne out of the familiar story of how acts of either altruism, religious duty, or both on the part of the occasional slaveholder, sometimes on the part of the spouse, or as a source of amusement for a young family member, led to rudimentary literacy acquisition for a few. Note the emphasis on efforts assumed to have been outside African American influences such as the efforts that ensued from their own motivations or acts of relatives, friends, neighbors, and significant members of their own community and organizations. The second image comes out of a similar genre that chronicles organized efforts made by outside governmental, secular, or religious entities. These may include the American Bible Society, the American Tract Society, itinerant plantation ministries, the Freedmen's Bureau, and others; their stories typically record the activities of such organizations and how their actions aided bound and free persons in learning how to read and write before, during, and immediately following the American Civil War. Again, there is stress on simple transmission of reading and writing skills rather than focus on relationships among the universal transforming nature of family lives, community ways of life, and literacy developments. There is a third image that appears to have been molded into oversimplified descriptions of how African Americans in the nineteenth century formed literary societies, seen as largely imitative of those societies initially founded and popularized by Benjamin Franklin and elite early Americans of the eighteenth and nineteenth centuries.

All the same, in their consequences, singly or together, the approaches leave, once again, fixed, socially invented images of the African American reader and writer that magnify an age-old problem in scholarship. That is to say, the dilemma of scholarly stance or, fundamentally—whose story is it anyway, the hunter's or the lion's? Overall, the descriptions leave little understanding about the theoretical, cognitive, and affective nature of literacy development as individual, family or community development.

In doing so, the modes of inquiry result in emblematic depictions of the literate African American reader and writer as an odd, passive recipient of written traditions, divorced or otherwise cut off somehow from his or her own rich oral traditions, without purpose or meaning, an awkward marionette, to be moved about strange stage to strange stage. No such single-dimensional, lifeless person or persons, of course, ever existed, except in social and historical imaginations. Literacy is cultural knowledge. Literacy knowledge is, therefore, never given, but taken, both consciously and subconsciously.

The ways in which literacy becomes a part of any group are truly dynamic. This is because individual, family, and community literacy behaviors are interrelated, mutually supportive developmental processes, and, while basic reading and writing acquisition is most certainly necessary to their growth, descriptions of their attainment alone lack analyses and comprehensiveness to explain the ongoing development of written and oral traditions within multiple, universal perspectives.

What is more, literacy learning and uses cannot be explained as solitary undertakings. Even one person all alone, engaged in a silent or an oral reading of ancient scrolls found in a cave on an island in the middle of an ocean is a social and cultural event, a recursive dialogue between author and reader, a virtual communication between the past and the present. Any literacy event requires the construction of oral or written text meaning through the use of prior explicit or tacit knowledge gained from social and cultural experiences. This includes metacognitive use of two or more of the following language cueing systems: graphophonic, syntactic, semantic, and pragmatic (Bohannan & Glazer, 1988; Clay, 1991; Goodman, 1967). If nothing else is certain in the study of human behavior, it is clear that we all are creations and creators of society, driven, in part, to repeat the same social behavioral patterns, changing and modifying them as we go, gradually altering them over time (Durkheim, 1918/1951). No one person or group, accordingly, is sole creator of society and its culture (Berger, 1963; Berger & Luckmann, 1967; Huggins, 1971).

In order to have use, literacy studies, either up close or from cultural or social distances, must account for links among a range of family and community language arts behaviors (reading, writing, listening, speaking, and viewing) and the quality of their intellectual and social lives. Missing this, we have no meaningful way to construct how families and communities affect literacy development. Conversely, we have little or no means of telling how literacy developments as social and cultural developments affect family and community lives. Explanation must then include analysis of connections between the aforementioned cognitive processes and the affective processes that give rise and meaning to them because it must be understood that to be literate means more than just the ability to read and write (Bloome, 1980; Bloome, Harris, & Ludlum, 1991).

Similarly, the number of nineteenth-century literate African Americans is unimportant to this discussion. Few Americans outside of New England were readers and writers during the period in question and, on balance, to be a reader or writer meant, in some instances, the ability to simply produce a signature on a document. Notwithstanding, we have acquired a body of literature on eighteenth and nineteenth literacy traditions of other groups of Americans. There cannot be two separate realities with regard to objective research. What is more important to know is the quality and function of literacy traditions within institutional contexts across time and space.

Consider the layered meanings underlying poet Countee Cullen's musings. He wrote:

Yet Do I Marvel

I doubt not God is good, well-meaning, kind.
And did He stoop to quibble could tell why
The little buried mole continues blind,
Why the flesh that mirrors Him must some day die, . . .
Inscrutable His ways are, . . .
Yet do I marvel at this one curious thing:
To make a poet black and bid him sing!

(Cullen, cited in Bontemps, 1969)

Cullen's words challenge us to contemplate the ultimate reasons all people speak for themselves, no matter what their objective social or economic circumstances, without self-conscious thought to the "other." At another time, jazz singer and songwriter Billie Holiday's practical, largely unapologetic words would perhaps unknowingly answer Cullen's words in the following heavily laden tones: "I do not got a legit voice, but I'm not going to change. I'm going to sing my way. You just feel it and, when you sing it, other people can feel something too. Without feeling, whatever you do amounts to nothing" (see Recording Arts, 2001, p. 16).

Holiday's notes are pure. Historically, all people are immutably endowed to tell their stories using song, dance, oral, written, or graphic texts, while setting their own stages, choreographing their own steps, writing their scripts, speaking, laughing, and crying out in their own dialogue neither seeking permission nor devising explanations framed to pander. While Holiday referred to the artistic quality of her voice, which she publicly and privately disparaged, one can understand her words at different levels. She demanded to know just whose voice was more legitimate than was her own and just who could ever possibly sing her pain and her joy better than she could. Most importantly, she challenged us with this task: tell our stories with purpose, meaning, and passion, or don't tell them at all.

The conscious and subconscious birthright to tell and retell life stories is the source of oral and written traditions, the beginnings and very firmament of human development. We need only to step back, examine largely spontaneous, authentic literacy talk along with manifest behaviors, and ask questions that might lead to evolving explanations of lives. If accounts of the development of African American literacy traditions are to be credible, then they must be authentic and multidimensional. Functionally, effective explanations are those layered with applied and theoretical knowledge of the developmental stages of literacy growth and other principles of literacy development in families and communities.

Scholarly explanations, therefore, are not flat planes, fixed, but revolving towers of many-sided mirrors on the objective realities of the world. Against the latter, the validity of literacy principles are tested to see if they remain robust, despite extreme, recurring, and mercurial social, economic, or other presumed obstacles to literacy growth. This includes obstacles that supposedly lie within and outside of readers and writers as members of families, communities, and larger social spheres. Sound research-based literacy principles suggest that, whether we are called former slaves, former slaveholders, or neither, in the aggregate, we all generate and make meaning from varied texts for reasons linked to our human and social conditions, and in theory we all learn to do so in developmentally predictable ways. Removal of literacy principles from their familiar, comfortable surroundings of conventional inquiry to examine them against the landscape of somewhat unknown territory is then truly a test of their strength that may pave new roads of inquiry.

The question is, now, by what specific approach or approaches to the examination of nineteenth-century African American literacy traditions can we find fresh interpretations of and ask new questions about literacy development, thereby contributing to existing comprehensive perspectives on common conditions for and stages of family and community literacy development? Answers are not simple because of the complex nature of literacy development and the role of written and oral traditions in social and cultural development. Here it is believed that literacy behaviors take root and flourish in multiple contexts, nurtured by more than one attendant condition. For this reason, their study warrants the use of a multidisciplinary approach. Singly, no discipline can provide multiple perspectives and evolving explanations. Hence, approaches to research applied in this work reflect modes of argument, consistent with historical, sociological, and anthropological modes of argument and inquiry consistent with historical, sociological, and anthropological research conventions, and developmental theories of literacy development applied to family and community literacy.

History, anthropology, and sociology must be about understanding many contexts for human behavior from group perspectives (Carr, 1972; Collins, 1988; Cook-Gumprez, 1986; De Castle & Walker, 1991). In the case of African American literacy development, however, there is the proclivity to study individual literacy attainment more so than family and community literacy traditions. Why is this the case?

One reason, as implied earlier, could be inadequate perceptions about the role of literacy in society or about the developmental processes of literacy learning, or misleading definitions of literacy. Major works abruptly dismiss notions of group African American literacy traditions—emergent or otherwise—based on the belief that since so few were able to read and write, literacy was inconsequential to the group. Because of their condition, it is assumed that African Americans obligingly attended to other more outwardly "relevant aspects critical to the quality of their lives." This assumes that, like glass, lives can segment into mullioned pieces to be examined in isolation pane by pane. It also assumes that language can be separated from what it means to be a people. Overall, for whatever reasons, problems related to the tendency to reduce study of African American literacy traditions to single achievements are better understood by exploring the possible results of applying solely individualistic approaches to the study of African American literacy developments within historical perspectives. Huggins (1971), as well as others, expressed concern over the study of African American lives as a study of heroes and heroines.

Studies of African Americans that take this direction are "weakened and methodologically flawed when researchers substitute rigorous analysis for study of individual African American historical heroes" (Huggins, 1971, p. 19). The result, he argued, is a "warped, distorted historical record" (Huggins, 1971, p. 19). This is because, once more, the social sciences must involve qualitative, quantitative, or some combination of both analyses of social group behavior from a broad base.

The implications are that, intentionally or unintentionally, past propensities to limit, if not to dismiss, focus of the institutionalization of nineteenth century African American literacy, has led perhaps to inordinate and misguided attempts to shine light on individual literacy achievement and to create heroes and heroines with whom the majority can identify. Descriptions of individual literacy learning alone do not have the power to explain the complex development of traditions.

While Huggins did not address literacy development, his argument, possibly influenced by Durkheim and others, implicitly supports the idea that we can study no form of human behavior apart from its societal influences. It is assumed that Heath's (1983) definition of literacy as cultural capital is subsumed in the statement. Therefore, by the same set of rules, one might say to discuss literacy traditions solely as individual developments would likely fuel what Huggins (1971) had called social myths and heroes and what sociologists Berger and Luckmann labeled social constructions of reality. In this circumstance, to do so creates a social invention of the literate African American hero or heroine who is a lone noble figure or a childlike soul caricature, rigid contoured cardboard cutout, and an anomaly apart from family, community, and oral tradition. Quite the opposite is true given the significance of storytelling, song, graphic symbols, and signs in all societies. The Ashanti, as have many literate and emergent literate people, used story-songs to tell about everyday life, death, ceremonies such as weddings and funerals, and to preserve the history of the Ashanti life and values (Fisher, 1953).

We cannot give countenance to narrowly defined literacy foundation explanations that begin and end with examinations of individual literacy attainment at the expense of sound inquiry based on scholarly understandings about the reader-writer as a member of wider society as well as research-based knowledge about reading and writing as a part of all the other language arts.

The foregoing further demands the question why the significance of the nineteenth-century African American family and community efforts in their literacy development is de-emphasized, unnoticed, or all too often summarily dismissed. Could it be that such slights begin with the belief that reading and writing are such sacred symbols of complex social and cultural development and achievement that they must be only cautiously associated with African American culture, but not, for sure, seen as a genuine part of that culture? Is there no room for even the possibility that the culture has had an impact on wider American written and oral traditions as much as the latter has had on the former? Few question the historical significance of the African American on the whole of American culture. For instance, can anyone deny the influence on American popular culture of African American music, song, and dance, or deny the impact of African American political thought, literature, and liberation theology on American intellectual, political, and cultural and thus the dialogue on American freedoms?

Huggins (1971) believed that individual achievements are strong, recurrent, themes because we all, perhaps, have a perceived need to embrace socially gratifying interpretations of the past. We especially hold on to those that focus on individual struggles and avoid mention of or smooth over past and present tensions among groups. He also wrote that stories of individual achievements and heroism are easier to digest than stories of multiple lives fraught with disappointments, setbacks, frustrations, interminable strife, and conflict. In brief, we all write and internalize what we want to hear or believe about our past selves, regardless of who we are or believe we are as people. Given this, historical accounts that spotlight individual literacy attainment among African Americans, enslaved persons, and free persons, may possibly be seen as more interesting and rewarding to think about than others. This may be especially true of those that are written to appeal to the American sense of story grammar and literary champions, clothed in literary themes that portray deep-rooted American values of individualism.

This may well have been the case in the past as seen in the reading interests of nineteenth century American and European readers. They purchased thousands of copies of slave narratives, regarding them as among the most original, exciting American adventure tales (Davis & Gates, 1985). The narratives characteristically told of capture, enslavement, bold escape from bondage, chase, subversive underground tactics, and finally freedom and the triumph of the human spirit (Davis & Gates, 1985).

Some of the fugitive slave accounts were as popular as if not more so than books inspired by the then widely read tales of the American West (Davis & Gates, 1985, pp. xv–xvi). To illustrate their point, Davis and Gates (1985) share the following record:

> [From] 1760 to the present, almost *half* of the Afro-American literary traditions was created when its authors and their readers were either slaves or former slaves. . . . Here is an example of how well they sold. Frederick Douglass' *Narrative* (1845) sold 5,000 copies in the first four months of its publication. Between 1845 and 1847, the *Narrative* sold 11,000 copies; in Great Britain, nine editions were printed in these two years. And by 1860, 30,000 copies had been sold. Solomon Northrup's narrative sold 27, 000 copies in its first two years of publication. Moses Roper's text went into ten editions between 1789 and 1850. And William Wells Brown's book reached its fourth edition in its first year of publication. (pp. xv–xvi)

Against this backdrop, it may be clear that critical examinations of how and why African Americans institutionalized their literacy traditions, passing them along to succeeding generations, contributing to the whole of American traditions, are potentially far more relevant and thought-provoking than descriptive accounts of literacy attainment, especially single literacy development. Consider yet another perspective through the widely known account of eighteenth century poet, Phillis Wheatley Peters.

As some may remember, Wheatley Peters was a talented poet; her work was one of the first two books of poetry published in America, and she was the first American poet to have achieved international recognition (Quarles, 1961; Shields, 1993). Ironically, Wheatley Peters, a New England slave, published her hugely popular works at a seminal time; the colonies prepared to formally declare independence from England.

An increasingly restless group of privileged Americans determined to release the business interests of the colonies from the bonds of English rule and build a sovereign nation loudly voiced their objections to their political and economic circumstances under British colonialism, which they compared to economic slavery. In an attempt to build a moral argument and an American ideology to fuel resistance to British domination, those of influence began a search for a national identity that would bring the colonies together as a formidable force with which to be reckoned (Kornfeld, 2001). Accordingly, they forced the belief that without symbols such as a national flag, an American archetypal poem, or a popularized American national song of praise, ordinary citizens would neither perceive a sense of nationhood nor would they willingly fight to achieve separation from England. Labeling those opposed to their plan Loyalists and themselves Patriots, they encouraged the artistically talented to effort their request for a popular American symbol (Kornfeld, 2001).

While Wheatley Peters's early writings, espoused conservative Loyalist views, they were well-received because they did, nevertheless, represent American views; however, it was actually her later works that praised Patriot separatist visions, adopted by the leadership class, that answered the call for a symbol of American idealism. Again her works were well-received; she was befriended by the likes of Benjamin Franklin, General George Washington, and others who admired her art and foremost its articulation of newly forming definitions of America. Her works were to be recognized as definitive of the American freedom cause (Shields, 1993).

Most accounts of Wheatley Peters's life and contributions inevitably begin with the story of her early literacy learning when as a young girl she was abducted and sold into slavery. Reportedly, she was about six or seven years old (Quarles, 1961; Shields, 1993). Early on in her life, she demonstrated keen intelligence that exceeded her chronological years; particularly, she displayed exceptional linguistic talents. In today's educational parlance, Wheatley Peters was a linguistically gifted child. She "learned to read and write in English and Latin within the first year or so of her coming to the American colonies" (Shields, 1993, p. 1252). Beyond this, she was to write widely acclaimed interpretations of epic English poetry at a young age, and she was to produce her own important works as well, with her first publication at the age of thirteen (Shields, 1993). It was discovered that about two weeks after she was brought to work for the Wheatley household, Wheatley Peters was writing Arabic symbols on chalk slate and on walls. Later, she was introduced to English and Latin print, which she mastered in a short time. While her poetry was considered noteworthy by most accounts, what was generally considered truly remarkable was, within the reasoning of the time, the amazing idea that she, an African slave, possessed the capacity to read and write at all.

For many this ends the story about Phillis Wheatley Peters; however, for any language arts practitioner, researcher, or parent for that matter, there is far more to consider in all of this. That Wheatley Peters was writing Arabic symbols approximately two weeks after her arrival raises questions of when, where, and most certainly from whom did she acquire the literacy knowledge and skills (Shields, 1993). A language arts researcher or educator would go a step further. Other questions would arise such as how was it possible that the child had developed an awareness of Arabic print, a concept of word, and fundamental concepts about the features and functions of print made connections between oral and written languages and incorporated all of this early literacy knowledge into her symbolic play in a few days' time?

For to do so would have been a rare feat and an unbelievable accomplishment, of course, even though she was, undoubtedly, a precocious and an exceptional child. This would be inconsistent with what we know today about early childhood cognitive and literacy development with respect to interrelatedness among literacy modeling, guided practice, and literacy play within a supportive, literate environment. Further, one must assume that she was profoundly affected by what was likely for her a host of incomprehensible experiences. All things considered, what is measured in any society to be an unspeakable act happened to this young child. She was seized, forcibly separated from her parents and community, held against her will, placed on a ship bound for a strange land, and upon arrival made to work in the household of strangers. Within days, she had suffered an abrupt and irrevocable change in her legal and social status. She must have been so terrified that, under such a state of affairs, neither she nor any young child would have had the capacity to achieve such developmental leaps. It is obvious that the learning took place long before this traumatic experience and developmentally in her early childhood.

Wheatley Peters, as Shields (1993) reports, was born a member of the Fulani people—a large linguistic group with a long history of Arabic written culture; this is not a minor element of this case. It is possibly an answer to many questions regarding this child's early linguistic abilities, and this is significant because, as discussed, she was more than likely an emergent writer and therefore a developing reader long before she met the Wheatleys. Current literacy research suggests that literacy play learning to listen, speak, read, and write are interconnected processes (Christie, Roskos, Enz, Vukelich, & Neuman, 1995; Graves, 1983). Arguably, Wheatley Peters was not only an emergent reader in three languages—English, Latin, and Arabic—she was linguistically talented in four, if one accepts that, given her age when seized, she had to have been a fluent speaker of her Fulani mother tongue. By the time a child is about five years old, he or she has the ability to comprehend as well as generate syntactically and semantically correct sentences in his or her mother tongue with no formal education. That child cannot, on the other hand, any more than can most adults, formally express all that he or she may actually know about the grammar of the language. Children who speak one dialect at home and another at school, and still another at church cannot essentially explain what it is they do to make sense of the syntax of everyday communications (Ehri & Sweet, 1991; Morrow & Weinstein, 1985; Strickland & Morrow, 1989). They aptly switch from rule-governed home talk to rule-governed playground talk to standard dialect that has its own set of rules. All of this places a completely different perspective on Wheatley Peters as a reader and writer and on the nature of her birth family and community who initially nurtured her earliest linguistic interests.

Historians, generally unfamiliar with early childhood affective and intellectual development, including relationships among literacy development and literacy play, allow the aforementioned implications to go unexamined; this may be somewhat understandable, but still these types of absences are still regrettable. It is equally regrettable that, in the case of Wheatley Peters, the record, for a multitude of reasons, is either obscure or silent on so many other portions of her life. Far less is known, for example, about this person as a literate African American child, adult, parent, member of her community, and poet than is known about how her captors paraded her around America and abroad as a wonder. What's more, it leaves much to learn about the role of African American families and communities as forces in the development of American literacy traditions from this nation's inception and during America's Age of Revolution. The role of African Americans during the American Revolutionary period is important to American history (Berlin & Hoffman, 1986; Davis, 1975; Norton, Gutman, & Berlin, 1986).

This also is important because, although to read, write, and be African in nineteenth century America was indeed heroic and even noble, it was not singular. Now, this is not to imply that eighteenth-and nineteenth-century literate African Americans were commonplace, for Wheatley Peters was an atypical American reader and writer. This is just to say it was not, of course, as Cornelius (1983, 1991) and many others have argued, truly believed by most at the time that it was against laws of nature for them to read and write, considering man-made laws and social practices meant to either bar or restrict access to learning, and thus undermine literacy rights. It was well understood that without these barriers, African American literacy would have led to a literate class of freeborn and enslaved Africans that would ultimately compromise slavery (Bond, 1969). Literate African Americans would not only undermine the slave institution, but also threaten to end the privilege of some at the expense and exploitation of others, an untenable situation that was bound to explode.

Literacy as cultural capital was increasingly absorbed into the African American experience in various stated and unstated ways. Huggins (1971, pp. 17–19) writes that "cultures either exist or they don't; they are never successfully [self-consciously] manufactured or promoted. . . . [I]f we really want to understand what [African Americans] have done and are doing, it is best to consider them in terms of the traditions they continue." The valuable links among language (written and oral) and human experience were lost on neither the European American nor the African American. This inextricably binds all to what became American literacy traditions. If literacy was important to some Americans, it was because its attainment and use became privileges denied others in that land.

In answer to the question posed earlier regarding which approach or approaches may lead to comprehensive explanations of the foundations of African American literacy as family and community developmental processes, it is, once more, a multidisciplinary approach that would be most useful here. It is by this means that inquiry can move the focus of the nineteenth-century literate African American away from images of strange and unusual figures toward familiar images of readers and writers, recognizable and universal to the story of human development as interconnected relationships among family and community. In foresight, this line of investigation of African American foundations of literacy as emergent, universal family and community efforts represents a fundamental shift in approach to African American literacy development explanations.

Possibly, this line of inquiry roots, deepens, enriches, or otherwise lends support to existing and future studies of the development of early African American family and community literacy traditions, ultimately expanding discourse on the role of African American family and community in literacy growth and school achievement, thus giving more depth to the thought regarding the foundations of American literacy.

A reasoned dialogue among past African American readers and writers from their own family and community perspectives is achievable. There is overwhelming evidence to suggest that nineteenth-century African Americans' social and cultural institutions were universal enough and substantial enough for them to have participated fully in the development and transmission of their own traditions (Genovese, 1976; Gutman, 1977; Levine, 1979; Stampp, 1956). One can only assume that the same families and other institutions were also major to the development of their literacy traditions.

The term *traditions* brings to mind many images and assumptions. In this context, traditions are learned ways of thinking, believing, and behaving passed along from one generation to the next primarily by way of the family and secondarily by other social and cultural institutions (Durkheim, 1951; Geertz, 1973; Goodenough, 1971). For example, studies suggest that African Americans, slaves and free persons, throughout the centuries tended to hold on to their old ways of thinking, believing, and behaving. These ways are manifested in their family values and kinship terms, and in their child-rearing, educational, and naming practices (Genovese, 1976; Gutman, 1977; Herskovits, 1941; Joyner, 1983; Levine, 1979; Litwack, 1961; Stampp, 1956; Stuckey, 1987; Webber, 1978). Neither forced migrations nor slavery destroyed their family and community ways of life, all of which remained dynamic throughout the nineteenth century (Billingsley, 1968).

This work defines literacy traditions as ways of knowing, behaving, and believing that are in perpetual motion. At the same time, language, written and oral, is indeed a multidimensional and comprehensive network of interrelated systems and affective processes, such as reading, writing, listening, viewing, and speaking, and attitudes toward, perceptions of, and interests in literacy. The foregoing systems and processes move through significant events, determined by complex and attendant intellectual, social, cultural, and historical conditions. With this in mind, literacy traditions examined in this work are epitomized by, but not limited to, any of the following examples: Bible reading, letter writing, signatures, recitation of the alphabet, poems or prayers, hymn singing, the use of symbols to perform mathematical operations, recognition of environmental print and graphic symbols, speeches, sermons, narratives, signs, map making, map reading, and the like. The foregoing examples, therefore, take into account emergent and mature literacy behaviors and the use of written, graphic, and oral texts that have significance to those who produced them.

Evidence of written and oral culture—books, periodicals, newspapers, writing paper, globes, maps, quills, and other such artifacts—endures in layers of extant literature produced by and about early African Americans. As in an archeological dig, these layers have been sifted in order to turn up material evidence of the types and uses of various community and family owned reading and writing materials, kinds of environmental print, and large and small group-participation structures for literacy-related family and community events. Speeches, sermons, slave narratives, testimonies, song lyrics, and many other contexts for oral language were included; these serve to remind all of the interconnectedness of written and oral language which makes up language arts traditions.

Family literacy traditions considered were those literacy behaviors that functioned, in a broad sense, to, intentionally or unintentionally, actively engage family members in rituals intended for the maintenance, well-being, and continuation of the family as a viable social unit. Similarly, literacy behaviors that constituted community literacy traditions were recurrent literacy activities that functioned to, intentionally or unintentionally, actively engage a cross section of distinguished and undistinguished people in the African American community in literacy-related events that were integral to community life and were intended for the maintenance, well-being, and continuation of the community.

The terms *nineteenth-century African American family* and *African American community* need clarification, beginning first with the concept of the African American family. Not long ago, historians and others questioned the existence of the nineteenth-century African American family, assuming the horrors of slavery and what followed destroyed this institution. These assumptions were based upon, among many other things, the premise that historically the African American family did not take on the nuclear-family structure commonly associated with European families. Decades of research, however, have led to an abundance of evidence to the contrary; there is little doubt that the African American family as an institution did endure as a synthesis of West African and American ways of thinking and behaving that was different from that of European Americans; however, the differences were not detrimental to the survival of the former group.

The West African influence on family development in America is evident in the structure of the early African American family. Like Gutman (1977), White (1985), and many others, it is assumed here that the African American extended family was not a mere response to the harsh social and economic conditions of the times, but likely a blending of Old World and New World ways of family life. The African American extended family, therefore, was not an aberrant form of its European counterpart. Even in the face of a wealth of research findings to suggest the opposite, the myth of the destroyed African American slave and free family is strong, so enduring that still today it is expedient to establish its existence before a discussion of family impact on any category of nineteenth-century African American social or cultural development can proceed. We now know that Africans characteristically brought with them their heritage of the extended family, which functioned to care for and protect their loved ones, as families will, from the outside forces that threaten to undermine their familial relationships and quality of life, and put an end to their very existence. African American family and community historically took on the responsibility of providing education for their youngest members through apprenticeships and other paths, including informal and formal collective efforts (Webber, 1978). Accordingly, many have argued, the adaptation of the foregoing West African family structure to new circumstances was, without doubt, the cultural capital with which African Americans purchased the means to successfully rise to the challenges of their new world (Billingsley,

1968; Blassingame, 1972; DuBois, 1908; Foner, 1975; Gutman, 1977; Herskovits, 1941, 1939; Hill, 1972). As with other groups, in times of strife and crisis—wars, famines, political revolutions, ethnic or religious persecutions—the family historically survives, and so it was with the Africans who were forced to arrive in a new world by the thousands. Each group who came to these shores had in somewhat different response to the challenges facing them that required them to reach inside their own collective memories to find their own unique answers (Billingsley, 1968).

Blassingame (1972) has analytically defined the nineteenth-century African American community as a cultural group without distinct geographical boundaries; African Americans base their community identity on their common historical experiences and racial identity. African American community is, therefore, similarly defined here as a cultural group of those with African heritage who—regardless of geographical location, legal status, or whether they were skilled or unskilled, educated or uneducated—consciously or unconsciously formed an identity and a bond based on their shared historical experiences and racial awareness, along with empathy and support for one another. Blassingame's definition enables this discussion of African American literacy development places their experiences and the study of these within a global perspective.

With the foregoing in mind, an attempt is made to formulate an understanding of nineteenth-century African American perspectives of family and community traditions through the analysis of writings that originated within the context of their family and community life. Therefore, formal and informal schools, churches, benevolent societies, mutual benefit societies, literary societies, and newspapers are examined. Additionally, attempts were made to describe and explain formal and informal rituals, symbols, and sacred objects as they relate to the topic at hand. The cultural meanings African Americans attached to their own symbols of literacy, signs, ritual behaviors, and artifacts, and literacy itself have been examined through African American narratives, songs, literature, letters, diaries, autobiographies, sermons, essays, and many other contexts for writing, reading, speaking, and listening.

In line with current research approaches in the social sciences, the worldviews of articulate families as well as voiceless families appear. Although many nineteenth-century African American families left an invaluable legacy of letters, diaries, journals, hastily written notes to family and friends, deeds, maps, and records of births, deaths, and marriages perhaps tucked away inside the family Bible, many more left little written evidence of their existence. What is more, an inestimable number of families either lost track of or produced no family papers, letters, photos, or other evidence of their lives. This, however, does not pose a problem without a solution.

Current methods for the study of family and community life at cultural and historical distances compensate for this by maintaining balance among the articulated and unarticulated, meaning among those who left copious artifacts, those who were less prolific, and those who left none. It is generally thought that to include only the most educated and well-known at the exclusion of those who followed ordinary life paths results in misleading and unbalanced views, fertile ground for the creation of myths and half-truths. Anthropologists, led by Malinowski (1961), and historians, following the paths taken by Blassingame (1972), Gutman (1976); Hofstadter (1944), Levine (1979), Stampp (1956), and many others have long ago argued the validity of approaches designed to study culture and history from the bottom up. This means justification for the study of African American literacy traditions, using existing African American sources that originated in their own nineteenth-century family papers and communities in conjunction with other records has been well established. Again, this study aimed to include as many perspectives as possible in order to build multiple images of early, literate African Americans as members of families and communities and, thereby, provide a comprehensive record of African American foundations of literacy. Decisions about whose voices should be heard in this work were not determined solely by volume, but by how well the combined voices of a people from diverse yet common backgrounds and experiences blend to form a full choir.

With regard to specific sources, selected letters from the vast collection generated by the ACS have been especially useful in learning about literacy attitudes, interests, and materials, and family and community life. The published letters and other artifacts are a record of the lives, times, and thoughts of ordinary and elite nineteenth-century African American families.

In order to provide multiple perspectives of the lives and times of early African American readers and writers, hundreds of personal letters written by enslaved and freed African Americans have been read and interpreted. The men, women, and children who wrote these letters, of course, never suspected that their words would be historically significant, which makes them valuable. Such letters as used in this study can be found in the Carter G. Woodson (1969) collection, *The Mind of the Negro as Reflected in Letters Written During the Crisis, 1800–1860.* These letters, as primary sources, are presented in Woodson's collection unedited and with little or no editorial comment. Historians have used this and other such collections extensively to answer many different research questions, and have viewed these as invaluable research tools. Also used in this study were letters written by African Americans before the Civil War, collected by Robert S. Starobin (1974) in his work, *Blacks in Bondage.* Again, the letters represent the writings of ordinary African American slaves and freemen in the 1800s. The letters of a free black family who lived Charleston, South Carolina during the years immediately preceding the American Civil War collected in Michael P. Johnson and James Roark's (1984) *No Chariot Let Down* have also been useful.

John Blassingame's (1977) *Slave Testimony: Two Centuries of Letters, Speeches, Interviews, and Autobiographies* has been an extremely important source for this work. Blassingame's collection provides, as do the aforementioned collections, the African American voice regarding family and community literacy development. Slaves freeborn and emancipated persons are represented. African Americans' organized efforts to promote literacy are reflected as well. The letters of the Skipwiths, an African American slave family, are collected in R. Miller's (1978) *Dear Master: Letters of a Slave Family* and in Bell I. Wiley's (1980) *Slaves No More: Letters from Liberia, 1833–1869.* Both works contributed greatly to the findings in this study. Both helped to provide images of the development of African American intergenerational literacy traditions and harbor a wealth of information regarding the types of reading materials available, literary genres read by families, popular titles, and the kinds of reading and writing activities that were necessary for family and community development, including leisure reading, religious instructional, first aid reference, and the like.

The sources visited suggest that African American conductors operated the Underground Railroad and carried out other anti-slavery and resistance activities by using a variety of forms of oral, written, and graphic communication, including what would be considered, in the 1800s, a state-of-the-art innovation in communication—the telegraph (Still, 1872). Letters and reports by African Americans in the North and the South, as well as those generated by the first generations of emigrants to Liberia, provide inventories that reveal the nature of reading materials that interested African Americans before and after the general emancipation.

Newspapers that operated as mouthpieces for abolitionist organizations supported by African Americans, along with newspapers owned and operated by African Americans that served as organs of their own benevolent and literary societies corroborate slave narratives and testimonies about the lives and times of slaves and free persons in the 1800s. Particularly helpful are papers printed in cities with large populations of free African Americans who widely supported their newspapers. African American readers responded to issues affecting them in letters to editors and interesting, informative articles. The biographies and obituaries that appeared in these papers were, in some cases, according to Dann (1971), the only existing sources of detailed information regarding individuals who lived either ordinary or extraordinary lives. Newspapers published excerpts from narratives as well as entire narratives of fugitive slaves and were sources for interesting statistics on the economic or educational status of African Americans, and reported census information. Advertisements offered information on the material lives of African Americans. Issues included literary contributions—short stories, poems, and essays—fashion news, women's and children's concerns, and social organizations' activities, along with pressing political matters. The use of nineteenth-century African American newspapers in this study has helped round out the profiles of normal African Americans and their lives from their own perspectives. Those read for this study include the following: *Freedom's Journal*, *Colored American*, *Rights of All*, the *Elevator*, and many others that operated at the time. Antislavery newspapers with African American contributors and a large circulation within the African American community were also consulted. The paper of abolitionist William Lloyd Garrison, the *Liberator*, and the *National Anti-Slavery Standard*, owned and operated by Lydia Maria Child and her husband, were read. These provided, as did the aforementioned papers, an inside look at the organizational life of African Americans in the nineteenth century because most of these papers were manifestations of African American resistance to slavery.

Many autobiographies and narratives written during the period studied have been read, including *A Black Woman's Civil War Memories* (Taylor, 1902) and the life and career of Ida B. Wells as portrayed in *Southern Horrors and Other Writing* (Wells, 1997). Wells's biography is based on the following three volumes of autobiographical writings and political essays published at the turn of the century: *Southern Horrors: Lynch Law in All Its Phases* (1892), *A Red Record* (1895), and *Mob Rule in New Orleans* (1900).

Slave narratives published as separate works as well as those collected in volumes have been most valuable. Arna Bontemps's *Great Slave Narratives* (1969) provided the original writings of James W. C. Pennington whose narrative entitled *The Fugitive Blacksmith, or, Events in the History of James W. C. Pennington, Pastor of a Presbyterian Church, New York, Formerly a Slave in the State of Maryland.* Frederick Douglass left volumes of writings that depict, among many things, the thoughts of African American slaves, freedmen, and leaders in the abolitionist movement. His well-known work, *Narrative of the Life of Frederick Douglass: An American Slave Written by Himself*, published in the mid-1840s has influenced this work.

Collected essays, excerpts from speeches and addresses, correspondence among abolitionists and politicians, sermons, newspaper articles, and other writings produced by Douglass were read to determine how the nineteenth-century African American organized his or her resources to promote literacy. R. J. M. Blackett's (1986) book, *Beating Against the Barriers: The Lives of Six Nineteenth-Century Afro-Americans*, provides biographies of the lives of James Pennington, John Sella Martin, William Howard Day, and Robert Campbell. Primary and secondary sources were consulted for this study, including personal documents produced by African Americans. Also consulted were works on the lives of such men and women as Richard Allen and Edward William Blyden, who was born in the West Indies and immigrated as a child to the United States, Henry Highland Garnet, Charity Bowery, Susan Boggs, Mary Frances Harper, Mary Ann Shad, John Mercer Langston, Martin R. Delaney, Peter Humphries Clark, Alexander Crummel, Henry McNeal Turner, Daniel Payne, and Isaiah T. Montgomery.

African American newspaper agents who traveled to large cities and remote areas exposed many urban and rural African Americans to reading materials, including antislavery pamphlets, books, women's and children's magazines, church newsletters, and newspapers. African American newspapers, churches, benevolent societies, and anti-slavery organizations sent out these agents, journalists, and lecturers (some of whom were well-known and drew large audiences) to gather news, promote the interests of sponsoring societies, and increase circulation of their publications. Fortunately travelers, sometimes widely published journalists, chronicled their experiences in detailed narratives, letters, or speeches printed in various papers in Boston, New York, and other large cities (Dann, 1971). These papers afforded an inside look at the concrete ways in which African American literacy was promoted, documenting educational opportunities and progress that spanned local, state, regional, and national levels, and, in the case of some well-known educational lecturers and abolitionists such as Frederick Douglass, Ida B. Wells, and immigrants to Liberia, the international level.

Observations of African American readers and writers by missionaries, American Civil War Union officers, and others offered interesting perspectives regarding the types of reading and writing behaviors in which African Americans engaged before, during, and after the Civil War. Much can be learned from these sources, especially how African American literacy was perceived by officers in command of African American troops, journalists, and most importantly by African Americans themselves. The diary entries made by Thomas W. Higginson, a Union officer in charge of an African American regiment and an anthropologist in his civilian life, for example, reveal interesting perspectives on African American soldiers as beginning readers, many encountering and handling, perhaps for the first time, written materials. Higginson writes how the soldiers spent hours of their free time—fatigued, muddy, and drenched in sweat—hunched over primers by campfire light, attempting to master the rudiments of print. Diaries, memoirs, ethnographies, and other means of recording human behavior have led to an understanding of the makings of African American family and community literacy traditions.

Fisher's (1953) contribution to thought regarding the development of African American community is his conceptualization of the historic significance of African American folk music, including spirituals, work songs, and gospel hymns as a reflection and documentation of the African America experience. His work, *Negro Slave Songs in the United States*, provides an analytical examination of authentic

African American song lyrics, chronologically arranged. His creative work was indeed helpful in providing yet another layer of knowledge regarding literacy development and community development, especially in making links between oral and written traditions.

As mentioned earlier, reliance upon African American sources to write about African American family and community life has long been a common practice in the social sciences. Social and cultural historians have used slaves' accounts of slavery to interpret past lives in ways relevant to this study (Blassingame, 1977; 1980; Davis & Gates, 1985; Miller, 1978; Perdue, Barton, & Phillips, 1975; Starobin, 1974; Yetman, 1984).

Webber's *Deep Like the Rivers: Education in the Slave Community, 1831–1865* (1978) is an example of a qualitative study in which the researcher relied on slave sources. Webber used John Dollard's *Criteria for the Life History: With Analysis of Six Notable Documents* (1935/1971) to guide his analysis of learning as cultural transmission in African American slave quarters. While Webber does not address literacy learning, he does unveil the nature of adult-child, teaching-learning relationships among African Americans that led to the transmission of other forms of cultural knowledge, and he does so thoroughly and with such sensitivity that inferences about these relationships have had special meaning to this study of family and community literacy development.

Articles collected in the work entitled *African Voices: the Life Cycle of Slavery* (Mintz, 1993) contributed to an in-depth look at the social and cultural phases of slave life from birth to death. Deborah Gray White's (1985) book, *Ar'n't I a Woman?: Female Slaves in the Plantation South*, imparts revealing and important details about the female slave life cycle and consequently adds to the understanding of the role of African American women in the slave family.

According to Billingsley (1968), the earliest group of scholarly, qualitative studies of the African American family is W. E. B. DuBois's ethnographic studies of the African American family, written from 1894 to 1915. Earlier studies of the African American family failed to use systematic ways to examine African American culture and society (Gutman, 1976; Billingsley, 1968). Instead, works were guided by popular and religious beliefs that reflected the prevailing views of the time. The credit for bringing scientific methods of inquiry to the study of African American family, culture, and community belongs to W. E. B. DuBois. In *The Negro Family* (1908/1968), DuBois's major emphasis is on the impact of West African heritage on African American family organizations, functions, and structures. Like a few of his contemporaries and others after him, he provided evidence to suggest African ways of life were not crushed because of slavery. The cultural survival thesis important to dialogue in the study of the African American family is reflected in many cultural, social, and historical works about nineteenth century African Americans (Aptheker, 1946; Davis, 1978; Genovese, 1976; Gutman, 1976; Herskovits, 1941; Huggins, 1977; Levine, 1979; Stuckey, 1987).

The most comprehensive study of the nineteenth-century African American family is Herbert Gutman's (1977) work, *The Black Family in Slavery and in Freedom, 1750–1925.* Gutman's extensive and innovative use of slave sources to provide an understanding of the African American family has made his work standard reading in the field.

The foregoing examples suggest that the creative use of multidimensional approaches to the study of African American family and community, and the use of authentic oral and written texts created within the nineteenth-century African American community lead to powerful, interesting, and comprehensive perspectives on the nineteenth-century African American family and community.

The sources relied on in this study were selected and examined in light of the research questions posed earlier in order to identify and classify various types of family and community literacy behaviors. In order for a family literacy activity to be considered, it had to be compatible with the aforementioned definition of literacy and the African American family. Accordingly, the reading and writing behaviors documented here are those that were ongoing, frequent, and integral to family life, and those that functioned to actively engage families in rituals intended for the maintenance, well-being, and continuance of the family as a viable social unit.

Recurrent community literacy behaviors were also selected and classified according to their common characteristics and possible contributions to this work. The criteria used to consider a community literacy event significant were whether it occurred with frequency, that it persisted over time, and that it meaningfully engaged a representative cross section of ordinary and extraordinary families in the community.

The expressed and implicit meanings that African Americans attached to their literacy behaviors as evidenced in their individual, family, and community literacy histories were identified. The frequency and pervasiveness of these expressions were noted. The expressions were grouped according to broader cultural meanings that emanated from the examination. The groupings or categories were named, using words recorded in the family and community literacy histories studied. Categories of broad cultural meanings that reflected the African American experience as a whole were considered cultural themes. Explanations of nineteenth-century African American traditions were grouped according to these categories of meanings. Expressions of these categories were discussed as they related to types or domains of a written tradition, including literacy events, rituals, symbols, signs, and sacred objects. Expressions of the categories of cultural meanings were also discussed in terms of the relationships between broad cultural meanings and domains of literacy knowledge and behaviors.

The types of reading and writing materials, again, mentioned by nineteenth century African Americans in their literacy histories are discussed. Inferences from the nature of the materials are made with regard to nineteenth-century African American literacy interests, values, and perceptions.

Finally, the historical contexts in which the mentioned literacy behaviors occurred were evaluated for their significance to African American experience. It is assumed in this work that if a category of meaning is not firmly grounded in the African American experience, it cannot truly be a significant cultural theme, or, in other words, a mirror that reflects, in this case, African American perspectives on the development of their literacy traditions in the nineteenth century

This work was informed by sociological and anthropological theories of social and cultural life: symbolic interactionism and life course perspective. Symbolic interactionism as an approach is a set of principles by which to examine and interpret the underlying cultural meanings of social behaviors through a society's symbols, such as its languages, ideas, and material objects. Symbolic interactionists, across disciplines, attempt to address long-standing problems concerning the mechanisms that hold societies together (Vinoskis, 1988). As an analytical framework, symbolic interactionism was first associated with Durkheim (1951), Cooley (1902), Goffman (1967), Blumer (1969), and others; it appears in many variations across fields. Cultural anthropologists, Geertz (1973), for example, have used aspects of symbolic interactionism to examine everyday rituals, believed to make up human interactions, as a means of explaining cultural behavior. A brief review of Durkheim's work provides background to better understand symbolic interactionism and its importance to this study.

Durkheim (1951), as suggested earlier, asserted that our social fabric continuously weaves itself into more or less the same patterns because of, in part, its self-renewing behaviors or rituals, such as religious and patriotic ceremonies and family traditions. All behaviors, he proposed, are essentially social in origin, not individual. Through his study of suicide as a social, not private, act, Durkheim (1951) asks us to consider how social status, gender, age, religion, and the like may influence the nature of suicide or other acts and decisions commonly considered private and individual. He was among the first to raise the question of whether any supposedly individual behavior is indeed individual.

Goffman (1967) took a slight turn in his interpretation of ritual behaviors. He broadened Durkheim's formal ritual theory by proposing that in addition to formal, large-scale, and highly visible rituals, society stays intact because there are also microlevel, natural rituals that are part of our invisible or implicit culture. Natural rituals, according to Goffman, occur in everyday life in the form of face-to-face interactions. Goffman's interpretation of interaction rituals explains how normal conversations and even very brief face-to-face encounters are rituals with their own mutually understood rules and conventions (Collins, 1988). Using the theater as an analogy for social life, Goffman categorized social interactions into two groups he labeled *front-stage* and *back-stage* behaviors. One tends to reserve the front-stage behaviors for social interactions carried out in public settings. In contrast, back-stage behaviors are those behaviors that are generally displayed solely in the presence of one's primary group, most likely either family or kin. To understand human behavior, according to Goffman, one must not only be able to comprehend observable, overt behaviors, but also to understand the underlying motivations for the behaviors.

With this in mind, discussion of the kinds and functions of rituals in society and culture give substance and meaning to the African American institutional and familial development of literacy. The ways in which a family as a group of interacting individuals used literacy—recording family statistics, bedtime stories, and religious activities, planning journeys, writing letters, passing on recipes, reviewing family documents, and performing many other functions—highlight the role of literacy rituals in family development at the face-to-face level. Additionally, how the family confronts the outside world or stands between loved ones and the world with regard to legal, religious, and other community matters involves essentially rule-governed contact, differentiated along age, gender, and social-class lines. Institutional rituals involving reading and writing embedded into community rituals such as festivals, weddings, literary groups, church, and the like are examples of other rituals important to this topic. For example, annual emancipation celebrations in African American communities are telling of how communities recognized their common historical bonds.

Overall, both informal and formal rituals are mechanisms for the development of social bonds, believed to form the base for solidarity between people. Rituals, or culturally prescribed ways of interacting, are considered a major source and means of perpetuating group ideas, feelings, folk beliefs, and sense of community. Ceremonies involve the coming together of people who share a common disposition and purpose. They center on what Durkheim has (1951) called sacred objects. Rituals engender feelings of group belongingness and commitment. In this respect, commitment to group rituals with their sacred objects and symbols has extrinsic rewards as well as its own rewards. On the other hand, disrespect for symbols, sacred objects, or other elements of a ritual can result in sanction and punishment for the offender.

In symbolic interactionism, the focus is on cultural symbols as a means of understanding social behavior. Oral language and other forms of human communication are scrutinized thereby to determine how these explain aspects of social behavior. Culture itself is defined in this line of thought as a network of symbols that have shared meanings. The cultural meanings that underlie group behaviors are more important than the behaviors themselves. In this investigation of African American literacy traditions it is believed that observation of social behaviors alone leads to simple categorization and description; however, examining how behavior is made evident by rituals, symbols, and sacred objects enables examination of what that behavior means to a group of people. It is further assumed that study of the underlying causes of the behavior go beyond mere description and that such inquiry is a useful vehicle for the construction of comprehensive explanations, which can lead to generalizations about and predictions of social behaviors.

The definition of the term *symbol* helps to explain symbolic interactionism. A symbol can be any object, idea, or person. Hence, a symbol's presence at an event would have deep meaning to insiders and perhaps only surface meaning to outsiders (Collins, 1988). Symbols also delimit group membership and boundaries. A charismatic leader, a flag, a scroll, a uniform, and patriotism are all examples of symbols deified and untouchable. Symbols that envoke intense emotions among those committed to them, and also among those who oppose them may be sources of endless dialogue and debate. In ritual theory, such rarefications are sacred objects. For example, two of the most widely recognized reading approaches at the time of this writing, the balanced literacy approach and the systematic phonics approach, are arguably sacred objects. Also sacred are the dialogue, patterns of teacher–student interactions, and artifacts such as textbooks, workbooks, professional journals, and the like that characterize each approach. Insiders and outsiders among both groups are quick to pick sides and draw battle lines around issues. The more sacred the object, the longer and more protracted the debate. Further, group differences are harder to resolve under the circumstances.

Since humans are social beings, it has been argued that their interactions are possible in theory only because social behavior is predictably guided by a set of mutually understood symbols whose meanings are constantly created, recreated, interpreted, learned, and negotiated within the interaction. Moreover, Durkheim (1951) suggests that whenever people interact the individual disappears and a new entity, the collective, emerges. Durkheim further suggests that the collective supersedes the individual and therefore individual thought can only be viewed as collective thought. With respect to notions of reality, the symbolic interactionist would assert that reality is a social construction (Berger & Luckmann, 1967). Truth is therefore fluid, evolving, and subjective. A key assumption is that people interact and define social situations according to the meanings they attach to their symbols. Differences in worldviews can be traced to symbols and their meanings.

Life course perspective as a mode of analysis is rooted in symbolic interactionism (Bertaux, 1981). As such, life course perspective analysis is a set of principles by which to examine the family as either a small group of related people who care for each other or an institution as it affects and is affected by social and historical developments (Elder, 1985; Hareven, 1978, 1982). The objective of this study was to construct an interpretation of what it may have meant to be a member of a nineteenth-century African American family who had, along with other such families, laid the foundations of African American literacy. For this reason, examined were relationships among individual, family, social, and historical development and literacy development.

The dynamics among these elements of individual, family, social, and historical development are important in life course perspective (Elder, 1981; Hareven, 1978). Concepts of time are, according to Elder (1981) and Hareven (1978), social constructions as well as chronological and biological realities because individuals play an important part in the development of their society. Society in turn plays a crucial part in the development of the individual. The same is true of relationships between family development and social and historical development. The meanings attached to childhood, adolescence, adulthood, retirement, and aging, for example, point to why this is debatably so. Individual time, family time, and chronological time are distinct but nonetheless interdependent measures that are commonly referred to in life course perspective. As parts of the whole dynamics of change, each of these measures of time are inseparably linked—understanding one process is, therefore, dependent on understanding the other processes (Tallman, 1986).

Symbolic interactionism and life course perspective as analytical frameworks are consistent with the research questions posed in this multidisciplinary work. Both are, therefore, also consistent with the stated purpose of this study: to provide a comprehensive explanation of the interconnected relationships among the African American family and other social and cultural institutions in the development and reinforcement of nineteenth-century African American literacy traditions. These analytical frameworks focus on the examination of the family life of people who lived in the past and make use of modes of argument based on anthropological and sociological principles. Conclusions drawn from such examinations can lead to the development of substantive generalizations about nineteenth-century African American family and community literacy.

As discussed earlier, social scientists had debated whether slavery and its aftermath destroyed the African American family. The following review of works presents in more detail both sides of that debate. Important to this work are those studies that demonstrate the universality, strength, and stability of the African American family in the nineteenth century, even under extremely adverse conditions. Why is this important to the study of the development of African American literacy? It is important to review both sides of issues related to the nature of the early African American family and community in order to support the basic assumption of this study: that the African American family was indeed functional before, during, and after slavery, and, therefore, played a dynamic, rather than passive, role in the creation, transformation, and transmission of their literacy traditions. The works reviewed in this section are arranged chronologically and grouped according to their major arguments, research traditions, and theoretical or value orientations.

The prevailing theme of early publications about African American family life was that slavery and its aftermath destroyed or prevented the development of viable African American cultural institutions. These themes are commonly associated with publications such as E. Franklin Frazier's *The Negro Family in the United States* (1948) and Nathan Glazer and Daniel P. Moynihan's *Beyond the Melting Pot: The Negroes, Puerto Ricans, Jews, Italians, and Irish of New York City* (1963). Daniel P. Moynihan's *The Negro Family in America: the Case for National Action* (1965), Stanley Elkins's *Slavery: a Problem in American Institutional and Intellectual Life* (1959), and Gunner Myrdal's *An American Dilemma: The Negro Problem and Modern Democracy* (1944) are also associated with the belief that slavery and its legacy destroyed the African American family. In an attempt to examine twentieth century African American social problems, Glazer, Moynihan, and others maintained that what they determined to be family instability in African American families in the 1960s was traceable to slavery in the nineteenth century. They believed that slavery more than any other form of oppression was psychologically and socially disruptive and destructive to the African American family, so much so that it had caused a chronic and lasting instability among African American families. Historians and others attacked these views as they were to challenge other negative myths about African Americans proposed in earlier times.

The earliest treatment of the American slavery institution, however, which was to have an impact on its historiography and, in turn, an impact upon conceptualizations of the African American family in the nineteenth century, is U. B. Phillips's (1969) *American Negro Slavery: A Survey of Supply, Employment, and Control of Negro Labor as Determined by the Plantation Regime*. Phillips supported his account with a large volume of plantation records, which presented slaveholders' perspectives on American slavery. His work emphasized the slaveholders' worldview, including culture, religion, and daily activities and accepted the slaveholders' accounts of how slaves were treated. Phillips, like many of his contemporaries, argued from the position slavery that was necessary for the survival of the African. He rationalized slavery to be morally defensible because it brought the African out of barbarianism and exposed them to Christianity and European civilization. Further apologists rationalized that slavery as an institution was basically unprofitable in the long run. Instead, slavery was a part of the social traditions of the Old South.

Life in the Old South was portrayed as idyllic for slaveholders and slaves alike; African slaves were paternalistically caricatured as content, well-protected children incapable of creating and maintaining a culture and existence without European-American domination. While this school of thought preceded Phillips, he was the one who skillfully and authoritatively incorporated the popular belief of African racial inferiority into the period's most comprehensive study of American slavery. Formally linking the notion of racial inferiority with the study of American history was to have serious consequences.

Phillips's work, considered the definitive interpretation of American slavery, was to become the standard text in American universities where it endured critically unchallenged for many decades. His publications influenced many historians such as James B. Sellers, who wrote *Slavery in Alabama* (1950), and Charles B. Sydnor, author of *Slavery in Mississippi* (1933), as well as others who adopted his descriptive framework.

Despite the foregoing, with the wave of new social and scientific findings in mid-twentieth century America, the Phillips's school of thought on American slavery became unacceptable. Scholars such as DuBois and Woodson had critically countered Phillips's interpretation before the 1950s, but their ideas were largely ignored until later.

Beginning in the 1950s, however, American attitudes toward race relations began to undergo change as a result of shifting political winds and a greater demand for objectivity in the study of African American society and culture.

Historian Richard Hofstadter's article, "U. B. Phillips and Plantation Legend," published in the *Journal of Negro History*, Hofstadter accused Phillips of relying solely on an unrepresentative sample of sources and being racially biased in his selection of facts. Oscar and Mary Handlin (1950), in their article, "Origins of the Southern Labor System" (*William and Mary Quarterly*), gave a similar critique of Phillips's work on slavery. Criticism of Phillips's interpretation came to an apex; Kenneth Stampp's (1956) *The Peculiar Institution: Slavery in the Antebellum South* proved an effective, direct confrontation.

Stampp's scholarly work depicted slavery as an economic institution that was indeed as highly profitable as it was cruel, oppressive, and exploitative to Africans. As such, Stampp's work suggested that American slavery was designed to maximize the interests of the slaveholding class in the South at the expense of enslaved Africans in that region. Stampp's neo-abolitionist approach to the study of American slavery continues to have a substantial impact on research on slavery today.

Following Stampp's break from tradition was Elkins's work, *Slavery: A Problem in America Institutional and Intellectual Life* (1959). His main emphasis was on the psychological impact of slavery on the African. He compared this impact with the psychological impact of Nazi concentration camps on European Jews. He depicted both Jews in the camps and Africans in plantation cultures as psychological victims, powerless to effect change in their circumstances.

One of the many constructs developed by Elkins to describe the personality of the enslaved and incarcerated is his use of the term *Sambo* to define what he interpreted as an acquired personality of both World War II Jewish prisoners and African slaves in nineteenth century America. He believed that in order to survive the objective realities of their oppressive systems the enslaved and incarcerated took on personalities of the oppressed. He wrote that the *infantilization* of the oppressed resulted in a Sambo personality, one that is docile, childlike, obsequious, and marginal to social and cultural processes. This interpretation was soon challenged.

Although major themes found in Elkins's work did not depart completely from those of his predecessors (especially Phillips), his work did make a significant contribution to the historiography of American slavery because his controversial book forced many historians to begin to study slavery, notably its effects, more critically. His publication, for example, inspired others to examine slavery from the perspectives of slaves, thus using slave sources such as literature, songs, diaries, narratives, and autobiographies to sustain their arguments. Others reacted by strongly rejecting his interpretations while at the same time adopting some of his methods of inquiry. Consequently, he exposed the need to reexamine slavery through the eyes of the enslaved. As more phenomenological studies appeared offering fresh perspectives, raising new questions, and arriving at novel conclusions, it became increasingly clear that one cannot fully understand American slavery by exclusively examining the slaver's perspectives; the experiences of the slaves must be critically examined from their points of view.

Soon it had also become clear that arguing whether American slavery was cruel or mild, a profitable economic system or an unprofitable social system, was senseless. Instead, scholars realized that seminal problems in American slavery studies began with failure to examine African slave culture and society from African American perspectives, using artifacts generated by slaves and freed persons.

In this regard, J. W. Blassingame's work, *The Slave Community: Plantation Life in the Antebellum South* (1972), is exemplary for its treatment of African American slave culture. He presented a unique perspective on the American slave culture, particularly on the family and community life of the African slaves in the South as well as the culture of the slaveholders. Using a variety of slaves' personal accounts as well as many plantation and personal records left by slaveholders and slaves, Blassingame examined the common experiences of slaves to discover how their experiences may or may not have shaped slave personalities. He found that many types of personalities existed that were a result of both the social system in which the slave had to survive and his or her African culture that continued to grow and evolve even in bondage. Blassingame argued that slaves hid their private lives from the slaveholder so that they could maintain complete control over their inner world. The Sambo image, if it ever truly existed, was what slaves wanted the slaveholders to see. Blassingame (1972), DuBois (1908), Herskovits (1941), Levine (1979), and many others asserted that Africans still held on to their own values, religion, language, and family patterns despite social obstacles. Blassingame found evidence of the existence of many more believable, authentic personalities that influenced the slave-slaveholder relationship. The *Nat Turner personality*, or the *rebellious African slave* personality, was ever present and widely feared

(Wood, 1988). Above all else, Blassingame found that the African American slave personality was as diverse and complicated as any and that the slave was a human first and a slave second, not an object shaped and created by the institution of slavery.

American history had undergone a revision; it was nearly impossible for any responsible scholar to attempt to restore old beliefs. Reinterpretations of the American slave system, the culture of the antebellum South, including both the slaveholders' and the slaves' world, proliferated as unconventional and sometimes controversial explanatory models evolved, bringing with them novel terminology, the inclusion of new modes of argument, and new questions, innovative methods, and problems. Research designs that incorporated traditions borrowed from anthropology, sociology, and other fields of study applied procedures for writing slave history from the bottom up, history from within, or slave history from slave sources.

Other works portrayed slavery as a brutal institution, largely resisted by Africans. Studies of slave resistance, resiliency, accommodation, community, and culture, as well as studies of how slaves developed strong family and other cultural bonds despite harsh conditions, emerged. Blassingame's work was followed by Eugene D. Genovese's *Roll, Jordan, Roll: The World Slaves Made* (1976) and Charles Joyner's, *Down by the Riverside: A South Carolina Community* (1983).

Genovese's dialectical model contributed greatly to our understanding of slave family and slaveholder relationships. The interdependency of racial and ethnic groups for survival in America (and particularly in the South), he maintained, resulted in a mixture of several unique European, African, and native cultures. African agriculture, mores, language, and customs, for example, are rooted so deeply within the American culture that they have strongly influenced and, it should be noted, have been influenced by European American culture and society.

Herskovits's (1941) *Myth of the Negro's Past* was important to the early development of the argument for African cultural retention. Herskovits argued that African American families, language, music, and art were directly related to West African culture. His early work on African cultural survival is supported by later works by Lawrence Levine (1979, *Black Culture and Black Consciousness*), Sterling Stuckey (1987, *Slave Culture*), Thomas Webber (1978, *Deep like the Rivers: Education in the Slave Quarter Community*), and Miles M. Fisher (1953, *Negro Slave Songs in the United States*). These works pointed to the necessity of using African American oral and written culture to fully understand African American history.

Forces both within and outside the social sciences contributed to the increasing number of studies of African culture and society. The social unrest and uncertain political climate of the 1960s and 1970s created conditions for the use of scholarly dialogue to help resolve social problems and inform political debate over societal issues. In large-scale studies of the status of African Americans in rural and urban areas of the North and South, investigators often cited the works of historians and sociologists to dictate and formulate social policies. African American families were often targeted for study.

The most extensive study of the African American family is Herbert G. Gutman's (1976) *The Black Family in Slavery and in Freedom, 1750–1925*. As a leading voice in African American history, Gutman's work is standard reading. The significance of Gutman's watershed study will be discussed in further detail following an overview of works about the African American family that preceded Gutman's work.

As a leading voice, one of the first groups of scientific sociological studies of the African American family includes the works of DuBois. During his time, many social scientists did not study African American life and thought systematically. Instead, work was guided by popular and religious beliefs. DuBois's overall work is distinguished by the fact that his scholarly efforts are largely responsible for bringing scientific methods of inquiry to the study of African American family, culture, and society.

DuBois's writings, from 1884 to 1915, represent the earliest qualitative studies of African American life (Billingsley, 1968). As a result of the level of his scholarship, his presence in America society, and the changing status of African Americans in this country, his publications were difficult to either avoid or let go unacknowledged (Billingsley, 1968). Scholars, therefore, began to go beyond the chronicling of racial myths toward a reexamination of their own problems and methods. In the end, they had to react to DuBois's work in a scholarly manner.

Works that acknowledged DuBois's contribution were in direct contrast to those by Frazier (1948), Moynihan (1965), and others who either ignored the universal human qualities of the African family or underestimated the resilience and strength of the African family during slavery and its aftermath. Previous works had repeatedly suggested that slavery and its legacy had left the African American culturally deprived, emotionally depraved, and morally corrupt. Beyond the themes of the African American family's resilience and strength is the importance of the theme of universality. Scholars increasingly recognized that while African American families were somewhat different from other American families, their differences were not pathological. Comparative studies of immigrant European American families and African American families suggested that there were more similarities and fewer differences between both groups than originally assumed. Myths about the African American families proved unlikely with the expanding of scholarly investigations of family as social scientists began to seriously challenge standard explanations of social achievement as definitions of culture.

As mentioned earlier, Gutman's comprehensive study of the last generation of African American slaves made a significant impact on the study of African American family life from a cultural and historical perspective. Gutman wrote mainly in reaction to social scientists like Moynihan and Frazier whose emphasis was on a cultural-deficit view of the African American family. He especially took issue with claims that the African American family was either destroyed or nonexistent during slavery and its aftermath. Gutman's study was to examine the nature of the African American family from 1750 to 1925, especially the critical years right before emancipation and the equally important years that immediately followed the end of the Civil War. Gutman argued that the last generation of slaves, would reveal comparative data on the strengths and weaknesses of the African American family during and after slavery, and if there was any evidence of the pathology that sociologists claimed there to be, Gutman theorized, it would be the most strikingly evident during this period.

Gutman examined 1863 to 1866 family and kinship records of African Americans from Virginia, North Carolina, Mississippi, Louisiana, Tennessee, and Kentucky in order to determine how African American cultural beliefs, values, and behaviors shaped their responses to their American experience. Gutman made use of evidence from the records of the Freedmen's Bureau and Union Army records. He also used census records that recorded marriages, births, deaths, household compositions, occupations, and other vital information that revealed much about African American family life in the nineteenth century. Among the many findings, Gutman's data suggest that in the decades that followed general emancipation, most African Americans lived in families headed by two parents, and African American marriages were enduring relationships that survived slavery and, later, freedom. No differences were found in the rates of voluntary termination of European American marriages and African American marriages. A noteworthy finding was Gutman's discovery that African American naming practices that included giving family names to their children suggested strong kinship ties among African Americans despite the ever-present threat of relocation of family members.

Gutman argued that previous definitions of the African American family had been misleading. In order to understand the African American family, he maintained, one had to broaden definitions of family to include the concept of the extended family. Most important, Gutman found no evidence to support the notion that slavery had caused a breakdown of the African American family nor did he find evidence of pathology among the families he studied. His findings undermined previous deficit views of the African American family. Subsequently, the study of the African American family took on new formations.

In summary, this chapter provided a rationale for and the direction that the book takes on the topic of emergent African American literacy traditions as family and community efforts in the nineteenth century. Explanations of concepts related to the African American family and community and their underlying assumptions important to this investigation stand out as signposts along this route. The conceptual and chronological vehicles are life course perspective and symbolic interactionism. Finally, this chapter examined works meant to analytically describe the travelers on this journey—the main characters of the story. The second chapter presents evidence of the concrete ways in which African American parents and other family members laid the foundations of their literacy traditions. Chapter 3 examines informal and formal schools operated by African Americans. Informal schools are referred to as *invisible institutions* because they were generally schools without walls and they often operated in secrecy. Formal schools, referred to in this study as *visible institutions*, were those schools that operated in full knowledge of the community, and had a curriculum, an identifiable source of financial support, trained teachers, and in some cases a board of community trustees. The fourth chapter examines nineteenth-century African Americans' organized efforts to promote literacy in their community, including literary societies, benevolent societies, church organizations, newspapers, community solidarity and national conventions. Chapter 5 provides an interpretive summary, analysis, and discussion of the findings of this study. Implications for literacy research and instruction are also considered.

Chapter 2

Family

Although unspeakable hardships and social-economic circumstances threatened to grind away at the nineteenth-century African American family's resolve to endure intact, it was indeed the family as an institution that was primarily responsible for the development and persistence of African American literacy traditions. Families increasingly applied powerful, old, new, or adopted oral and written strategies that proved useful, if not essential, to all that mattered to the continuation of their family ways of life.

Driven to experience their intellectual freedoms as well as their natural rights to maintain lasting relationships and raise and educate their children, the families used the same wit as cunning and timeless as any learned from their West African brother, Anansi, the quintessential Everyman and trickster. Renamed Brother Rabbit in America, Annasi appears in West African folk literature sometimes as a common man, at other times as a spider. In African American tales he is most often a rabbit. No matter what his form, he serves the same purpose for the storyteller. Bother Rabbit always finds a way to outdo and outsmart his large foes, Brothers Bear and Fox. So armed with these dispositions, skills, and knowledge, African Americans removed some encumbrances to their intellectual growth and independence. Often, like Brother Rabbit, they were to carry out their triumphs in plain view of the unsuspecting. More often, they succeeded in secret, and always they operated at great risk and tremendous cost.

The African American literacy histories examined in this chapter suggest that to be literate was a family trait. Parents or extended-family members fueled and supported literacy learning and functions. Thus, family involvement was, it is argued, important to the development of the first generations of African American readers and writers. The following strategies kept their literacy traditions robust: uprooting families to immigrate to Liberia or relocate to free territories; sending children away to be educated by relatives or kin; developing alternative, collaborative, and informal learning opportunities within the community; supporting private, religious, and public or free schools through benevolent societies or churches; and using Sabbath schools. Ultimately, the nature of African American family life provided a catalyst for the institutionalization of reading, writing, and the other language arts behaviors within varied contexts.

Analysis of the descriptive data about emigrants to Liberia collected by Shick (1971) supports the foregoing. The records suggest that during the years 1820–1843 approximately 4,400 African Americans left for Liberia, transported by more than fifty ACS-sponsored ships with such names as the *Harriet*, *Independence*, *Liberia*, *Strong*, *Jupiter*, *Elizabeth*, *Nautilus*, *Luna*, and *Orion*. Some frigates such as the *Luna*, *American*, *Saluda*, *Jupiter*, *Nautilus*, and *Doris* made more than one trip, carrying passengers, mail, books, building and agricultural supplies, tools, and the like to and from Liberia. The names of some ships, not included on Shick's extensive, detailed lists, are scattered throughout the body of literature about or produced by African Americans during this time.

Upon close examination of passenger registers, one can infer that nearly all of the people traveled in extended-family groups or primary-family groups, in other words, intact households. Aboard the 1829 *Harriet* voyage, the 1820 *Elizabeth* voyage, and the 1821 and 1828 *Nautilus* voyages, for example, one can find evidence that there were, in most cases, at least 2 or more adults of the same age group, and sometimes an elderly family member and children. The 1829 *Harriet* register lists 101 passengers with 46 passengers, or almost one-half of the travelers, identified as readers, writers, or spellers, ranging in age from six-year-old Francis Payne to forty-nine-year-old J. Turner. Two adults are registered as illiterate; the literacy status of the remaining passengers is listed as unknown (Shick, 1971).

The point of origin for the majority of people in this group was Virginia with the remaining from North Carolina, Washington, D.C., and Maryland. The record presents 46 literate passengers aboard the 1929 *Harriet*; 8 passengers were under the age of twelve and 34 passengers who were twelve years old and older are listed as literate. Other ACS papers and sources suggest that the number of literate families who came in the same year or even on the same March 29, 1829 voyage may have been higher. Letters, books, poems, and other written artifacts documented that year appear in ACS papers. For instance, it appears that in July of 1829, about four months after the arrival of the *Harriet*, sixty-year-old Abouhl Rahhahman and his fifty-five-year-old wife were among those possibly aboard; however, their literacy status is recorded as unknown even though it is well known and documented that Rahhahman wrote fluently in Arabic and English. One can only speculate as to why the Rahhahman family's literacy status was listed as unknown at the time they were registered. Published in the July volume of the *African Repository*, Rahhahman's autobiography tells about his forty years of marriage during which he and his wife together endured capture from Africa, ensuing enslavement, emancipation, and finally their Liberian emigration. Earlier, on May 5, 1829, Rahhahman sent the following letter to Ralph Randolph Gurley who served as the secretary of the American Colonization Society for approximately fifty years. Rahhaman wrote:

> Rev. Sir: I am happy to inform you that I arrived safely in Africa, with my wife, and found the people generally in good health, you will please inform all my friends that I am in the land of my forefathers. (*African Repository*, July 1829, Vol. 5, p. 158)

Joseph J. Roberts, twenty-two years old, and his two younger brothers were among the families from Virginia who traveled on the 1829 *Harriet* voyage. All three men were freeborn persons from Norfolk, Virginia. The eldest Roberts received a liberal education in Virginia. Of his brothers, one was a member of the clergy, a bishop, and the other a physician. Joseph Roberts, after serving as Liberia's governor, went on to become the first elected president of the young nation.

John Brown Russwurm came from privileged means, as did Joseph J. Roberts. He went to Liberia in late September the same year the Robertses arrived aboard the *Susan*. He arrived November 15, 1829 (Singer and Ruddell, 1969; Stockwell, 1868). Brown Russwurm is remembered, among many other distinctions, as the first African American to have earned a college degree from Bowdoin College in Brunswick, Maine, and as the third African American to have earned a college degree. Brown Russwurm is also remembered as coeditor of the first African American newspaper, *Freedom's Journal*, founded in 1827. After a dispute between prominent African American leaders and himself over his support of the ACS, which he had earlier opposed, Brown Russwurm, in 1829, immigrated to Liberia where he established the newspaper *Liberia Herald*. Later, Brown Russwurm was to also assume a leadership position, becoming the Liberian Republic colonial secretary from 1830 to 1834. Following this, Brown Russwurm served as governor of the Maryland colonization (Beyan, 1991).

Although Roberts and Brown Russwurm were not representative of all Liberian emigrants, they did represent the type of African American sought for Liberian emigration by the ACS. The ACS considered educated, free African Americans suitable for recruitment to Liberia based on their potential to spread Christianity and promote "civilized" ways of life in Africa. For example, in a letter dated August 12, 1847, John Drew wrote:

> I can say confidently that about 12 person will meet the packet at Norfolk about the 1st of Septr. (namely) myself 60 years of age. Mary my wife 47, B. Lewis 27, Delila his wife 24, my Son Peyton 21, my daughter Sophia C, 18, my Son Rufus 14, my daughter Evelina 11, my daughter Julia 8 B. Lewis, Son Wm. 7, his daughter Mary 3, John Quinichett about 40, which makes up the 12—(6 males & 6 females;) Smithea and family are rather uncertain, though if he should come, he has 6 in family, himself about 30 years old, his wife Mary Jean about 30 and has 2 Daughters, & 2 Sons. There are 2 others talks of coming—Willie Carter about 35, and John Cousins about 22 or 3. There is between 50 and 100 persons around us here, that seems to be very much in faver of migrating to Liberia. (*ACS Papers*, January to March 1847, No. 248)

While some aboard the 1829 *Harriet* voyage, particularly those from Virginia, were freeborn persons who had received a formal education and a measure of wealth, and had not experienced legal slavery, others came from ordinary beginnings. Others paid for their passage to Liberia by buying their labor from slaveholders. B. W. Mann greatly wanted to leave Richmond, Virginia to settle in Liberia. The slaveholder, John Cosby, set the price of his freedom at $400. Mann and Cosby agreed that the former would earn this sum of money by hiring out his trade. At the time of the writing of his letter, Cosby received from $75 to $80 a year for Mann's factory work. It appears that Cosby released Mann to work at the Hiram B. Dickisons Tobacco Factory, located on 14 Cary Street, Richmond, Virginia, and Mann's wages were to be given to Cosby until the $400 debt was paid and Mann's freedom won. Instead, Cosby continued to collect Mann's wages without freeing him. Mann was later to receive 75 cents a week to pay his expenses while living in the city of Richmond (Woodson, 1969).

Literacy was a vehicle that drove the dual mission of the ACS. Agents of the organization sought whole families and significant members of African American communities with the hope these would bring a stabilizing effect to the colonies. Those who were literate (identified as those who could read, write, spell, or had a liberal education) were particularly valued because they could spread God's word (*ACS Papers*, Vol. 1, p. 116).

Many African Americans who were of the freeborn class emigrated because they were promised that they would be allowed to freely establish (or reestablish) businesses and develop their own social, political, and educational institutions. Recently emancipated persons and those of lesser means were sometimes told that they had to leave for Liberia within twelve months of their manumission or suffer reenslavement.

Among all the passengers who left America for Liberia between 1820 and 1843, for example, many were relatively young—the mean age was 20. The largest number of immigrants, 1,608 or 36 percent, was from Virginia, followed by North Carolina with 691 people or 15.6 percent, Maryland with 392 people or 8.9 percent, and Georgia with 241 or 5.5 percent. People categorized as "at-large" account for 6.5 percent. Not surprisingly, the largest number of emigrants came from southern, agricultural states. Northern states such as New York, Pennsylvania, Ohio, Connecticut, Rhode Island, and Delaware registered the fewest number of emigrants. It is likely that persecution of African Americans because of harsh enforcement of laws prohibiting the teaching of reading and writing to African Americans, as a result of slave insurrections and uprisings by literate

African slaves like Nat Turner, in some places may have affected patterns of Liberian immigration. Later, there were those who expressed alarm over the passage of the Fugitive Slave Act of 1850. The repercussions of this for the emancipated and freeborn were tremendous as reports of the capture of freeborn and emancipated families who believed they were safe in new territories before the new law was enacted became widely circulated.

Many families, it appears, saw the ACS movement as a way to find homeland, freely reestablish their lives, and finally be able to exercise rights they were unable to express in America. In a letter written January 20, 1849, Peter Butler of Petersburg, Virginia, spoke for the many saying, "Go to Liberia so as I may . . . educate my children and enjoy the right of man. . . . I wish to go very much and carry all my family which we are four in the family" (Woodson, 1969, pp. 93–94). His message leaves no doubt that family, education, the pursuit of happiness, and freedom were one and the same.

A freeperson and a family man, John Robinson was recommended for Liberian emigration sponsorship in a letter from S. Wesley to Reverend William McLain. It is apparent that he was a valuable candidate based on many qualities, including literacy. Robinson of Baltimore, Maryland, Wesley wrote, was a respected local leader in his community and he was the head of a large household. He and his wife had five children, eight grandchildren, and a son-in-law who was the guardian of a group of orphaned children. All family members, including extended family members were literate (Letter from S. Wesley to Reverend William McLain, *ACS Papers*, April to June 1852, No. 96). It is the latter quality, along with Robinson's leadership qualities, that most interested the writer and ACS member Wesley. Other correspondence suggests that more than one person spoke on his behalf.

The occupations of the aforementioned literate *Harriet* passengers and those of the other vessels were diverse: bricklayers, stonemasons, cabinetmakers, farmers, shoemakers, a cooper, a blacksmith, a millwright, a schoolteacher, nurses, and a physician. In all, the record of emigrants for the period 1820–1843 lists about fifty different occupations with many requiring special knowledge, acquired by apprenticeship to artisans and skilled labor. One can infer that those who left took with them many skills valued as the building blocks of any society. Some worried that the removal of these families from the African American community would lead to a drain on their American communities. One can reasonably assume from all this that reading and writing among many of the families discussed up to this point, meaning those found in the Shick (1971) data set and other sources, literacy was indeed a family trait. Passengers under the age of twelve and listed as literate came from families in which older family members were also literate. Intergenerational literacy, it can be assumed, was, in part, fostered by family life.

Discussion of the role of the African American family in literacy development continues at this point with a critical account of the literacy behaviors of the Skipwith family, who lived in the nineteenth century as slaves and free African Americans. The correspondence between family members and John Cocke, owner of the plantations they worked and later supporter of their immigration to Liberia, is rich in detail. Inferences about African American family literacy made from these letters, along with the insights of historians R. Miller (1978) and B. Wiley (1980) with regard to John Cocke's personal life, the culture of plantation slave labor, and family life help construct an understanding of the influence of family on literacy development.

The Skipwiths lived on the Hopewell plantation in Alabama, owned by John Cocke, who operated more than one large plantation. The following account concerns those who lived primarily on the Hopewell plantation. Because Cocke owned another plantation in Virginia, he was, apparently, absent for long periods from Hopewell (Miller, 1978). Unable, therefore, to keep watch over the daily operation and overall management of his estate—planting; tending livestock; repairing equipment; supervising the sewing of seasonal clothing for slaves; managing slaves, workload, and the division of labor; hiring and letting go overseers—he turned over such responsibilities to his head house servant, Lucy Skipwith. Skipwith used her position well. She was thought of highly by the Cocke family and considered an effective leader who was capable and trustworthy. The overseer reported to Skipworth who wrote monthly to Cocke to inform him of the state of his affairs and those of slave families on the Cocke plantation and on nearby plantations. She also kept him abreast of developments in the lives of key community people (Miller, 1978; Wiley, 1980).

Skipwith was a dominant figure in the lives of her family, the Cocke family, and those of other slave families on the plantation (Miller, 1978; Wiley, 1980). Her regular and detailed correspondence is telling about how complex relationships developed between slaveholders and slaves that sometimes led to a series of compromises on the part of the slaveholder, and, on a few occasions, ultimately benefited slave families. Specifically, Skipwith's literacy behavior underscores how some African American slave families artfully used every available resource and opportunity to not only protect their children's quality of life, but also enhance their children's and their own intellectual development.

Cocke placed Skipwith in charge of the Hopewell plantation's Sabbath school, infant school, and night school. Her constant complaints to Cocke about the mistreatment of slave families by an overseer eventually led to the dismissal of the overseer (Miller, 1978). Skipwith was then entrusted with the responsibility of finding the overseer's replacement. She hired another overseer, Mike Smith, who was more to her liking. Skipwith believed that Smith was a kinder person than was the former overseer, and Smith, she believed, was more willing to listen to how she thought things should be done on the plantation. She liked and respected the young overseer she had secured, and based on her letters to Cocke it appears that the respect was mutual. Smith willingly accompanied Skipwith to assist her in the teaching of the families in addition to other responsibilities related to the running of a large and profitable agricultural estate. Skipwith felt that Smith was a very good teacher. Speaking highly of him to Cocke, she wrote: "Smith takes a delight in assisting me in the Sabbath school, and is never absent from there, he is very good to learn any body any thing that he can" (Letter from Lucy Skipwith to John Cocke, Hopewell Plantation, August 25, 1860; see Miller, 1978, p. 233). The mention of the word *anybody* in the language of the time, was a reference to race or social class. This phrase appears in nineteenth-century newspaper articles as a colloquial term that preceded the term *whites only*. Public notices and advertisements for church services or for help wanted were carefully worded to distinguish between who was and who was not invited to come or inquire.

Skipwith hired a clergyman from town, C. B. Eastman, to teach math. She was pleased with Eastman's work and especially with how he found ways to engage his students. For example, she mentioned that Eastman's idea to hang a chalkboard in the infant school, created excitement among the children and encouraged them to practice their handwriting and spelling. Skipwith stated that both she and the children had learned a lot about math during Eastman's time with the plantation infant school. She was especially excited about her increased knowledge of mathematics. She wrote: "I learnt more in Arithmetic while mr. Eastman was hear than I ever thought of in my life, and I have a great love for it. I would give anything if I had any one to instruct me farther in it" (Letter from Lucy Skipwith to John Cocke, Hopewell Plantation, May 19, 1855; see Miller, 1978, p. 198).

Skipwith's own enthusiasm for learning, especially math—not surprising given her position as a household servant—was crucial to her duties and was not lost on her youngest child, Maria. Skipwith's daughter did well in that subject. Eastman, in turn, rewarded her accomplishments with prizes of a book and a chalk slate. Skipwith believed that Maria learned as much, if not more, arithmetic than her other students, including Maria's older cousins Albert and George even though, Lucy stated, "[Maria] never made a figure untel she was Taught by [Eastman] and she can now Add multiply and Subtract" (Letter from Lucy Skipwith to John Cocke, Hopewell Plantation, May 19, 1855; see Miller, 1978, p. 198).

Skipwith taught reading and writing at the plantation infant school and the Sabbath school. She rewrote instructional reading materials so that they rhymed, making them easy for children to remember. The memorization of lengthy Bible passages, including the Ten Commandments, was considered a burden for many learners, young and old, during this time (Robinson, 1977). Obviously with this in mind, Skipwith found ways to make sure the religious reading materials appealed to children and were written at their levels of understanding. She maintained that this would enable the children to apply their learning to their daily lives. She boasted that since she introduced her approach, the children had developed a deeper understanding of their own behaviors and had a greater understanding of the written word. She believed that before her modification of the texts, the children did not understand the relationship between having to read and memorize the Ten Commandments and their own behaviors. She stated that this changed when she took the time to make the words meaningful to them (Letter from Lucy Skipwith to John Cocke, Hopewell Plantation, August 31, 1857; see Miller, 1978, pp. 215–216). Her method of teaching is a remarkable example of sound, holistic practices that include an attempt to use developmentally appropriate, predictable texts.

Skipwith sent Cocke a copy of one of her writings, requesting that he have it printed into small tracts, or booklets, presumably so she could distribute copies to her students and their families. In her letter dated August 31, 1857, she wrote:

> I send you these verses which I have taken from the 10 Commandments. I wish you would have them printed for me in a small track. . . . I will now bring my letter to a close hopeing soon to hear from you. Lucy Skipwith

The 10 Commandments

Thou no god shalt have but me 1st
This Command I give to Thee
love me then with all thy heart
Never from my words depart
Thou no golden gods shalt have 2nd
gods of sliver do not love
Seek the true the liveing Lord
For I am a jealous god
Thou shalt not take my name in vain 3rd
Sinful words thou shalt disdain
guiltless live before my face
And I will be thy hideing place
Remember thou the Sabbath day 4th
Never work nor even play
The god of Heaven will ever bless
The man who keeps the day of rest
Honour thou thy Mothers words 5th
Never break they Fathers laws
They who does their Parents will
Long upon this earth shall dwell
Thou no murder shall commit 6th
With the murders do not set
Lest thou learn his wicked ways
And live in Sorrow all thy days
Thou no wicked deed shall do 7th
Righteousness shalt thou persue
Let your actions all be right
And like the morning star be bright
Thou shalt see by this Command 8th
Honesty do I demand
Every human being should feel

That it is a sin to steal
Thou shalt always speak the truth 9th
To aged and the youth
False witnesses do I despise
Ile drag them downwards from the sky
Covetousness here thou see 10th
Is a great offence to me
Thy neighbours goods thou shalt not crave
Thy neighbours goods thou shalt not have.

(Letter from Lucy Skipwith to John Cocke, Hopewell Plantation, August 31, 1857; see Miller, 1978, pp. 215–216)

What is also so remarkable about Skipwith's modification of Bible literature and how it was used in her schools is that what she wrote may have had an impact beyond Hopewell. One can infer by Skipwith's casual request that asking Cocke to arrange to have her text published into a small tract was but one of many such requests. She did, after all, not explain much about how she would use the tracts nor did she specify how many she needed and when she expected to receive them. Cocke, it can be assumed, was familiar with all this; it was routine. Skipwith, presumably barred by custom from making such arrangements on her own, needed his assistance. It is unlikely that printers credited her on her works. According to literature about nineteenth-century children's books and periodicals, often the small books were produced without author names (Rachman, 1999–2001; Robinson, 1977). The American Tract Society and other nineteenth-century organizations mass-produced pamphlets written by ordinary people with young children as the intended audience. Most of the works were largely didactic precepts and stories written to teach children morals and godly behaviors, such as kindness toward others, obedience to their elders, daily recitation of prayers, cleanliness, and other virtues. Illustrations were romantic and idyllic, depicting angelic children engaged in activities exemplary of righteous and good children. The text was written in simple rhyme and verse meant to appeal to the young. Social and church groups as well as parents bought these for their children. Churches circulated the small books for children to accompany Sunday school lessons (Rachman, 1999–2001). It is interesting that Skipwith contributed to that American literary tradition—whether her particular reading materials ever made their way into the general American audience of children is unimportant. What is important is that, decidely, she, as Huggins (1981) stated earlier, continued this American tradition, making it uniquely her own and that of the Hopewell families, and especially the children who lived and worked there. Her behavior is consistent with that of other amateur writers of the time who began to write specifically for children. Parents read such pamphlets or books to their children. Skipwith read *Pilgrim's Progress* aloud to the children. This book, which Skipwith most likely found on the shelves of Cocke's library or asked him to purchase, is one of many read to children to teach them to be upright and virtuous. It was believed that this would lead to the development of a strong American nation (Rachman, 1999–2001).

In addition to her teaching activities, Skipwith filled her letters with proud news concerning the educational progress of her daughters, Betsey and Maria. She and others considered Maria to be the infant school's most capable student. In fact, Maria's school achievements were a familiar topic in many of Skipwith's letters. She was definitely every bit the proud mother and teacher when she talked about both of her children.

She also wrote often about the progress of adults and other children in her charge, expressing mixed emotions regarding whether she was having an impact on some of them (Miller, 1978). While in her letters she invariably opened up the topic of the plantation school by writing, "I am going on with my school as ususual, and my Children are still improveing," she expressed less optimism at other times (Letter from Lucy Skipwith to John Cocke, Hopewell Plantation, May 19, 1855; see Miller, 1978, p. 198). For example, on July 20, 1855, Lucy wrote:

> I am still going on with my School and I can see improvement in the Children every day there is two of the little girls that I think will write very well by Christmas, and three of the Boys. I hope that the rising generation will be wiser than the old set I do not get on with my night School so well at preasant. the nights are so short and the Children are so sleeppy when they come from work, that I cannot keep their eyes open no time, and it will soon be picking Cotton time and when they get through with their Cotton at night it will be too late to keep them up, as they will have to rise very early.

> (Letter from Lucy Skipwith to John Cocke, Hopewell Plantation, July 20, 1855; see Miller, 1978, p. 201)

Later in November of the same year, again she wrote: "my school Children are improveing." However, this time she regretfully added that at least those who actually "come to School every day [are doing well] but I can but do little with the others" (Letter from Lucy Skipwith to John Cocke, Hopewell Plantation, November 18, 1855; see Miller, 1978, p. 205). By May 30, 1856, Skipwith brought up the subject of the impact of the children's labors on their learning as she, in obvious frustration, wrote:

> My school Children have improved but little since you went away the largest of them are out at work and those that I have every day are very small, Just learning their letters. I will do the best I can with them at night Scholl. (Letter from Lucy Skipwith to John Cocke, Hopewell Plantation, May 30, 1856; see Miller, 1978, p. 206)

On July 5, 1856, Skipwith's dispirited comments about the future of her infant school not only show how difficult her challenges were and how seriously she took them, but how genuine was her concern for her students, children who physically and psychologically suffered more than their share of adult burdens. One of the children had died the day that she wrote to Cocke, and several children had died during the week from various fevers and illnesses. At the time of her letter, she predicted that several children yet suffering from an outbreak of a disease she did not name in her letters may not last through the week. In another reference to dismal school attendance for the foregoing and other reasons related to the children's labor on the plantation, Skipwith wrote:

> I am very much disincuraged with the pressant prospsect of my school it seems to be falling every day. In week days I hardly ever have more than two Children and they are very small, and at my night schooll there is so many of them and I have them such a little while that it is little that I can learn them. (Letter from Lucy Skipwith to John Cocke, Hopewell Plantation, July 5, 1856; see Miller, 1978, pp. 208–209)

Skipwith continued this message, however, on a brighter note, admitting that "my greatest Chance to learn them is on the sabbath. my sabbath school goes on very beautiful" (see Miller, 1978, p. 209). Regardless of how many times Lucy expressed her sense of failure, for the most part she wrote about the achievements of the children with pride, referring to them as her little scholars. For example, she was proud when at a regional religious revival the Hopewell plantation children compared favorably to other children in the area in their reading and reciting of Bible scripture (Letter from Lucy Skipwith to John Cocke, Hopewell Plantation, November 11, 1854; see Miller, 1978, p. 197). On one early occasion, Lucy told Cocke:

> I am going on with my school as usual, and my Children are still improveing. as they are going on reading so well, I am Teaching them to write, and some of them can make letters very well. I am inhope that some of them will write by the time you come out here I keeps up a night school for the instruction of the Children that work out in the Farm. they seem to improve very slow in reading, but they improve makeing figures very much and they seem to have a great love of it. (Letter from Lucy Skipwith to John Cocke, Hopewell Plantation, May 19, 1855; see Miller, 1978, p. 198)

In 1863, in the midst of the Civil War, Skipwith faced other problems in keeping her school operating regularly, one of which involved her personal safety. The overseer, Smith, gave up his job and moved away to attend a nearby college (Miller, 1978). Without a steady overseer on the plantation, Skipwith was wary. She worried about the safety of her students and herself if she continued to hold daily classes. About this she wrote, "some white people in the neighborhood has said that they would punish me if they caught me at it," and Skipwith went on to add that she was "afraid to carry it on [the Sabbath school] unless some grown white man was liveing [t]here." Lucy concluded her thoughts on the whole matter writing, "I will commence Teaching again as soon as this talk dies out" (Letter from Lucy Skipwith to John Cocke, Hopewell Plantation, August 15, 1863; see Miller, 1978, p. 254).

Besides discussing how well her own children and the other children in her charge were doing in school, Skipwith's monthly letters contained a wide array of other themes. An ever-present topic in her writing was her daily ritual of reading of the Bible aloud. She gathered families, including her own, every morning for what was called family prayers, and read aloud a passage from the Bible, then led the group in prayers and singing. Apparently this was an early morning practice encouraged in religious instructional manuals and reinforced by some slaveholders; this practice appears in other accounts. Lucy was placed in charge of family prayers and therefore often listed in her reports to Cocke those chapters of the Bible that were read during a given time period. For the month of August 1854, for example, Skipwith read aloud from Matthew chapter fifteen to the third chapter of Luke. By November 1854, it appears that she had read aloud from where she left off to the fourth chapter of John. The following year, 1855, as mentioned earlier, Skipwith read aloud the book *Pilgrim's Progress* to the plantation children. It is likely that she read popular literature for her own enjoyment as much as for the enjoyment of the children.

In addition to her writing about her reading aloud, Lucy wrote about planting matters and referred to newspaper reports on the extent of damage to local crops from bad weather. She reported to Cocke on the damage to his crops and the crops of nearby plantations caused by storms. She commented on an unusual cold spell one growing season, stating that the "thermometer was at 48 and 50" much of the time and at other times it had been "cold enough to keep a fire going all day" (Letter from Lucy Skipwith to John Cocke, Hopewell Plantation, April 28, 1860; see Miller, 1978, p. 227). References to everyday literacy functions like reading a thermometer are present in her letters. Skipwith's letters, in fact, read like a good book. She did not write just to inform, but she regarded writing as a literary experience. In other words, Lucy Skipwith wrote because she loved writing, she read because she loved reading. What is more, her writing informed her reading and her reading in turn informed her writing. Had she written only to inform Cocke about the affairs of his estate, her letters would not be nearly as valuable as they undoubtedly are to future readers.

Skipwith also kept an account of the value of or prices received for livestock or farm goods either traded or sold (Miller, 1978). She kept track of the number of yards of cloth that was needed for the sewing of seasonal garments, informing Cocke of surpluses and shortages in her supplies and equipment. On one occasion she informed him that the sewing of seasonal garments for the plantation workers had to be delayed because the loom was in such disrepair that she would have to wait until it was either fixed or replaced (see Miller, 1978).

On May 30, 1861, Skipwith sent Cocke an article from the *Religious Herald* about the Hopewell plantation. The article, which had first appeared in another publication, was reprinted in the April 25, 1861, issue of the *Religious Herald* (see Miller, 1978). Even though the journalist Brame wrote in praise of the Hopewell plantation's Sabbath School run by Skipwith, Lucy criticized details in the article pertaining to the number of African Americans working the plantation. She wrote: "I send you a piece that Mr. Brame has had published in the R.H. about this plantation, thinking you may not have seen it" (see Miller, 1978, p. 237). She went on to tell Cocke that the article contained some insignificant inaccuracies: one being that Brame had miscounted the number of people working on the Hopewell plantation.

Since this was such a minor error, one wonders what Lucy's real intentions were in her letter to Cocke. Given Lucy Skipwith's wit and sarcasm, as will be demonstrated later, it may well be that she was not as put out with the *Religious Herald* journalist's error as much as she let on. Instead, maybe she actually wrote Cocke to inform him about the article, on the chance that he really did not see or hear about it—consider the underlying meaning of the words "thinking you may not have seen it." Sending the letter to Cocke, it appears, was her way of ensuring that he did indeed read the article and could make a comment at a later time, without her having to come right out and say what she wanted him to know. Keeping in mind that the article she sent to Cocke was a reprint, she obviously felt that it was about time her efforts were acknowledged by Cocke.

It could also be that she wanted to tell him that the only reason the school was mentioned in the first place was that she, Lucy Skipwith, was doing such an excellent job that her efforts were applauded once again in a widely read newspaper, yet she had not heard from him regarding his thoughts on the matter. According to Miller (1978), Cocke thought himself to be a religious man. It is very possible that he purchased a subscription to this popular periodical for each of his residences. If so, it is unlikely that he had not seen or heard about the newspaper story that made public Skipwith's accomplishments and the success of his plantation school; perhaps Skipwith's note was little more than a jab on her part. Given her wit and humor, that she might have written to let him know she was aware that he must have known about the article and yet had failed to comment on it or otherwise acknowledge and praise her work and fame is quite likely.

Humor, sarcasm, sadness, anger, and other emotions were discernible in her letters. On several occasions, she made sarcastic quips about the work habits of one man on the plantation who always, in her opinion, managed to do less than his share of work. She also wrote about the lives and deaths of other slaves and conflicts between individuals. In one letter, for example, she wrote that an elderly worker, Shadrack, died in his room on July 30, 1855. She reported that he had "gone to bed as usual and died about midnight with his Bible across his chest opened to his favorite passage, the 20th chapter of the acts" (Letter from Lucy Skipwith to John Cocke, Hopewell Plantation, August 28, 1855; see Miller, 1978, p. 203). The foregoing quote raises interesting questions about Lucy's motives for writing. Does she write solely to inform Cocke of Shadrack's death and his steadfast religious devotion, or to show that Lucy, in accordance with Cocke's expectations of her, has maintained a pious community? She was expected to do so and being in charge of the souls of so many meant that she had to make sure they were able to read the Bible for themselves; it was because of her efforts that many of the families could read. It is difficult to know. It does, however, suggest in yet another form that Lucy Skipwith, like most writers, wrote for multiple purposes related to life, death, work, love, learning, eating, nature, and a multitude of other human matters.

When the overseer, whom Skipwith had later influenced Cocke to dismiss, threatened to harm her if she continued to send letters about him to Cocke, Skipwith promptly and angrily wrote to Cocke telling him about the man's behavior (Miller, 1978). She added a damaging note about the morality of the overseer's wife, too, because the woman had suggested that her husband give Lucy 500 lashes for writing letters about them and then refusing to show them the letters (Miller, 1978). Lucy knew that any question of immoral behavior on his plantation would incite an angry and swift response from Cocke who wanted to be known for his piety. She therefore gave Cocke information about the overseer's wife that she knew would surely lead to dismissal of the overseer (see Miller, 1978). She wrote not only that the woman couldn't control her own children who ran wild and were rude and disrespectful to their own mother, but also to condemn the overseer's wife's foul language and her habit of chewing tobacco and taking laudanum. Laudanum was an addictive narcotic in the form of a tonic made from opium and alcohol and taken for what, Lucy decided, were questionable medicinal purposes. Skipwith's complaints eventually led to the overseer's dismissal from the Cocke plantation and the hiring of Smith (Letter from Lucy Skipwith to John Cocke, Hopewell Plantation, July 28, 1859; see Miller, 1978, p. 223).

Skipwith, with characteristic dignity and grace, intervened on behalf of her daughter, Betsey. A teenager, Betsey was to be sold because her behavior at one point had caused gossip among those in the slave and slaveholder communities. Cocke decided to sell Betsey as an example to others because he did not like the idea of scandal. Betsey had created numerous problems before, but was forgiven, presumably because she was Lucy's daughter (see Miller, 1978). Just when Cocke had made up his mind to sell Betsey and Lucy realized he would not change his mind, Lucy presented him with a logical alternative to his original plan that involved the nursing care of her aging parents who lived on another Cocke plantation (see Miller, 1978).

In a series of letters, Skipwith convinced Cocke that if he was indeed determined to send her daughter away from Hopewell, it would be to his advantage to send her only as far as his other plantation so that she could take care of Lucy's ailing parents (see Miller, 1978). Lucy made the case that sending her daughter to take care of her aging parents would be a wise decision. Betsey, Lucy argued, could replace her grandmother's labor, and, at the same time, no one else from the labor force on the other plantation would be needed to care for the elderly couple. In the end, it was agreed that Betsey would be sold, but kept within the confines of the Cocke family's plantation, and so Betsey left the Hopewell plantation (see Miller, 1978). This practice of replacing labor often served to settle arrangements for elderly slaves, a form of social security and a practice upheld by slaveholders who would otherwise sell aging elderly slaves or turn them out after a life time of servitude to live on their own. Families used this practice to hold on to and care for their loved ones. Frederick Douglass wrote about his memories of the misery of the practice of *turning out* and told of the grievous consequences for victims and their familes (Douglass, 1993).

Skipwith and Smith treated the plantation's sick or injured people. Therefore, having found a medical book in Cocke's medicine chest, Lucy became interested and shared it with the overseer. They both read it before treating people and administering medicines. In a letter to Cocke, Skipwith wrote that she appreciated having found the book and, in the same sentence, she coyly asked Cocke whether he was planning to continue running the plantation without a doctor (Letter from Lucy Skipwith to John Cocke, Hopewell Plantation, April 28, 1860; see Miller, 1978, p. 228). This was a wise decision. Cocke must have soon answered her question, for in subsequent letters Lucy's discussions included mention of a local doctor's visits to plantation women and children (Letter from Lucy Skipwith to John Cocke, Hopewell Plantation, July 21, 1860; see Miller, 1978, p. 231).

Without question, literacy was a tool Lucy Skipwith used well to successfully guarantee her position as an indispensable servant, authoritative figure, and effective leader to her family, the other slave families, and the slaveholder (Miller, 1978). In turn, she used her influence to protect the well-being and enhance the intellectual development of her family and other enslaved families on the Cocke plantation (Miller, 1978). Skipwith's greatest contribution is her life as an example of a nineteenth-century parent, writer, reader, and teacher. Lucy's behaviors are telling with regard to the role of a strong, capable parent or a significant adult within the community assuming leadership and authority to create a literate environment for themselves and their families.

If the account of the Skipwith family's literacy tradition ended with Lucy Skipwith, her children and grandchildren, her students and their parents who lived on the Hopewell plantation, it would be only half-told. Too much would be unexamined because reading and writing behaviors studied in only one setting cannot fully explain a literacy tradition, nor can generalizations be made about the reading and writing behaviors observed in only one setting. To offer a multidimensional, holistic explanation of African Americans' literacy traditions, this examination must be continued in order to demonstrate that the reading and writing behaviors observed in the setting of the Hopewell plantation were indeed the foundations for the Skipwith family literacy traditions. To do this, it is necessary to ask whether these behaviors existed outside of the environment first examined. It is important to determine whether literacy remained a part of the lives of the people once they left the confines of the plantation and the constraints of slavery. At this point, therefore, it is important to continue with this investigation to see how well their traditions stood up to cultural strains imposed by the passing of time and changes of environment.

Continuing the account of this family's literacy history away from the Hopewell plantation, and accounts of others like them, can serve to strengthen the argument that literacy traditions are primarily developed, supported, and transmitted through the institution of the family, regardless of where that family, because of social or historical circumstances, resides. The Skipwith family's worldview, which shaped their ways of thinking and behaving, including how they educated and disciplined their children, built their homes, and made their livings was formed by their African heritage and their experiences in America.

It will be argued here that when the Skipwiths and other families like them moved away from the Hopewell plantation and similar settings with their worldviews firmly and fully intact, they reestablished their way of life in their new land. In doing so, they brought with them what was most important to the continuation of their established family lives, including their literacy traditions. The Skipwiths and the other families who went to Liberia in the mid-1800s recreated their communities in Africa, giving their settlements names such as Maryland. The capital of Liberia, in honor of President James Monroe, was named Monrovia. Similarly, streets in Petersburg, Virginia were named in honor of Joseph J. Roberts, the first African American governor and later the first elected president of the Republic of Liberia (Jackson, 1927). There was a constant flow of communication between families separated only by distance. This flow of communication between families is evident not only in their letters, which are discussed below, but also in the African American institutions that they recreated.

African American social and cultural institutions that were created in America to promote and support families' educational efforts were promptly reestablished in their new home, using the same organizational names, constitutions, activities, and the like. If the Skipwith family literacy tradition along with the literacy traditions of other African American families survived, then evidence of this would most certainly have to be demonstrated in their literacy histories in the first years of their migration when the traditions were most likely to be robust and relatively unaffected by time or other strains. It is in this moment that one might truly and clearly see the defining characteristics of their family literacy tradition.

Some of the Skipwiths who were manumitted in the early 1830s emigrated to Liberia. They wrote letters back to America to keep in touch with their relatives, friends, and former slaveholders. The continuation of this African American family's literacy traditions and those of extended family members and other families most likely known to the Skipwiths are discussed in this section. The significance of their literacy stories is that they kept their legacy of literacy vital through their commitment to reading and writing and as a result of the integral nature of literacy in their family life, regardless of the passage of time, changes in environment, and the natural attrition of family members.

The Skipwith family who left for Liberia in 1833 was headed by Peyton (Lucy's younger brother) and Lydia Skipwith. It appears that they took along with them their six children, Diana, Felicia, Martha, Matilda, Napoleon, and Nash. One of their daughters, six-year-old Felicia, however, fell victim to cholera aboard the ship *Zebra* before reaching Liberia. By some accounts, Felicia, while aboard the ship, accidentally fell on a large nail that pierced her leg and led to a serious and infection that may have precipitated her bout with cholera. Extended family members who later joined the Skipwith family included the Faulcons, Cannons, Sterdivants, and the Nicholases (Miller, 1978; Wiley, 1980).

Because Peyton Skipwith was a stonemason by trade, he and his family were joined, in January 1838, by sixteen-year-old John Hartwell Faulcon, who had been apprenticed to him. Soon after, Faulcon's mother, Susan Faulcon, arrived in Liberia along with her other son, George. Her young daughter Agnes, like Skipwith's daughter, apparently did not survive the arduous voyage. At the time of Susan Faulcon's arrival, other members of the Skipwith extended family came to settle in the West African colony. Robert Leander Sterdivant and his three children, Diana, Rose, and William Leander, arrived in Liberia on June 7, 1842, aboard the *Maripose*. Along with that group came Sterdivant's brothers, Peter Jones and Richard Cannon. Skipwith's cousins, James Nicholas and Julia Nicholas of Norfolk, Virginia, came also. Julia Nicholas was said to have been a permanent member of the Skipwith household (see Miller, 1978). All of the mentioned emigrants had been formerly enslaved by the Cocke family; John Cocke and his sister Sarah Faulcon manumitted them and supported their emigration to Liberia (Miller, 1978; Wiley, 1980).

In the first few years of their arrival, the two oldest Skipwith children, Matilda and Diana, were schooled at home by Peyton Skipwith. When Baptist missionary schools were established, Matilda attended formal school while the younger children remained at home to be schooled by their father. By 1837, four of the Skipwith children were enrolled in formal schools (Letters from Peyton Skipwith to John Cocke, Monrovia; see Miller, 1978, pp. 61, 66, 72, 74). Diana and Nash were sent to a Baptist missionary school run by Mr. Lewis Johnson. Johnson was, in Diana's opinion, "very studious," and "one of the best school masters in the town." (Letter from Diana Skipwith to Sally Cocke, Monrovia, August 24, 1837; see Miller, 1978, p. 87). Matilda and Napoleon, who were older, were sent to a Baptist missionary elementary school that was run by Mrs. Ivens (see Miller, 1978, p. 87).

John Faulcon enrolled in a Methodist missionary preparatory school, financed by the Ladies Benevolent Society of New York City. Mr. B. V. R. James was in charge of the school. By 1849, Faulcon was enrolled in the Alexander Classical High School (Miller 1978; Wiley, 1980). This school, financed by the Board of Foreign Missions of the Presbyterian Church, was also based in New York (Wiley, 1980). The Alexander Classical High School director, H. W. Ellis, was a former slave who grew up in Virginia and Tennessee and had lived as a young man in Alabama. He developed scholarly interests early in life and was literate in English, Greek, and Latin. Ellis, accompanied by his wife and daughter, was sent to Liberia in 1847 as a missionary. His mission was to establish a high school. This he did, and the school was opened in 1847 (Wiley, 1980). By 1849, the same year that Faulcon said he enrolled, Ellis reported that he had at that time some "16 promising students, whom [he had] been teaching ever since January 1, 1849" (Letter from H. W. Ellis to Reverend William McLain, Monrovia, November 20, 1849; see Miller, 1978, p. 228).

In the first years of the school, it appears that students such as Faulcon attended school from 8:30 A.M. to 2:00 P.M. Ellis stated that the students were involved in classroom instruction for about five hours a day. The students, Ellis reported, were given a short recess from the classroom and a longer afternoon break from the school building each day. Ellis estimated that most of the students studied on their own for one or two hours and, therefore, spent seven to eight hours a day involved in school work. Ellis reported that the students were excellent learners and had "read through the Historia Sacrae, . . . Greek, besides other sciences" (Letter from H. W. Ellis to Reverend William McLain, Monrovia, November 20, 1849; see Wiley, 1980, p. 228).

Peyton Skipwith's letters covered a wide range of topics, including agriculture, the price of farm products and livestock, the educational progress of the Skipwith children and that of John Faulcon, along with news regarding his stone masonry business. His services were much in demand as, he wrote, he was the only master stonemason in the colony. Skipwith's letter was corroborated by other letters to ACS in which writers mentioned that more stonemasons were needed because Monrovia's only stonemason's construction schedule was so crowded that they expected delays in the building of a particular school. Skipwith's letters reflected his reading interests. He was a man burdened with the difficulties of forging a living with his hands, raising and educating his family, serving as a master stonemason to young apprentices, taking care of his sickly wife, and at the same time coping with all the hardships expected in living in a new nation. He leaned on religion to define his emotions and actions. It is not clear whether this was because he was a religious man or because his writing reflected common nineteenth-century parlance, or both. It could also be that the Skipwith and Cocke families both used this type of language when writing because the colonization movement was seen to be a civilizing, religious mission that was to bring Christianity to Africa. Given the serious, emotional content of his letters, it is probably a combination of all of these underlying reasons that account for the letters' linguistic style and content. His comments often contained references to the Bible and he used quotes from the Bible to punctuate his statements. On the death of his daughter Felicia, for example, he referred to the Book of Job. He wrote: "I have lost Felicia but I thank god that our loss is hur gain as Job Sais the lord gave and he taketh I thank god that he has mad it possible that we may meet to part no more" (Letter from Peyton Skipwith to John Cocke, Monrovia, February 10, 1834; see Miller, 1978, p. 58).

Peyton Skipwith's letters provide an inside look at his family life. His writings suggest ways that the family used literacy to maintain and protect their way of life. In his June 25, 1846, letter, Skipwith wrote to Cocke,

> You desired to know whither we stood in kneed of Bibles. this we do not kneed so much as we do other Books. we have

> aplenty of bibles here. . . . If you [want to] you can send some valuable Books for my family such as History . . . writing paper [and] quills. (Miller, 1978, p. 83)

In March 1835, Skipwith wrote about the death of Lydia, his wife, stating "I lost my wife she died on July 2d 1834" (Miller, 1978, p. 59). Skipwith also wrote about his own failing health. Apparently, he was going blind and suffered from pains associated with laying stone, making it difficult to run his business without the aid of his son, Nash.

Skipwith and his wife sent their children to school regularly, and they were pleased that the children did well. The children also attended Sunday school (Letter from Peyton Skipwith to John Cocke, Monrovia, May 20, 1839; see Miller, 1978, p. 79). Skipwith appeared also to be satisfied with his apprentice, John Faulcon. He wrote that Faulcon was learning the stonemason trade well and that the young man "upon the whole [was] a very fine boy, and suit[ed him] well." He continued on with his praise of his apprentice to say that he thought John Faulcon would, "if he continues thus, make a useful man" (Letter from Peyton Skipwith to John Cocke, Monrovia, April, 27, 1841; see Miller, 1978, p. 79). It is difficult to know Skipwith's feelings toward Faulcon, whether Skipwith is truly proud of Faulcon or he is just reporting progress. He acknowledges academic progress on the part of Faulcon, but seems to be reserved, if not cool, in his appraisal of him as an apprentice stonemason. His use of the word *if* makes one wonder. It could be that Faulcon was more interested in academics than he was in the stonemason business, as might be inferred from a letter he wrote to Cocke in which he does not really mention his work with Skipwith or a future in stone masonry. He may have agreed to go to Liberia ostensibly to learn a trade under Skipwith, but in truth wanted to take advantage of educational opportunities unavailable to him in the States.

On the other hand, it might be that again Cocke, as with others in his position, manumitted slaves with a missionary zeal to bring Christianity to Africa, making it necessary to stress the ability to read the Bible as instrumental to that goal in conjunction with working hard with one's hands. The foregoing may in part explain underlying attitudes in the letters.

For whatever the causes, in addition to asking if the families were in need of Bibles, it appears that Cocke had asked Skipwith about Faulcon's academic progress. In response, Skipwith must have asked

Faulcon to write to Cocke, thinking that in this way Cocke could make his own judgment. Faulcon apparently complied and mailed the following note:

> Dear Sir: By this you May Learn that I am well. . . . In your last letter to Mr. Skipwith I was informed that you wanted to See my hand writeing and composietion. This you May take for granted to be my own writeing. I have joined the Classical School under Revd. Mr. H.W. Elles. Also I am a member of the Junior debating Socity. Last Febuary I delived an address on chimesty. . . . I just bought a Lot few weeks ago. Now I am about to put me up a Small house if the Lord Spares me Longenugh. . . . John H. Faulcon . . .
>
> My Love to Mother sisters Brother aunts and uncles friends also every Body on your plntation. (Letter from John H. Faulcon to John H. Cocke, November 22, 1849; see Miller, 1978, p. 6)

Evidence that Peyton Skipwith's children, Diana, Matilda, and Nash, were indeed readers and writers is seen in their own writings over an extended period. Diana wrote letters to the family and friends who remained in America. Her father was a constant subject of her letters along with news about her brothers and sisters. She wrote about the educational advances in the colony, telling about its four then recently established schools, and she talked about the her brothers' and sisters' missionary school education. She also wrote of her own writing and inquired about the Hopewell plantation school. She specifically asked about the handwriting of her friend and cousin Betsy Moore as a hint that Betsy should take the time to write to her. It also appears that she like Faulcon wrote to provide a writing sample of her academic progress. It could be that she was asked to do this. She wrote:

> Please to rite me a word if the school is goin now and if Betsy can rit good and tell her that she would send her love to me if noth[ing] els. . . . This is some of my one hand riting. Do yo think I improv or not? (Letter from Diana Skipwith to Sally Cocke, Monrovia, August 24, 1837; see Miller, 1978, p. 87)

In another letter, Diana wrote:

> Tell betsy that I reseave the hankerchief. Tel her for me if that was her hand riting She can right wel enough to rite to me for I dos want to get a letter from her verry bad. (Letter from Diana Skipwith to Louisana Maxwell Holmes, May 8, 1838, Monrovia; see Miller, 1978, p. 90)

By 1840, Diana, still a student, taught Sunday school for the Baptist church. Her letters reflected her interests in vegetable gardening, growing fruits, local newspaper stories, and family gossip. She inquired about the well-being of her loved ones in Virginia and asked about Betsy's pending marriage plans. She wrote a catalogue of the customs of the indigenous people of Liberia and sent it to Sally Cocke, John Cocke's daughter. On a number of occasions, she sent Sally seeds that she had collected and packaged. She wrote descriptions of the contents of the packets and detailed instructions on how best to plant and care for the seeds, advising that if her instructions were followed carefully the seeds would grow well and that the Virginian climate would be suitable for raising the African plants. She also sent copies of a speech delivered in Monrovia by African American educator Edward Wilmot Blyden (originally from the West Indies). The speech was most likely sponsored by the Dr. Blyden Literary Union, a literary society founded by African Americans and later reestablished in Monrovia (Johnson, 1906). Additionally, Diana enclosed in her father's correspondence several editions of two different newspapers, the *Liberia Herald* and the *African Luminary*, both founded and printed in Liberia. Finally, she regularly requested writing paper because so little was available in Monrovia (Letter from Peyton Skipwith to John Cocke, Monrovia, November 11, 1839; see Miller, 1978, p. 72).

Skipwith's daughter Matilda wrote many letters, dated from October 23, 1844, to February 23, 1861, to family and friends in Virginia. Having lived with much tragedy in her life, Matilda wrote letters that seem gloomy compared to those of her sister Diana. Matilda was married to Samuel Lomax, and together they had three children, Lydia Ann, Eliza, and Adala. She occasionally mentioned their reading and writing progress, but only in the briefest of terms, in which she simply stated that she sent them to school and that they were quickly learning to read and write, rarely much more than those few words. Her letters tell about the deaths of family members living in Liberia, which included her first husband; her second husband;

her father, Peyton Skipwith; and her beloved sister, Diana (Letter from Matilda Lomax to Sally Cocke Brent, October 23, 1844; see Miller, 1978, pp. 100, 101; Letter from Matilda Lomax to John Cocke, Monrovia, September 30, 1850; see Miller, 1978, p. 105). She sent news of the death of her uncle and Peyton Skipwith's brother, Eramus. Eramus Skipwith, according to Miller (1978), could read and write. It appears that, however, he had either grown too ill from aging to write on his own or was perhaps otherwise disabled, because Matilda wrote that he had dictated to her five of his latest letters sent to Virginia (Miller, 1978). Matilda also wrote about her teaching activities, as well as news of armed conflicts between African American colonists and the indigenous people of Liberia.

Nash Skipwith, Peyton's oldest son, took over his father's stonemason business when Peyton Skipwith died in October 1849 (Letter from Nash Skipwith to John Cocke, Monrovia, November 2, 1849; see Wiley, 1980, p. 68). Although a young bachelor, Nash, it appears, undertook responsibility for educating his sister Matilda's children after the death of her second husband, as well as three of his siblings from his father's second marriage (Letter from Nash Skipwith to Mrs. John Cocke, Monrovia, November 2, 1849; see Miller, 1978, p. 96). On behalf of himself and the children, Nash Skipwith wrote the following request:

> Writing Paper and Some Steel Pens and Some In Velps with Gilted Edges. . . . 1 Large Dictionary, Webster; first and 2d, 3d, 4 Volum of Alison History and other such Valubil Books as will soote my studdy. . . . I would Rather have this book than to have the other things for my convientcy but I hope you will Send them all, for god Sacke. Yours, Nash Skipwith. (Letter from Nash Skipwith to General John Cocke, Monrovia, May 15, 1851; see Miller, 1978, p. 98)

In January of the following year Matilda writes that her brother Nash, like his father before him, had died on October 27, 1852, from a three-day illness brought about from a condition related to his work as a stonemason, one she referred to as "a strain in lifting a rock" (Wiley, 1980, p. 73).

From the beginning of Liberia's creation in the early 1800s through the time the Skipwiths lived there, reading and writing materials had been among the first families' most requested items: "Next to livelihood, health, and religion, learning seem[ed] to have been their greatest concern" (Wiley, 1980, p. 101). Nash's letter is exemplary of many settlers' written requests. The complete title of the history book written by Alison that Nash Skipwith referred to in his May 15, 1851, letter was *History of Europe from the Commencement of the French Revolution in 1789 to the Restoration of the Bourbons in 1815*. Its four volumes were written by Sir Archibald Alison and published in the years 1842 to 1844 by Harper and Brothers in New York (Wiley, 1980). As can be seen, at the time of Nash's request, the book was a relatively recent publication, being not yet a decade old. Reading, it would appear, was an ongoing interest and activity while in Liberia.

The foregoing account suggests many answers to the questions asked earlier in the study regarding the specific ways the African American family was important to the development of their literacy traditions, the underlying motivations for reading and writing, and the nature of their literacy traditions themselves. The role of the family in the development of their literacy traditions as it has been illustrated in the example of the Skipwith family, suggests that family life was indeed a catalyst for reading and writing activities. Family members took active roles in educating their children and the children of extended family members. One can infer, by their actions and words, their underlying motives for learning to read and write and the nature of their behaviors or the function of literacy in their lives. Literacy functioned to enrich and give meaning to their lives, as a tool for academic growth, and as a form of leisure activity. In addition, literacy was a means to keep in touch with family and to strengthen family bonds, all of which is evident in the ways these family members made regular academic progress, wrote letters, and read novels, textbooks, and newspapers as part of their daily lives.

Just as the Skipwiths and members of their extended family transported their literacy traditions with them to their new homes, other families who settled in the now-expanded African American community demonstrated through their words and behavior that they too continued their efforts in the making of their literacy tradition. Others demonstrate that they also carried along with them their reading and writing values, interests, and attitudes.

Skipwith's relatives, and families probably known to the Skipwiths, apparently also enjoyed reading to be informed, as a recreational activity, and for intellectual stimulation and growth. A boy, Daniel W. Nelson, wrote a letter to a Charles Andrews for his mother,

Peggy Potter of Monrovia. On the same piece of paper, Nelson wrote another letter, this time on his own behalf and addressed it to Andrews's wife Sarah. He told Sarah about his schooling and requested the following materials: "smiths geography, smiths Arithmatic smiths grammar and some Pencils and a slate and some Pens and paper and Ink. . . . send some books of all kinds" (Letters from Peggy Potter and Daniel W. Nelson to Charles Andrews and Sarah Andrews, December 29, 1847; see Wiley, 1980, pp.104–105).

This thank-you note for books received was sent to Virginia:

> We also received the books which you sent, Thos that were in the box & a packet of some very interesting readers. . . . we do severally and jointly send our thanks to you for your bountiful kindness to us all. Uncle Robert, father, uncle John, Peter & myself were all Present when the books were distributed. John Page, Junior, uncle Robert's eldest son . . . Thomas Parker, . . . my brother . . . all got books. (Letter from Solomon S. Page to Charles W. Andrews, Monrovia, April 22, 1849; see Wiley, 1980, p. 105)

Solomon's uncle, Robert M. Page, the man referred to in the foregoing letter, had at another time requested, in his words, "a family medical book" that would help him better understand a type of medical treatment called Tom Seigun that was, at the time he wrote, popular among laypeople (Wiley, 1980, p. 112). Samuel Thompson popularized the treatment in America in the book *A New Guide to Health*, published in 1822 (Wiley, 1980). Page's son John who, as his letters imply, had been suffering from a long-term illness was also interested in health books, and judged that "some good Books such as an Family medical Book on Tom sowign . . . would be more usefull than real doctor medicine" (Letter from Solomon S. Page to Charles W. Andrews, Monrovia, April 22, 1849; see Wiley, 1980, p. 112). That is a strong statement on the role of reading in this man's life. In the same correspondence, he expressed his thanks for books he had already received, which included the following titles: *The Life of Reverend John Newton Doddridge*, *Rise and Progress*, *Life of Solomon*, and *City Cousin* (Miller, 1978, p. 112). Families also requested pamphlets, magazines, and newspapers. Like Diana Skipwith, others attended public lectures and obtained copies of the lectures.

Henry B. Stewart, a carpenter and a minister from Savannah, Georgia who had emigrated to Liberia, demonstrated a strong commitment to education. He, his wife, and their eight children left from Savannah for Liberia May 14, 1849. They arrived, having traveled aboard the ship *Huma*, on June 27 of that year. Stewart, like the Skipwiths, Faulcons, Ellises, and others mentioned, came ashore a firm believer in education and reading as a family activity. "My children," he later wrote, "are all going to school and are doing well, 4 of them are making Rapid progress in grammar and Geograph[y] & Atlas, Aritmatick & other parts of learning" (Letter from Henry B. Stewart to Reverend William McLain, Monrovia, October 20, 1849; see Wiley, 1980, p. 283).

In another correspondence Stewart again wrote of the progress of his children and told the reader that the settlement had "Som very good teacher so far as they can go. . . . We like to go farther in our Studies . . ." (Letter from Henry B. Stewart to Reverend William McLain, Monrovia, September 20, 1950; see Wiley, 1980, p. 284). In 1860, Stewart and his wife sent their fifteen-year-old son, Thomas Stewart, back to America to be educated at Oberlin College in Ohio.

Just as they must have done before they came to settle in their new home, Stewart, his wife, and their children filled part of their leisure time reading magazines, newspapers, and books sent to them from American friends and Baptist church missionaries. In the excerpt below, Stewart specifically named the *African Repository* as one of his favorite newspapers. He suggested that reading was an activity his family had always enjoyed, which further lends support to the inference that the family's reading and writing traditions were well established before they arrived. In a thank-you letter for reading materials sent, Stewart wrote:

> The Papers & Reposatory Came Safe via Monrovia, Per Schooner Lark in advance of the Stevens. Myself and family are all in the Enjoyment of good health; may it find you the Same . . . it is indeed a very great Satisfaction To me for the variety of inteligences in these paper & more Especily So as my family is Large and is very fond Reading. . . . All the Reposatory has been Received, and I herewith Send my Subscri[ption] for the present year, $1.00. (Letter from Henry B.

> Stewart to Ralph R. Gurley, Monrovia, August 10, 1860; see Wiley, 1980, pp. 302, 304)

In another letter, Stewart mentioned a donation of 224 books to his church from the Massachusetts Sabbath School Society. Stewart, at one point, appeared to be seriously concerned over the fact that schools for emigrant children had been established in his area, but no schools existed for indigenous children. Having earlier established the Congregational Church in Greenville, Liberia, Stewart requested aid from the Baptist church that sponsored his settlement in Liberia to help establish a school, to be run by his church, for the indigenous children in his area. He had also sent away for "books and papers mail and newspapers, the *Independent*, *New York* and the *New England Puritan*, and the *Boston*" (Miller, 1978, pp. 298–299). He asked that the materials be sent by way of the British route while apologizing by saying, "I know that that Rout is Expensive but it [the newspapers, books, and papers] will serve to Enliven & Cher the minds of my Congregation" (Miller, 1978, p. 290). It can be assumed that he meant that the reading materials would be used for intellectual as well as leisure activities by church members who were a long way from their homes.

Stewart promoted literacy among members of his Congregational Church through church-initiated and -supported social and educational programs. As pastor of the Congregational Church, he adhered to the current religious belief that salvation could come only to those who were able to read God's words for themselves. This is explicit in the following:

> I am happy to Say that many of our brethern in the ministry Labours to impress upon the mind of their People that a Right & corect Knowledge of Divine truth is essential to Salvation. This is strick conformity to the commission given by the great head of the Church, Go ye therefor and teach all nations, teaching them to observe all things whatsoever I have Commanded you. . . . The Prospects Cheers our hearts for the future when we See the Unitired Effort put forth by the Citizens in their Pesevarance in the Literary instruction of their Children. The Sabbath Schools of all our Churches will testify that our aim is to perpetuate the Blessings and knowledge of Christian Religion to our Children. (Letter

from Henry B. Stewart to Ralph R. Gurley, Monrovia, July 16, 1858; see Miller, 1978, p. 301)

Stewart continued his letter by noting that churches in the area were beginning to offer educational opportunities to indigenous children and that many were making rapid progress in their "Second Syllable & Repeats the Lord's Prayer" (Miller, 1978, p. 301). Apparently, the Sunday schools were using an alphabetic method to teach reading and the Bible as instructional reading material. This method was widely used in America beginning during the Colonial period.

In a subsequent letter, Stewart wrote that his church school and Sabbath school had received donations from various friends and organizations in New York, Massachusetts, and Rhode Island. He had received those that appear on his following list:

> 150 Bibles & testaments . . . Arithetic, Grammars, Dictionarys, Speling Books . . . 6 Volumes of henry's Commentary . . . 50 plymouth hymn Book and Sabbath School Collection, Punchard Views of Congregationalism, the Congregation[al] Quarterly, Vol. 1, Lock Compliation Book, Sermon of Dr. Preston, history of Christianity first three Centuries, and many others too numerous to name. (Letter from Henry B. Stewart to Reverend Ralph R. Gurley, Monrovia, August 10, 1860; see Miller, 1978, p. 302)

With regard to families in the Greenville settlement, Stewart wrote:

> The people of Greenville are By no means [unconcerned about education and They want to] improve the[ir] Deficency in Early Life. Corse of Lectures on Weake nights on Different Subjects of General interrest, on Domestic acconomy, on agriculture, Civil Government and the importance of Education . . . I was pleas in Lisening a few Evening ago to a very anamaty discussion. (Letter from Henry B. Stewart to Reverend William McLain, Monrovia, September 26, 1851; see Wiley, 1980, p. 287)

As can be concluded from the foregoing, ships such as the *St. Elizabeth* and the *Liberia Packet* regularly made stops in Liberia and with good reason. Letter writing was a must for emigrant families and their numerous sponsors who supported their settlement in Liberia, especially members of the ACS.

With regard to the families' needs, basic items, which included seeds, tools, cloth, building materials, and so forth, were either scarce or nonexistent in the settlements, so they depended upon goods imported from the States. Some exchanged coffee, palm oil, and other products for needed goods. Letter writing was, therefore, taken seriously because it was an important link to others across the distances. And letter writing took careful forethought on the part of the families.

Letters written and received by the Skipwiths, Pages, Potters, Stewarts, and others were at times carried by the English Postal Service, whose cargo ships did not always arrive and depart on fixed schedules and most likely made only two trips a year. However, the colony did have regular service since several vessels were available for the transportation of passengers, mail, and cargo (Johnson, 1906). African Americans' interest in the shipping services between Liberia and America in order to keep in touch with family members is implied in S. Wesley Jones' correspondence:

> I see in public journals a proposition laid before Congress by a gentleman from this State by the name of Bryan, for the building of four large steamers of the first class, to ply between Liberia and the parts of the United States, for the purposes of carrying the mails and passengers. (Letter from S. Wesley Jones to the *African Repository* XXVI, pp. 276–277; see Woodson, Monrovia, 1969, pp. 68–69)

Even with regular service, settlers would have had little notice of when a ship would depart, sometimes less than an hour or so; therefore, by habit, they always kept mail and packages ready and waiting to be carried to a ship. Carefully conceived and often lengthy messages that logged in detail their daily activities are testimonies to this. Also telling of the seriousness of their intent is that despite spelling and other mechanical errors, the letters bore a characteristic style and format, and they were generally well worded. Few nineteenth-century individuals were, in fact, capable of writing as well as those represented thus far (Robinson, 1977). Additionally, it should be noted that the wider American public did not generally meet today's standards for spelling and grammar because, for the most part, standards were not widely known. American standards of spelling and grammar and other conventions were recent innovations set by Noah Webster in his primers at the urging of Benjamin Franklin and others leaders concerned about the establishment of an American English standard distinguishable from British English (Kornfeld, 2001; Robinson, 1977). Quite often, several different spellings of certain words were found to be acceptable.

In addition to personal writing, the families also wrote letters to agents of the ACS and to editors of the *African Repository* and other periodicals to be considered for publication. They sent and received bundles of newspapers written and edited by African Americans. Diana Skipwith's husband Moore James and her brother Nash were at one time printers for the newspaper *Liberia Herald*, printed in Monrovia. The *Liberia Herald* was a newspaper founded by John Brown Russwurm, a well known African American journalist who cofounded America's first African American newspaper, *Freedom's Journal*, in 1827. Russwurm resigned from *Freedom's Journal* and immigrated to Liberia. Diana sent copies of that paper to Virginia. Settlers wrote advertisements to antislavery newspapers and periodicals, requesting the whereabouts of family members displaced by slavery and war in America. Offers to buy family members from slaveholders appeared in the ads of such papers. Reports to agents of the ACS and benevolent societies, which supported the colonization effort, were also regularly sent.

The amount of mail that was shipped between the African American community in Liberia and their family and friends in their former communities provides evidence of the strength of their literacy traditions. It also suggests that African American literacy was strongly linked to family life and that traditions were passed along from place to place and from one generation to the next. The specific ways in which the family served as a vehicle to transport that tradition is important to the basic questions asked in this study.

A rough inventory, taken in 1851, of the types and kinds of books available to settlers in Monrovia revealed that with regard to private family libraries, "nearly all those of Monrovia have tolerable libraries, and several have extensive libraries" (Miller, 1978, p. 229). The value they attached to written traditions can be seen in the pervasiveness of their ownership of reading materials. The same inventory is telling of the literacy values, interests, perceptions, and attitudes of nineteenth-century African Americans. It was observed that the majority of Monrovia's leading citizens were first-generation former slaves whose children were highly motivated to achieve. Liberian youth, who were the benefactors, if not the catalyst, of a growing intellectual climate in the early period, had been known to say that Liberia in its early development needed a highly educated citizenry and, therefore, "many . . . were . . . using every means in their power for intellectual development" (Miller, 1978, p. 229). Nineteenth-century youth encouraged by their elders placed a great deal of emphasis on education that was to go beyond that of their mothers and fathers who, in many cases, had received only a basic grammar school education (Letter from H. W. Ellis to Reverend William McLain, November 20, 1849; see Miller, 1978, p. 229).

Ellis wrote in his report to the ACS that, in his opinion, the children in the Monrovia area had the "best opportunity to equal" their literate counterparts living in America (Miller, 1978, p. 229). Among many things, his judgment was based on his inventory of books for public use within the Monrovia area. In this regard, he found that for the approximately 1,000 African Americans who lived in Monrovia at that time, there were a good number of books available. The Alexander Classical High School housed 2,000 works, which included "all kinds of books, maps, globes, philosophical aparatus." Among the three other schools he inventoried, two of the preparatory schools had about 150 books and the third had about "300 books of the best kind" (Miller, 1978, pp. 228–229).

It would appear, then, that reading and writing behaviors were very much a part of the daily lives of the African Americans discussed thus far. Moreover, it would appear that the literacy traditions that were already firmly in place prior to their leaving their former homes, like their other family traditions, survived the journey and continued to evolve.

Families such as the Skipwiths who emigrated from America to Africa and the Skipwiths who remained in Virginia have had similar family literacy histories in that the families made strong efforts to educate their children whether in Africa or in America. Susie King Taylor's family, particularly her maternal grandmother, strongly supported her education. Taylor was born a slave on August 6, 1848. Until she was seven years old, she lived with her parents, Hager Ann Reed and Raymond Baker, on the Isle of Wright, about 35 miles from Savannah, Georgia. Her mother asked permission for Susie to live in Savannah with her maternal grandmother, Dolly Reed. Reed, a free woman, was literate and made a modest living trading farm products, and doing laundry and housekeeping (Taylor, 1902).

After the Civil War, Reed managed to put money for her old age into the Freedmen's Savings Bank. Some of her earnings went to pay for Susie's education. Susie was sent everyday to the home of another free woman, Mrs. Woodhouse. Since African American schools in Georgia were illegal, Susie and the other 25 or 30 children attended secretly, walking through the streets one at a time, carrying their school books hidden from view. After studying for two years with her teacher Mrs. Woodhouse, Susie studied with an African American nun, Mary Beasley, and was later tutored by Mrs. Reed's landlord's son (Taylor, 1902).

Susie remembered that when she was a girl during the Civil War she saw posters hung in the streets of Savannah that depicted what she described as horrible portrayals of Yankees with words of warning to African Americans to the effect that the Yankees were like beasts and if African Americans were to side with them they would be slaughtered for food. Frightened, Susie asked her grandmother to explain the pictures and slogans. By some accounts, Taylor's grandmother was semiliterate. Notwithstanding, she did interpret the posters. She told Taylor that the Confederates did not want African Americans to join the side of the North, so they used propaganda to scare them. As a young adult, Taylor's interests led to her career as an army nurse and teacher in an African American regiment during the Civil War (Taylor, 1902).

Abram Middleton, freeman born in 1828 in South Carolina, was taught to read and write by his slave father. He went on to study at Baker's Institute in Charleston. He and his brother, Benjamin W. Middleton, served in the South Carolina House of Representatives (Holt, 1977).

A former slave, Edward W. Culberson was a dairy farmer who learned to read and write informally. His wife had received a formal education and worked as a school teacher after the Civil War. The decision of their son, Luther Porter Jackson, to become an educator was strongly influenced by his mother. Jackson earned a B.A. and an M.A. from Fisk University and a Ph.D. from the University of Chicago (Porter, 1950).

Christopher Harrison Payne was born in 1848 of free parents in Red Sulphur Springs, Monroe County, in a part of Virginia that is now West Virginia. His mother, who was born a slave, learned to read and write and was determined that Christopher also acquire the tools of literacy. Payne wrote that his mother taught him to read and write when he was very young. He recalls that by the age of ten he had read the entire New Testament (Penn, 1891; Simmons, 1986; Woodson, 1969).

Similarly, Frederick L. McGhee's father, Abraham McGhee, who was born a slave, was literate. McGhee freed himself and worked during the 1860s as a blacksmith in Aberdeen, Monroe County, Mississippi. McGhee's father taught him to read. Later McGhee moved from the South to Chicago and earned a law degree (Logan & Winston, 1982).

Another man, Benjamin Holmes, learned to read from his father. His mother offered Holmes monetary incentives to learn to write. She paid him a coin for he each letter of the alphabet he learned to form correctly (Blassingame, 1977).

Logan Oscar J. Dunn was born a slave in 1821 in Louisiana. His mother operated a boarding house in New Orleans. Dunn's mother paid residents of her house to teach Dunn basic reading and writing skills. Since the boarders of the Dunn house were theatrical people, scholars have assumed that Dunn may have learned from these people the art of oration, for which he became well-known. Dunn, a wealthy property owner who was involved in politics, became a leading figure in New Orleans society (Blassingame, 1977; Christian, 1945; Perkins, 1943).

Another prominent African American figure in the nineteenth century, Isaiah Montgomery, was taught to read by his father, Benjamin Montgomery. Isaiah's mother was also literate. Both of his parents held slave status; however, they lived as *half free*. Half free persons were those who worked for wages and paid a portion of their earnings to their slave owners. In Benjamin Montgomery's case, he purchased his wife's labor. She was then able to stay home with their children. She, therefore, schooled Isaiah and his siblings in their home, located above the Montgomery family business, a store. The family lived relatively privileged lives, free from the daily domination of their slaveholder. Isaiah was an excellent reader, and, as a young boy, his mother sent him to collect mail and newspapers for their family and other families in the area. Where they lived, mail was collected in a location that was best reached by boat. Isaiah took neighborhood friends, both black and white, along with him for the daily mail run. His friends rowed the boat while Isaiah read aloud the latest stories from the local newspapers. They enjoyed hearing the news before anyone else in the neighborhood could (Herman, 1988).

Similarly, James C. Farley's parents were slaves before the Civil War. The Farley family lived in Prince Edward County, Virginia. In the 1850s, Farley's mother was a storekeeper, and he played and worked alongside her during the day. His mother taught him to read, write, and perform basic arithmetic. She later allowed him to attend public schools that were available to African American youth during that time (Simmons, 1968).

Daniel Payne's childhood experiences in a supportive, literate environment shaped the course of his life. Payne was born in 1811 in South Carolina to free parents, London and Martha Payne. His parents died in 1820, leaving him in the care of his great-aunt. Payne's great-aunt sent him to a private school operated by free blacks in Charleston. He remembered that his parents held daily morning prayers and hymn singing. He maintained that his own love of literature and the desire to read the Bible and to become an avid reader stemmed from his early childhood experiences with his parents (Payne, 1968; Smith, 1994; Strange, 1967).

Dudley Pasteur was born free in 1841. However, after his third birthday, he and his mother, Sarah Pasteur, were sold as slaves. Pasteur's father was a slaveholder, and it was he who arranged the sale. Growing up a slave in New Bern, North Carolina in the 1840s and the 1850s, Pasteur spent his early childhood years with his mother who not only nurtured him, but also taught him to read and write. These skills were put to good use in his life as a manufacturer of barrels, real estate owner, and leading figure in local politics. Included among the many positions Pasteur held locally were internal revenue collector and city marshal. He also held a seat on the common council. Pasteur served his state as a representative in the North Carolina House of Representatives from 1870 to 1874 (Foner, 1993).

One former slave woman who enjoyed reading the *Anti-Slavery Standard* told that she had learned to read from her father at an early age. The tradition appeared to continue. The interviewer observed the woman's two sons reading while lying down on the grass in the yard, and she stopped to have a lively debate related to something they read.

Using his Bible as text, an elderly slave taught freeborn John Malvin to read and spell when Malvin was a child in the mid-1790s. John Malvin's mother, Dalcus Malvin, was a free woman and his father was a slave. Malvin's father was a skilled carpenter who also worked as a clerk for his owner. Malvin learned carpentry from his father. Throughout his life as an abolitionist, educator, and businessman, Malvin fought against laws that prohibited blacks from formal education in the early 1800s (Berry & Blassingame, 1982).

The details of Susan Boggs's family life as a slave in Virginia in the 1850s suggest that her life was extremely difficult. Boggs was devoted to her only son and made many sacrifices to educate him and to protect him from the harshest realities of slavery. In addition to work Boggs did as a slave, she worked to provide a better future for her son. With regard to her own learning, Boggs expressed her predicament as a slave and a young mother in the following words: "I had my son taught to read and write while I was there [in Virginia] in a secret school, but I was always so busy getting a little money to pay for it, that I never learned myself " (see Blassingame, 1977, p. 421).

Many parents sent their children to protect and educate them (Drew, 1856). Boggs learned that her son, who was twelve years old, had been sold. To spare him, she quickly arranged to have him taken to Canada. Because of this initiative, Boggs's slaveholder had her jailed until as he could find a buyer for her. A buyer was found, and she was indeed sold. Many years later, Boggs bought her freedom and joined her son and his wife in Canada. Boggs spoke of the cruelties of selling children away from parents and the physical abuse of slave children that she had witnessed in her lifetime. She implicitly stated that because of these occurrences, many African American children during the antebellum period would have lived lives of lost opportunities had it not been for their parents who tried to protect and educate them whenever possible. On her own life she reflected:

> I often think if I had sense, and had my intellect like people that were brought up and had learning, what money I could make! I could set down and think of everything I have seen and write a book. I could make a living writing a book of what I have seen. You see what a bad thing it is for people not to have no learning. But I did have a great deal of head work in getting away. (see Blassingame, 1977, p. 421)

As with Susan Boggs, most African American parents had neither time nor opportunity to learn to read and write, but many did try to seize whatever opportunities they could to secure the possibility of a literate future for their children and grandchildren. Mrs. Lewis Bibb of Kentucky, a free woman, could not afford the cost of tuition required to send her children to schools run by freed blacks in the 1830s. She therefore sent her children to school once a week on Sundays. At Sunday schools, as they were sometimes called, children were taught reading and writing skills in addition to scripture. Later the Sunday school movement became popular in urban areas (Borchert, 1982). The schools were held in churches and were operated by volunteers. The schools were meant to attract those who neither attended church nor were able to go to school during the day (see Blassingame, 1977). Slave families in many areas had Sundays to themselves and some took advantage of the opportunity of the Sunday school to expose themselves and their children to the once-a-week reading and writing lessons. Again, the theme of parents saving their children from living lives of lost opportunity is a common one in former slave accounts (see Blassingame, 1977; Borchert, 1982; Boylan, 1988).

Making up for their own past losses by attempting to gain some measure of control over their children's fate as readers and writers was another common theme found in nineteenth-century African American parents' life histories. The Ross family, the Hill family, the Bruce family, and the Jefferson family are exemplary witnesses of the foregoing statement. George Ross, for example, stated in an interview that took place in Canada in 1863 that as a slave he was "never blessed with the privilege of educating" himself, but that "his children were able to read and write very well" (see Blassingame, 1977, p. 408).

In a longer testimony, Jennie Hill told about her life history, and included key moments in her life related to literacy learning. Hill, born in 1837, was enslaved from birth in Howard County, Missouri. Her family worked on a sheep farm, where she learned to weave cloth. She stated that as a child she was inspired by stories read to her about young Abraham Lincoln's experiences learning to read and write. She commented: "I ate all that information for there was nothing in this world I wanted more at that time than an education. But Abraham Lincoln was president of the United States. He was a white boy and I was just a slave" (see Blassingame, 1977, p. 592). Hill expressed pride in the fact that she and her husband had a real marriage ceremony performed by "another slave . . . who could read and write and knew something of the Bible" (see Blassingame, 1977, pp. 591–592). She continued, stating the man who married them "said the same marriage ceremony for us that [she and her husband] had to say over again when [they] were freed" (see Blassingame, 1977, pp. 591–592).

Hill and her husband had three children. Two years after the general emancipation, she and her husband went to Kansas, because they were "determined to give . . . [their] children the education which . . . [the parents] were denied" (see Blassingame, 1977, p. 593). When interviewed in 1933 at her home at 663 North Water in Wichita, Kansas, Hill recalled that even though education for enslaved African Americans was a rarity, her mother had managed to learn, as did Hill later. Her mother's literacy skills were manifested by the recording of Hill's birth in the family Bible. She stated that few slaves knew when they were born for their "mothers had no way of recording their births. . . . They had to guess at their ages" (Blassingame, 1977, p. 590). At the time of the interview, Hill was 96 years old and was still a reader who especially liked to read about "modern" changes in the world and "political situations" (see Blassingame, 1977, p. 590).

Born in 1848, former slave Anderson Evans was interviewed in 1932 at his house on 835 North Elm Street, St. Louis, Missouri. When he was young, Evans did not have a chance to learn without fear of punishment if found out. Reading and writing skills were acquired late in his life, and Evans admitted that he found reading to be his "chief source of comfort in his old age" (see Blassingame, 1977, p. 587). His told the interviewer that his Bible was very important to him and that he had read it in parts many times over. "To keep myself informed," he stated, "I have been a subscriber for forty years to a newspaper. It tells me all I need to know about what is going on" (see Blassingame, 1977, p. 588). Evans was determined that he would learn to read his correspondence himself. When his children, who could read and write, became adults and moved away from his home, they wrote letters to him and his wife. Unable to read, the Evanses were frustrated because their children's letters had to be read to them. Evans went to the postmaster in his area to get a copy of the alphabet, which he painstakingly copied over and over again. He eventually taught himself to spell and write well enough that he could correspond with his family (Blassingame, 1977).

Parke Johnson was not literate and had always regretted that fact. In his interview in 1880, he stated that he had been enslaved in Virginia. He had made his living as a shoemaker in that state since the emancipation. He had also been a carpenter and a farm worker during the antebellum period. After the Civil War, Johnson became an outspoken advocate for public education for African American children. His own children were educated on his farm. Johnson built a schoolhouse on his land and hired an African American woman to teach his children (Blassingame, 1977).

Nancy Bells was enslaved in Kentucky from her birth in 1835 until her liberation in 1853. One year after she had been freed, she and her husband Carey Bells, along with 22 other manumitted African Americans, sailed to Liberia on the ship *Sophia Walker*. The group arrived in Liberia July 30, 1854. The Bellses returned to the United States years later. They lived in Newport, Kentucky where her husband successfully ran for a seat on the city council but was not allowed to serve. The Bellses educated their two daughters at Fisk University in Nashville, where they studied music, majoring in voice. Both children were among the first group of the historical Jubilee Choir that traveled the country, singing African American spirituals (Blassingame, 1977).

Henry Bruce and his brothers and sisters lived with their mother. Although their mother was neither a reader nor writer, she set aside time in the evenings for her children to work together on reading and writing lessons. Their mother strongly encouraged the older children to teach the younger children (Blassingame, 1977).

Madison Jefferson was born in Virginia in 1841. His mother sent him to an evening school. He too remembers staying up until midnight or later to practice reading and writing (Blassingame, 1977).

Before his death, John Miller of Philadelphia, who was literate, arranged to have a Quaker woman by the name of E. W. Cope educate his youngest daughter, Philena Miller. Miller wanted his daughter to attend school in town to learn how to read and sew. After his death, calico cloth for the child's school dress and other clothing appropriate for wearing in town were purchased, and Philena was sent to Philadelphia to be schooled by Cope (Woodson, 1969).

Former slaves interviewed in the 1860s, Cox, Andrew Frehew, and William H. Howard, educated their children at Oberlin College. All three men had purchased their freedom and that of their families. Cox worked as a steward aboard a riverboat, purchased land, and built a house. All five of his children graduated from school. Cox also purchased the freedom of his two nephews, one of whom was attending Oberlin College at the time of the interview (Woodson, 1969).

In the aftermath of the Civil War, life was chaotic and hard for many American families. Adjustments to the end of the war as well as adjustments to freedom were difficult for most slave families. After the war, Mrs. Fitzpatrick, a former slave, found herself alone with twelve children, struggling as a worker on a farm. She was paid in corn, potatoes, syrup, and little else.

Fitzpatrick's son Jessie was dissatisfied with the circumstances under which he found his mother living. At the age of nineteen, Jessie became head of household. He moved the family to another farm near Tuskegee Institute, where he enrolled as a student. He studied and took care of the farm with the help of his brothers and sisters. Since his mother was too exhausted from doing farm work during the day to conduct family prayers, Jessie took over the responsibility of evening devotional prayers. He educated his brothers and sisters who showed interest, and he took care of the family until his death. After Jessie died, Fitzpatrick's next oldest son, Ransom Johnson became head of household. Johnson attended Tuskegee Institute and is also credited with having educated a number of his brothers and sisters (Blassingame, 1977).

Similarly, Timothy Smith took over the care of his mother and seven sisters and brothers toward the close of the Civil War. He had been placed in charge of his slave owner's farming business during the war and was asked to remain in charge of affairs after the general Emancipation in 1863. His skill as a manager and knowledge of the farm placed Smith in a position to negotiate the conditions of his stay and those of his family. An agreement was reached, and Smith and his family were paid one fourth of the plantation's profits. He also made an agreement that the former slave owner arrange schooling to help Smith keep the accounts. Smith wisely negotiated for schooling in the evenings for his brothers and sisters. Having successfully created conditions that would allow himself and his family to receive an education as well as be employed, Smith enrolled in a public school at night. The school was quite a distance from the farm, so, by 1869, Smith had begun to stay with an uncle who lived closer to town. He went on to graduate from Hampton Institute in 1875 and taught school in Virginia and West Virginia (Blassingame, 1977).

Lorenzo Ivy's father was an important supporter of his education. In the mid-1840s Ivy's family became aware that certain members of their family would be sold apart from one another. Their slaveholder wanted to benefit from the huge profits to be had in cotton and expand his wealth by moving his interests, including his slaves, from Virginia to the deeper South. Ivy and his mother lived on one plantation as did two of his aunts. Ivy's father and his aunts' husbands lived on a neighboring plantation. Alarmed by the possibility of losing their beloved wives and children, the men fought for the right to buy their families before the move to the South. They brought their cases before the owners of each plantation in order to reason with them that the slave owners should honor a long-standing, verbal agreement between both plantation-owning families. All concerned understood that in event of a move or sale, the affected enslaved families could be sold only between the two plantations. While the slaveholders saw this agreement as a means of creating a reliable, stable work force, the slave families saw it as a means by which their families would stay intact. Ivy's father argued successfully and the agreement held, at least for Ivy and his mother. He lost his aunts, who were moved deeper south away from their husbands. Ivy and his mother, however, were purchased by his father's slaveholder, and he remained with both of his parents through the end of the Civil War (Blassingame, 1977).

By April of 1866, the family moved into town. His father, who was a brick layer by trade, hired Ivy and other young men from the plantations to work for him. This move enabled Ivy to take advantage of educational opportunities to attend schools established for former slaves. He worked for his father at a wage of six dollars a month. Ivy went to school at night and then to a day school. When his father moved the family to Tennessee, Lorenzo, his brother, and his sister went to Hampton Normal Agricultural School. Ivy was graduated in 1874 and taught in Virginia for some time. In 1893, he was appointed the principal of North Danville Public School in Danville, Virginia (Blassingame, 1977).

In addition to brothers, sisters, parents, and grandparents' efforts to educate children, uncles and aunts also played a key role. Alexander Tardieu, a resident of Bordentown, New Jersey, took on the duty of supporting his nephew, William J. Simmons and William's mother, Ester Simmons. Two other Simmons siblings were also taken in. As fugitive slaves from Charleston, South Carolina, the Simmonses sought refuge in New Jersey with Tardieu. Tardieu, who was literate, taught the Simmons children how to read and write. Simmons was later apprenticed to a dentist and worked as a dentist's assistant until he enlisted in the Union Army. He completed his studies at Howard University and became a prominent educational leader in Kentucky (Blassingame, 1977).

Similarly, Mary Smith Peake, born free in 1823, spent part of her youth living with her aunt, Mrs. John Paine, in order to take advantage of free schools available in the area. Under Paine's care, Peake reportedly received a "solid public school education" in the city of Alexandria. By 1846, however, Alexandria was reclaimed by the state of Virginia, schools for free blacks were abolished, and Peake returned to Norfolk to live once again with her mother. In later years, Peake held positions as a schoolteacher. She opened her own infant school and managed to keep her school open through the end of the Civil War. Her school was recognized as an outstanding institution by the Freedmen's Bureau, which led to her institution being the first school in the nation to receive federal funds for public education (Berry & Blassingame, 1982).

Children in slave communities who had either been sold away from their parents or otherwise orphaned often lived with a surrogate parent, that is, an older slave would assume the role of parent to the child. James Pennington who was separated from his parents most of his life lived with an elderly couple whom he called Mother and Father. When, as a young man, he decided to escape slavery by any means possible, he first discussed his discontent and his intentions with his surrogate parents before making his move. For him the couple were his family (Blackett, 1986). Similarly, Jordan Winston Early, who was sold separately from his parents, referred to an older slave woman who raised him as Aunt Milly. His aunt and uncle were significant in his life. While in their care, he learned to read and write from other significant adults who were members of the slave community. His aunt's husband, whom he called Uncle, taught him astronomy (Aptheker, 1946, 1951; Berry & Blassingame, 1982).

One avenue nineteenth-century African Americans used to protect and unite with family members was the Underground Railroad. Families depended on African American conductors of the Underground Railroad to extend aid to, unite with, and discover the whereabouts of family members who had moved away voluntarily or forcibly.

African American family literacy played an important part in the successful operation of this organization. William Still was an African American abolitionist and an important conductor of the Underground Railroad. Correspondence between Still and the families suggests that Still was meticulous, thorough, caring, and effective in his dealings with the families who depended upon his experience and sought his advice and aid. Letters written and received by Still were laden with symbolic language. Letters and telegraph messages were often used to inform passengers and their families, waiting for them on the other side, of the Railroad's plans for their travel into free territory. Messages were signed by conductors and others who used pseudonyms. Travel routes named Lightning Train, Reading Road, Israel, Jericho, the U.G.R.R. Company, and Road Camden Circuit, are among the many names that appear in the literature. The following are examples of types documents generated by the activities of the Underground Railroad:

> Friend Still: I suppose sir that you have seen those five large and three small packages I sent by way of Reading, consisting of men and children. They arrived here this morning at [8:30] and left twenty minutes past three. Lately, we have formed a Society here, called the Fugitive Aid Society. This is our first case, and I hope it will prove entirely successful. (Joseph C. Bustill to William Still, Harrisburg, March 24, 1856; see Woodson, 1969, pp. 560–561)

The letter continued with this request for written instructions for future contact and information regarding the organization's operations by way of telegraph:

> When you write, please inform me what signs or symbols you make use of in your despatches, and any other information in relation to operations of the Underground Rail Road.
>
> Our reason for sending by the Reading Road, was to gain time; it is expected the owners will be in town this afternoon, and by this Road we gained five hours' time, which is a matter of much importance, and we may have occasion to use it sometimes in the future.
>
> In great haste, Yours with great respect, Jos. C. Bustill (see Woodson, 1969, p. 561)

The letter below is from a slave who was known to Still, but did not want others to know his status as a fugitive. This message suggests that ordinary slave families (as implied by his twice calling himself a "poor individual") sought the help of the Underground Railroad using messages written in symbolic language:

> To Mr. William Still:—Dear Sir—Please do me the favor as to write to my uncle a few lines in regard to the bundle that is for John H. Hill, who lives in Hamilton, C. W. Sir, if this should reach you, be assured that it comes from the same

> poor individual that you have heard of before . . . I hope you understand sir, this is from a poor individual. (From a slave secreted in Richmond to William Still, Richmond, VA., October 18, 1860; see Woodson, 1969, p. 561)

Slaves wrote to Still asking for his help in arranging the passage of a husband, wife, or child to a free state. Still helped one slave named Peter who later turned out to be his own brother from whom he had been forcibly separated for forty-nine years (see Woodson, 1969). As a result of his personal tragedy, Still began conscientiously to keep a daily journal of his Underground Railroad activities along with slaves' narratives of their experiences with the Railroad, relevant newspaper articles, legal documents generated by the organization's activities, letters from abolitionists and former slaves, and biographical sketches (Logan & Winston, 1982, p. 573). His journal, published in 1872, has been a major contribution to the body of literature regarding the role of African American conductors and the slave passengers of the Underground Railroad (Logan & Winston, 1982). Still's work also stands as a powerful statement about African American family life and the extent to which African Americans attempted to protect their families and their family way of life during the antebellum period.

People were aware of Still's journal and they asked him to make use of it to locate family members, as seen in this example:

> Mr. Still Please Look on your Book and you will find my name on your Book They was eleven of us children and all when we came through and I feal anxious about my Brothers. I left home. (Letter from Nat Ambie to William Still, Auburn, New York, June 10, 1858; see Woodson, 1969, p. 569)

The need of African Americans during this period to protect family members and family ways of life from the objective realities of a slave society had a direct impact on literacy traditions.

Free African Americans who came from elite backgrounds learned to read and write in highly literate environments. If neither schools nor tutors could be had, then children were taught in the home. In some cases, both parents had received a formal education, which was quite an accomplishment for a family in nineteenth-century America. Whenever possible, children in such families traveled with parents who were members of literary societies, delivered and attended public lectures, attended conventions, held public office, owned land and businesses, and exposed the children to famous abolitionists like Arthur Tappan, Frederick Douglass, and William Lloyd Garrison. Their family papers, including autobiographies, diaries, books, articles, speeches, and other personal and professional or scholarly writings, that have been used to form the very basis of American thought and informed dialogue on democracy and freedom, are held in special collections. Further, their portraits are commonly seen in textbooks (Dann, 1971; Foner, 1975; Franklin, 1980a; Levine, 1979; Litwack & Meier, 1988; Sweet, 1976; Winch, 1988). The children themselves went on to become well-known leaders in America. The Cummels, Fortens, Grimikes, DeBaptists, Shadds, and many others belong to this group of African Americans.

Ida Wells wrote of her childhood family reading experiences and revealed much about her family's reading interests, attitudes, and values. Wells wrote:

> my earliest recollections are of reading the newspaper to my father and an admiring group of friends. He was interested in politics. . . . Our job was to go to school and learn all we could. . . . My mother went along to school with us until she learned to read the Bible. After that she visited the school regularly to see how we were getting along. . . . She was not forty when she died, but she had borne eight children and brought us up with a strict discipline that many mothers who have had educational advantages have not exceeded. (see Royster, 1997, p. 14)

Thomas Braddock had the means to educate his children well. He was a successful builder and carpenter. As an owner of real estate he also earned a substantial income from his rental properties. He was known to have personally collected a library of books that was most likely invaluable to the education of his children. Braddock's will is indicative of how he and other free blacks respected education. He was very explicit about how his estate was to be executed in order to educate each of his children in the event of his death. The document, in part, reads:

> Educate my children, the boys until they arrive to the age of sixteen then I wish my executors to bind them to some useful and proper trade, and the girls I wish them to be put to the milliners or mantua-making business, but I wish them to be

kept regular at school until they are put to proper trades. (see Schweninger, 1990, p. 138)

Sarah Thompson Garnet, the wife of Henry Highland Garnet, was born in 1831 in Queens County, Long Island, New York. Free-born African Americans, such as Sarah, had been attending schools in New York since the 1700s. African free schools, established in 1787, had graduated many famous nineteenth-century African Americans. Garnet, however, did not live close enough to such a school to attend daily. Her grandmother, Sarah Hobbs, taught her in her home instead. Later, she was permitted to take up studies in normal schools located near New York City (Brown, 1972).

Mary Frances Watkins was also born of free parents in Maryland in 1825. She lived with her parents until their death and was educated at home by them. Her uncle, Reverend William Watkins, operated a school for free African Americans and Mary Frances Watkins continued her education in his school while under his care. She later became a teacher and an administrator for her uncle's school. The school survived for 15 years. Watkins became an important leader in the abolitionist movement (Brown, 1972; Davis, Redding, & Joyce, 1991; Still, 1872).

The Shadd children and other African American children could not receive an education in Delaware. The family, therefore, moved to Pennsylvania where schools that enrolled African American children had long been established. Mary Shadd was enrolled in a Quaker boarding school located in West Chester, Pennsylvania. Shadd and her brother are well-known for their work among slave fugitives in Canada. Shadd, who founded and edited an antislavery newspaper, also became an influential journalist of the antebellum period (Litwack & Meier, 1988).

William and Eliza DeBaptist's oldest son George was apprenticed to a barber and their youngest son Richard was schooled at home by a free black teacher. A Scottish-Irish Quaker, Richard Dillingham, was also retained. Richard DeBaptist along with children of other elite, free blacks were schooled by Dillingham in the DeBaptist home. DeBaptist completed his early education in Detroit under the guidance of Reverend Samuel H. Davis. He attended the University of Chicago and was ordained in 1860. DeBaptist served as a schoolmaster and pastor for the Negro Baptist Church in Mount Pleasant, Ohio until 1863 (Hartgrove, 1916).

Alexander Crummell's parents used their considerable resources to their children's advantage. Crummel, who became a nineteenth-century African American leader, attended African Free Schools in New York City. His parents hired teachers to tutor their children privately. His classmates included Patrick and Charles Reason, Isaiah De Grasse, James McCune Smith, Samuel Ringgold Ward, George T. Downing, and many others (Moses, 1989).

Not all wealthy nineteenth-century African Americans parents had easy access to formal or informal educational opportunities for their children. Schools for their children were closed and destroyed (Berlin, 1974; Berry & Blassingame, 1982; Genovese, 1976). In many cases, therefore, although parents had the means to educate them, doing so publicly or even privately presented a supreme risk to the lives and emotional well-being of their children. Some privileged parents, those from Louisiana, for example, sent their children abroad to study in Paris or other cities in France in order to avoid the day-to-day hardships of educating an African American child in nineteenth-century America. Others used the court system in attempts to win the right for their children to attend public schools on the basis that their property taxes were paid regularly to support public education (Berry & Blassingame, 1982; Birnie, 1927; Bullock, 1978; Franklin, 1980; Genovese, 1976; Huggins, 1977; Mabee, 1979; Woodson, 1969).

The literacy histories of the families examined suggest that regardless of where they lived and the difficulty of their circumstances, African Americans were indeed persistent throughout the nineteenth century in their efforts to educate themselves and their families. It can be concluded from their demonstrated commitment to literacy education that their literacy traditions, like their other traditions, survived space and time. This indeed is the test of tradition. For in the main, those nineteenth-century families discussed lived lives that had constant interruptions because of laws passed by those who sought to own them, war, involuntary termination of marriages, separation of children from their parents, forced migrations, violence or threat of violence, laws restricting their access to learning, and many other personal, social, and historical tragedies.

Notwithstanding, the efforts to educate their own children made by these families during the crisis, regardless of any obstacles they encountered or the limitations of their financial resources, led to the creation of a generation of readers and writers on two continents. Such were the beginnings of African American literacy traditions.

Chapter 3

Visible and Invisible Institutions

The latter part of the nineteenth century saw the formation of the black educational institution. Early African American schools, as both visible and invisible institutions, emerged locally, regionally, nationally, and internationally to support the family's efforts to provide a literate future for their children.

However, with formal schools run by free blacks being too few in number, vulnerable to terrorist attacks, and beyond the reach of many, such schools were not an option for a great many enslaved and free African Americans. Therefore, early on, many looked to each other to create alternative and unconventional routes to literacy learning for themselves and their children. As sojourners in this respect, each walked along somewhat different paths toward literacy. Whether one's path led to clandestine teaching and learning that took place in a house, a cabin, a wooded spot, a church basement, or down by a riverside, such literacy events were African American forerunners of or rehearsals for the development of their own formal community schools and institutions of higher education. Regardless of whether in slavery or in freedom, they fought to educate themselves (Brown, 1972; Bullock, 1970). With respect to African American struggles to become literate following mass emancipation, Genovese (1976) maintains the following:

> The freedmen's efforts to educate their children provide one of the most moving chapters in American social history . . . the extent to which blacks with few resources and little experience scraped to pay for schools and teachers stands out like a miracle. (p. 565)

There is ample empirical evidence to support the assumption that African Americans successfully made extreme, historically unprecedented commitments to educate their children in the nineteenth century. Evidence that has been gathered from the oral and written accounts of slaves, slaveholders, clergymen, teachers, missionaries, and travelers regarding African American formal and informal schools is presented in this chapter.

The teaching experiences of abolitionist and former slave Frederick Douglass confirm Bowery's testimony and that of numerous others. In 1833, Douglass operated a school without the knowledge of slaveholder William Freeland. Freeland held two men enslaved, Henry and John, and he hired other planters' enslaved laborers to work for him, one of whom was Douglass. After providing reading instruction to Henry and John, others from the neighboring slave communities wanted to learn as well, so Douglass decided to meet regularly with all who were interested at the house of a freedman. In the summer, Douglass mentioned that they did not need the shelter of a house because the shade of an old oak tree served just as well. He soon had as many as forty men and women in regular attendance on Sundays, and he stated that most managed to find and bring to the meetings old spelling books (Andrews, 1969; Douglass, 1993). In this manner he operated his Sunday school. Douglass also spent three evenings a week during the winter schooling some of his fellow slaves. In his opinion the people met with him regularly for one main reason:

> These dear souls came not to Sabbath school because it was popular to do so, nor did I teach them because it was reputable to be thus engaged. Every moment they spent in that school, they were liable to be taken up, and given thirty-nine lashes. They came because they wished to learn. . . . [T]heir minds had been starved by their cruel masters. . . . They had been shut up in mental darkness. . . . I taught them, because it was the delight of my soul to be doing something that

> looked like bettering the condition of my race . . . [and] I have the happiness to know, that several of those who came to Sabbath school learned how to read. (Douglass, 1993, p. 84)

Of all the men and women whom Douglass taught, he mentioned just one of them who actually used reading and writing as a means to physically escape enslavement. Presumably, this was accomplished by that person writing himself a pass to leave the area (Douglass, 1993). This serves to accentuate his point that slaves' motives for learning to read were largely intellectual.

A Quaker missionary found that even in the most isolated places, African Americans were zealous learners in the years immediately following the Civil War. One missionary wrote about a company of African American soldiers who were serving duty in a remote place. She wrote that "their zeal [to read] needed no quickening" (Swint, 1966). After several reading lessons, the same missionary asked an African American solider whether he believed that his knowing how to read would make him a free man. His response was a firm "no." He implied that for himself, being truly free meant much more than being a reader; however, he did believe that being a reader was in itself a form of freedom (Swint, 1966).

Father Joshia Henson, who was once a slave, provided his perception of his own literacy learning as an intellectual awakening. About learning to read he wrote:

> It was, and has been ever since, a great comfort to me to have made this acquisition; though it has made me comprehend better the terrible abyss of ignorance in which I had plunged all my previous life. It made me also feel more deeply and bitterly the oppression underwhich I had toiled and groaned; but the crushing and cruel nature of which I had not appreciated, till I found out, in some slight degree, from what I had been debarred. At the same time it made me more anxious than before to do something for the rescue and the elevation of those who were suffering the same evils I had endured and who did not know how degraded and ignorant they really were. (see Genovese, 1976, pp. 562–563)

The observations of Elijah P. Marrs, a northern traveler to the South, provides yet another glimpse of how informal learning took place in slave communities. He remembered vividly seeing a literate old slave, on one plantation where he had stayed, who taught his fellow slaves to read after ten o'clock at night (Genovese, 1976). It is probable that John Malvin was taught to read by an old slave in his community perhaps in this same manner, as were Henry Bruce, his siblings, and Madison Jefferson. Levi Choppin and Samuel Ringold were both taught to read by a parent, despite the fact that this too was illegal.

The risks for such secret teaching practices were great, as can be surmised from the confessions of one African American clergyman from Georgia. As he lay dying, he whispered to those in attendance that he had always grieved over the fact that he had been responsible for the death of so many slaves because he had taught them to read and write (Berry & Blassingame, 1982). African Americans did everything possible to teach others how to read and write. While men like Frederick Douglass, Father Henson, and many others were well educated and intellectually gifted, most involved with informal schooling were not as exceptional, but were indeed dedicated to the idea of literacy. In fact, most plantation schools, according to Genovese (1976), were conducted by literate slaves who had only rudimentary educational knowledge. However little experience these early informal educators had, they nonetheless generously and heroically shared what they knew with their fellow slaves.

African Americans took extreme chances in their endeavors to promote literacy in both slave and free communities. For example, Christopher McPherson, a freeman and successful businessman, established a night school for African American children in Richmond, Virginia, in 1811. The teacher whom he had hired was forced to leave that city after McPherson tried to publish the success of his school and solicit potential students in a local newspaper, over protests about the propriety of his doing so (Schweninger, 1990). When McPherson persisted, his school was shut down, and he was summarily arrested and jailed (Berry & Blassingame, 1982; Schweninger, 1990).

Another incident in Richmond, Virginia, points to the difficulties facing the early development of African American educational institutions. A Richmond, Virginia, newspaper in the early 1800s published an article in which it was charged that African American children were receiving reading and writing lessons and that they had also been spotted carrying school books to their church on Sunday. Not long after the article appeared, a group of Richmond city policemen stormed the African American church. They found that the rumors and suspicions were true; the children were indeed learning basic reading, writing and math skills (Berry & Blassingame, 1982). The school at the church was discontinued.

African American public and private schools were invariably met with some form of confrontation (Woodson, 1968). There were verbal harassment of both African American and European American teachers in the streets, dismissal of European American teachers from their church registers, fines for those who attempted to teach African Americans, mob violence toward European Americans and African Americans, and lynching of African Americans. Instances of African American schools having been forcibly shut down, teachers beaten, books and buildings burned, and classes dissolved were reported in almost every city around the country (Woodson, 1968). Following the slave insurrection led by Nat Turner in 1833, many schools were forced to shut their doors. Nat Turner, Denmark Vesey, and Gabriel Posser, three literate African Americans, all led rebellions, so the fear that educated African Americans were a danger to the existing social order fueled passions regarding the education of African Americans both free and enslaved, particularly in the 1830s and 1840s (Oakes, 1975; Woodson, 1968).

Yet such experiences did not discourage African Americans from establishing formal and informal schools. In any given community there were, reportedly, underground schools housed in churches, homes, city buildings originally intended for other uses, and a host of other physical arrangements. School buildings built, owned, and financed by African Americans were also available to some children (Woodson, 1968). In most cases, an individual out of necessity had to try over the course of his or her entire life, a combination of informal and formal schooling, as can be seen in the experiences of G. W. Offley.

Offley, a free black man from Delaware, made various attempts to learn how to read and write. Berry and Blassingame (1982) described his attempts in these words:

> [He learned how to read and write by spending] . . . a few weeks a night from an old Negro preacher, exchanging boxing and wrestling lessons with the son of a slaveholder for the ABCs or food with poor white children for reading lessons in Delaware, and then regular lesson from sympathetic whites in Hartford, Connecticut. (p. 47)

Like the experiences of Offley, the ordeals faced by former slaves George Teamoh of Virginia and Edmund Calisle of South Carolina demonstrate further that paths to African American literacy took many twists and turns, but, in the end, most who learned to read and write did so by sheer perseverance. Each learned to read and write in the face of overwhelming odds. Circumstances were such that most literate nineteenth-century African Americans learned a bit here and a bit there. And they were wise if they kept knowledge of their reading and writing activities away from slaveholders. They'd learned with friends or family members to either practice or share their literacy knowledge. Slaves' narratives tell about their having carried around for days, hidden somewhere in their clothes or under a hat, old schoolbooks they had found such as the *McGuffy Reader* or Noah Webster's blue-back spellers, which were extremely popular and widely available (Robinson, 1977; Woodson, 1968). They did not want slaveholders to find them with reading and writing materials, but they wanted to have the materials nearby whenever they could find a few moments to study. James W. C. Pennington mentioned that in order to avoid detection, he carried his speller under his hat for days at a time, and, between lessons from literate others he met in his travels, he practiced spelling, reading, and writing (Blackett, 1986; Bontemps, 1969).

This poem, written by educator, poet, and abolitionist Frances Ellen Watkins Harper prior to the Civil War, captured the plight of African American learners during the antebellum period:

Learning to Read

Our masters always tried to hide
Book learning from our eyes;
Knowledge didn't agree with slavery—
'Towould make us all too wise.
But some of us would try to steal
A little from the book,
And put the words together,
And learn by hook or crook.
I remember Uncle Caldwell,
Who took pot liquor fat
and greased the pages of his book,
And hid it in his hat,
And had his master ever seen
The leaves upon his head,

He'd thought them greasy papers,
But nothing to be read.
And there was Mr. Turner's Ben,
Who heard the children spell,
And picked the words right up by heart,
And learned to read 'em well. . . .
An, I longed to read my Bible,
For precious words it said;
But when I begun to learn it,
Folks just shook their heads.
And said there is no use trying,
Oh! Chole, you're too late;
But as I was rising sixty,
I had no time to wait.
So I got a pair of glasses
And straight to work I went,
And never stopped till I could read
the hymns and Testament.
Then I got a little cabin
A place to call my own—
And I felt as independent
As the queen upon her throne.
(see Davis, Redding, & Joyce, 1991, pp. 206–207)

In summary, African Americans in the nineteenth century used a variety of strategies for providing structured, systematic schooling for their children. Other types of informal learning opportunities were less deliberate. Literacy learning in many cases was an outgrowth of long-established social and cultural activities.

A long-established social and cultural activity in the slave community was the camp meeting. An African retention, the camp meeting took on new meanings in the African American community. Men and women in West Africa held separate meetings. In Africa, the meetings were held in secret. Meetings were forums for group decision making in which men and women played equal roles in determining nearly all the leading institutions as were manifested by the functions of the *Sande* and the *Poro*, or the female and male social and educational institutions (Beyan, 1991; Fisher, 1953; Raboteau, 1980).

In America, the meetings were also held in secret to discuss plans of action regarding escape, family problems, problems with an overseer, the passing down of information from one generation to the next, religious worship, and other concerns of the slave community. Former slave Early W. Jordan learned to read at camp meetings (Berry & Blassingame, 1982). It is more than likely that others did also. One could, then, argue that literacy learning was one of many reasons for these meetings in slave communities.

In fact, it may be difficult to separate informal schools, such as those run by Douglass and others, from camp meetings. Fearing insurrection, slave owners prohibited camp meetings; however, they were held covertly anyway. According to Fisher (1953) meetings that took place outside the view of slaveholders in densely wooded areas were called together by the singing of spirituals, which originated in the slave community, for a multitude of purposes. Such meetings were not without risks.

> On Sundays . . . I have seen the Negroes up in the country going away under large oaks, and in secret places, sitting in the woods with spelling books. The brightest and best men were killed in Nat's time. Such ones are always suspected. All the colored folks were afraid to pray in the time of the old prophet Nat. There was no law about it; but whites reported it round themselves, and if a note was heard, we should have some dreadful punishment; and after that, the low whites would fall upon any slaves they heard praying or singing a hymn, and often killed them before their masters or mistress could get to them. (Interview of Charity Bowery by Lydia Maria Child, *Emancipator*, April 5, 1848; see Blassingame, 1977, p. 267)

The spiritual "Steal Away" is believed to have been written by Nat Turner in the mid-1820s, and had reportedly been used repeatedly as a *signal song* or call to a secret meeting. The use of the signal song was intended to minimize the risk of being found out. A leader of the community would signal a call to meeting by singing, which would be picked up by another and another until all were aware that a meeting had been called at a previously agreed upon place. The call–response pattern of singing, in which one person sings out a message and the group repeats or otherwise responds in turn to the leader's call, is characteristically African and African American. The following words are from the spiritual "Steal Away":

Steal away, steal away,
Steal away to Jesus,
Steal away, steal away home,
I hain't got long to stay here. (see Fisher, 1953, p. 66)

The last part of the message, "I hain't got long to stay here," suggests a person on the run who must meet one last time with members of the community, family, and friends.

The camp meeting served as an opportunity for the informal learning of African American culture and traditions. Literacy traditions were also learned and practiced in this setting and in similar informal or invisible settings. Participants in such invisible classrooms took charge of their own learning and supplied, through various means, their own reading materials. With regard to supplying their own reading materials, a Mississippi slaveholder reported that slaves on his land could read and write because of their own initiatives. The interviewer recorded his words as follows:

> [T]here ent one of my [slaves] but what can read; read good too-better'n I can at any rate. 'How did they learn?' Taught themselves. I b'lieve there was one on 'em that I bought, that could read, and he taught all the rest. (Raboteau, 1978, pp. 240–241)

The slaveholder continued his account to say that African Americans bought their own reading materials from peddlers. He remembered that the people mostly bought religious books. Nowhere in his discussion is it mentioned how slaves were able to purchase these books. Harvey Graff's (1968) work, *The Literacy Myth*, and Knight's (1953) *A Documentary History of Education in the South before 1860* support the idea that rural blacks bought religious books from peddlers during the antebellum period.

If the slaves hired out their time, worked on an overtime system, or worked on their own plots in addition to work done for their slaveholders, then the foregoing discussion is a compelling account of just how much they must have enjoyed and valued reading. In many cases, slaves, with or without the slaveholder's knowledge, produced their own provisions. On Sundays or in the evenings after having completed assigned work, they tended their own gardens, berry bushes, and, in some cases, poultry and livestock to supplement their allotted diets and provide for their families. People of the slave community, with or without permission, fished, hunted, or trapped for furs as well. In some areas, they were able to successfully compete with small farms in local markets by selling of their own products (Andrews, 1996; Berlin, 1980; Dew, 1974, 1994; Genovese, 1976; Lewis, 1979).

Labor historians, using plantation records, provide detailed accounts of slaves who benefited financially through a system of overwork. In some cases highly skilled laborers who worked more than a certain number of days or hours in a day were paid for their labor. Money owed to them was entered into a ledger and paid to the laborers on a regular schedule. Some placed their earnings in bank accounts managed by the slaveholder who kept records of their transactions (Dew, 1994; Lewis, 1979). These African American men and women most certainly kept a record of their earnings. To not think so would assume that they were not quite capable of doing so. The laborers used their wages from overwork to supplement their families' basic needs or to provide a few luxuries.

This, along with any currency they might have been able to acquire by hiring out their labor in off seasons, was used to buy or trade for much needed cloth for winter clothing, leather, food staples, seed, and other necessities. Some were able to live relatively better than those who did not have such advantages. Even with these labors, however, many led miserable lives, ill fed and ill clothed. Without these pains, on the other hand, many would not have survived. Therefore, it can be argued that if people in the slave community owned any books at all besides the Bible, they were purchased at a very dear price.

In some places, it had been reported that religious groups handed out so many Bibles that almost every slave cabin had a well-worn copy (Blassingame, 1977). Further, narratives of former slaves suggest that even illiterate African Americans in such areas were well familiar with the contents of the Bible (Raboteau, 1980). It was not unusual for many to memorize whole books from the Bible, reciting them from memory. They would then look for key words throughout the Bible to build a sight vocabulary. The capacity to recite verbatim long excerpts from the Bible was most likely accomplished by having listened to whole passages being read or recited so many times that they were memorized by the group.

Raboteau (1980) tells of the experiences of Charity Bowery, who struggled to learn to read by memorizing whole passages from the

Bible. Her respect for the written word was so great that even as a fugitive she carried with her a copy of the Bible and late at night in the woods she would search pages for key words she had learned from others. Bowery, according to Raboteau, found immense comfort in being able to recognize the word *Jesus* on the pages. Resourceful and determined slaves used whatever printed matter they could to learn to read.

Indeed, important documents such as a former slave's bill of sale, a birth certificate, or the recording of births, marriages, and deaths in the family Bible were known by heart by all family members. For example, one woman interviewed proudly showed a letter written by her former slaveholder as proof of her age, place of birth, and the date and circumstances of her manumission. As the letter was read to the interviewer, members of the woman's family and some of her neighbors gathered around to listen, silently mouthing its contents, which they apparently knew from memory. When the reader made an error in reading, the correct word was supplied by a listener. Young children listened and participated in what the interviewer assumed to be a common practice of a group reading of family documents (Blassingame, 1977). Similarly, an old man who had bought his freedom when he was younger proudly kept his own bill of sale ready to show visitors in his home. Others held on to their bills of sale and manumission papers for many years and generations.

Literacy events, then, were not only reading and writing activities well grounded in family or community rituals, but also opportunities for informal learning for young and old alike. Also, the same printed matter served as reading material for informal literacy learning among adults and children alike. Both adults and children would engage in reading and writing activities important to the community. For example, a turning point in the literacy history of Sella Martin highlights this point. Martin recalled that once as a boy, when it was rumored that he, though a slave, could read, he was challenged to prove he could by a group of older men from the slave community. They told him to read a newspaper article aloud. Since he was young and an inexperienced reader, Martin was nervous about his performance. His telling of the event suggests that he had initially regarded his learning to read as a mental game he played. It was an intellectual challenge that he hoped some day would lead to his writing himself a pass in order to escape the bonds of slavery. But, mostly, he acknowledged, he considered what he was doing to be only playing or pretending to read. He was not yet certain that he was in fact a real reader, and implied that if given a random reading passage, he was not confident that he could even read the first line (Blackett, 1986).

As the men stood waiting, Martin stared at a newspaper article about Henry Clay, a leading statesman who had dominated American politics from 1820 to 1848. Martin wrote that, after recognizing Clay's name and other key words, he surprised himself by reading the passage smoothly and coherently enough to please his listeners. They congratulated him for being such a smart young man. Almost every evening after the incident, Martin recalled, the kitchen, where folks from the slave quarter gathered at the end of the day, was always full of people waiting for him to read aloud letters, literature, newspaper articles, the Bible, and any other writing that was important to individuals and the community as a whole (Blackett, 1986).

In this manner, slaves like Martin were exposed to literacy and some learned to read and write from each other. It is interesting to see here that neither Martin's inner desire to read nor his struggle to acquire the tools of literacy were sufficient in themselves to make him a real reader in his own eyes, but it was the slave community that made him realize that he was indeed a reader. He became a confident, able reader from being regularly and purposefully engaged with print within a meaningful, social context. Specifically, he received recognition and encouragement for his endeavors from significant people in his life who listened, praised, and observed his progress, but were also dependent on his ability to read and write. Thus reading and writing events were collaborative acts.

There were many other largely invisible contexts for informal schooling borne out of social and historical circumstances. Literate African Americans, directly or indirectly, modeled the reading and writing process to adults and children in their communities and families. They, thereby, consciously and unconsciously promoted literacy acquisition, values, attitudes, and interests. Learning was collaborative and in many instances literacy events took place while highly motivated participants were engaged in meaningful and purposeful activity, which is as important, if not more important, than learning through formal, direct instruction. Extended family life and community life, therefore, served as fertile ground for informal literacy learning.

The diary entries of Thomas Wentworth Higginson (1971), who was in charge of an African American regiment during the Civil War, provide some of the most detailed accounts of African American soldiers' lives and thoughts during that war. Relevant to this discussion are Higginson's ethnographies of literacy learning among African American soldiers which provide yet another window on literacy learning outside formal schooling. His reports give an inside view of a camp meeting that might, at another time, have taken place in secret. Higginson's example, like those discussed thus far, demonstrates clearly what some of the key ingredients are to the success of beginning readers and writers. The soldiers created for themselves a collaborative, risk-free environment in which they struggled to learn. They set their own purposes for reading, and engaged in real reading tasks. Colonel Higginson, an anthropologist in civilian life, observed and recorded his observations of soldiers learning to read and write from each other. He wrote:

> Some smoked silently; some cleaned their guns; some sang or prayed; some told stories or traded jokes and anecdotes, filling the air with shouts of laughter, often at their officers' expense. One group sat listening intently to words being spelled from a primer. This simple act . . . was a feat 'which always commands all ears, -they rightly recognizing a mighty spell, equal to the overthrowing of monarchs, in the magic assonance of cat, hat, pat, bat, and the rest of it. . . . Their love of the spelling-book is perfectly inexhaustible, -they stumbling on by themselves, or the blind leading the blind, with the same patience they carry into everything. (Higginson, 1971, p. 24)

One evening Higginson wrote of another literacy event that was a common ritual he observed among the men:

> Strolling in the cool moonlight, I was attracted by a brilliant light beneath the trees, and cautiously approached it. A circle of thirty or forty soldiers sat around a roaring fire, while one old [man] Cato by name, was narrating an interminable tale, to the insatiable delight of the audience. (Higginson, 1971, p. 11)

As the old man skillfully told his tale of his escape from slavery, Higginson made the following observation:

> This [was] their university . . . every [one] before me, as he turned over sweet potatoes and peanuts which were roasting in the ashes, listened with reverence to the wiles of the ancient Ulysses. (Higginson, 1971, pp. 11–13)

In his December 11, 1862, journal entry, Higginson wrote of having witnessed another occasion in which the camp meeting appeared to be an informal university. His anecdote once again began with a description of a typical evening camp activity. To protect themselves from the cold at night and prepare their evening meals, the soldiers built scaled-down versions of African huts from palm leaves. Each hut was a "neatly constructed booth" designed to contain "cook-fires" (Higginson, 1971, p. 13). Some huts were made large enough to hold several men. On one particular night, Higginson watched as a large group of men gathered in one hut and sang African Methodist church songs. At some point during the singing, extemporaneous speeches were made. The event began when one soldier called out "Give me another song, boys, and I'll give you a speech" (Higginson, 1971, p. 13).

Higginson went on to write that seven speeches were given that night and that "every speech without exception" was eloquently delivered. "Perhaps," he wrote, "the most eloquent speech was given by Corporal Prince Lamkin." Lamkin gave a historical commentary on the Civil War, and on the Fremont campaign and Lincoln's presidential campaign with brilliant historical references (Higginson, 1971, pp. 13–14). Higginson's anecdote told of how Lamkin began his speech by reminding his fellow soldiers that "he had predicted this war ever since Fremont's time, to which some of the crowd assented." Having thus established his authority to speak on the issue, Lamkin continued for some time giving his interpretive account of Fremont's campaign. Following this, he gave his political opinion of what he thought should be the reaction to Lincoln's election by slaves in Florida and other related political topics. Such speech events and storytelling rituals as these were evidence of a strong African oral tradition.

In the African past, men like Cato and Lamkin would have been community storytellers-historians. As living textbooks, their songs, dances, myths, tales, anecdotes, and speeches, some humorous and some informational, would have contained the history of their people, including social mores and customs to be handed down to the next generation. The camp meeting for the slave was indeed a university grounded in a strong oral tradition, a prerequisite in preparation for formal educational experiences and the development of a written tradition. Many African American Civil War troops like the First South Carolina Volunteers under Higginson's command benefited from such collaborative literacy and emergent literacy events as those described in this study and came out of the experience readers and writers.

African American perceptions of learning and the vocabulary of literacy found a way into their already well-established oral tradition, which included their storytelling, shout prayers, sermons, secular and spiritual songs, rhythms, and chants. For example, one spiritual sung during this period suggests that learning on earth was ordained by God as preparation for the hereafter when earthly knowledge would then be put aside in order to be with the Holy One. The words of the popular spiritual are:

God got plenty o'room, got plenty o'room,
Way in [the] kingdom,
God got plenty o'room my Jesus say,
Way in [the] kingdom.
Brethren, I have come again,
Way in [the] kingdom,
To help you all pray and sing,
Way in [the] kingdom. . . .
Daniel's wisdom may I know,
Stephen's faith and spirit sure.
John's divine communion feel,
Joseph's meek and Joshua's zeal.
There is a school on earth begun,
Supported by the Holy One.
We soon shall lay our school-books by
And shout salvation as I fly. (see Fisher, 1953, p.128)

Yet another spiritual clearly points to the influence of a culture of literacy on African American spirituals during the antebellum period. Fisher (1953) notes the appearance of literacy language in the songs of slaves. On this, he wrote of an African American man in Danville, Virginia, who made a song about his reading of *Missionary Brinckerhoff*, a then-popular booklet of doctrines of 1864.

Evidence of a written tradition among African Americans following emancipation can be seen in the spiritual "Joshua Fit the Battle of Jericho." The song ends with the words "I got my ticket, leaving the thicket, and I'm heading for the golden shore." Many other references are made to having a gospel ticket or a written pass into heaven. Mullin's (1992) discussion of African American religious activities may, in part, explain the appearance of the word "ticket" in spirituals. According to Mullin, missionaries rewarded members of their congregations by giving them a color-coded card for each catechism learned. The cards were regarded as tickets necessary in order to board "the train on judgment day." The cards, according to Mullin, were held on to for life and people were often buried with their collection of cards in their coffins. The catechism cards, or tickets as they became known as, became more than what they were intended to be, and were transformed into sacred objects.

Lucy Chase and her sister Sally worked as missionaries in contraband or refugee camps to protect and provide relief aid to the thousands of African Americans displaced by the Civil War. Chase wrote that they found many African Americans, who had learned to read and write while enslaved, living in the camp. Furthermore, she reported that these individuals were not only able and willing to share their knowledge, but in fact had been doing so for some time. Chase described Jane Washington, a Craney Island woman and former slave living in the camp, as an able reader. Washington was asked to help by teaching some of the camp children until the mission school could be erected and classes started up. She responded by stating that she believed she could be of service as she had been teaching her own children and had already been teaching some of the camp people to read (see Swint, 1966).

Washington learned to read informally when she was young. She recalled that while she was growing up the men in her community would come home "tired from with their labors, sit in their doorways, with their open books, till dusk [drove] them to the fire-light and they [were] joined at their fire-sides by their little ones, with whom they 'Stumbl[ed] along right smart'" (see Swint, 1966, p. 63). In this way she had learned. Another woman in the same camp indicated that she knew how to read, and, like Washington, had already been teaching a large group of African American refugees in the contraband camp to read as well (see Swint, 1966).

In a cabin on Craney Island, described as well kept, an old African American gentleman talked about the "pay school" that he kept before the war. He had twenty students, but lost them to the free schools that missionaries established on the island when "the peace came." As for his own learning, he said that he taught himself or, in his own words, "picked it up by slant," meaning he learned informally (see Swint, 1966, p.144). The missionary commented that when the grandson of this informant that the child "read with elegance" (see Swint, 1966, p. 144).

Child-created play songs heard around that same refugee camp were themselves testaments to the camp's culture of African American literacy knowledge, attitudes, and values. Camp children chanted the following words:

> Oh happy is the child who learns to read
> When I get over
> To read that blessed book indeed.
> Chorus:
> When I get over, when I get over
> 'Twill take some time to study
> When I get over. (see Swint, 1966, pp. 125–126)

Various unconventional routes to literacy learning were taken by nineteenth-century African American families. The families were resourceful in finding learning materials and members of their community to provide informal instruction or to work with them collaboratively. Informal schools and opportunities such as those discussed made it possible for many African American adults and children to acquire and practice rudimentary literacy skills and strategies.

The previous discussion of the various paths to literacy learning traveled by African American slaves and freemen raises questions about the material culture that supported their literacy traditions. As mentioned, slaves were able to acquire, through various means, reading and writing materials. They purchased, at a dear price, religious reading materials. They used materials found in the libraries of slaveholders and slaveholders' children. Additionaly, they were supplied materials from a variety of secular and religious organizations, and obtained antislavery literature and newspapers wherever and whenever possible. They also used the Bible as literature and family letters and documents as text for learning to read and to practice reading.

One book that was frequently mentioned in the literacy histories of African American soldiers, schoolchildren, and adult readers was Webster's blue-back speller. The Webster's blue-back was actually titled *Grammatical Institute of the English Language, Part One*, was printed in 1793. In 1787, his second book, titled *The American Spelling Book*, was published. The two books were the most available books to African Americans, and to most Americans, for that matter, because they were the only American spellers of the time, and together they sold about 80 million copies between 1793 and the end of the nineteenth century. Webster's spelling books dictated how reading, grammar, and spelling were to be taught for over one hundred years. It emphasized rote memorization using the alphabet method. This method required one's first experiences with print to be the memorization of the sounds of letter chunks in lockstep order. For example, the letter chunks *at*, *ag*, *am*, and the like would be expected to be learned in isolation. Once they were mastered by the student, he or she could move on to lists of one-syllable words, then two-syllable words, and so forth up to sixteen-syllable words. Webster's spelling books also contained lessons on "history, reading and grammar, religion, and Poor Richard's precepts" (Hodges, 1977, pp. 2–3).

The significance of Webster's spellers to this study is that it was the one textbook most mentioned in the literacy talk of the nineteenth century by African Americans in general and especially by adult emergent readers. In Chapter 2, on the role of the families, for example, Nash Skipwith asked for the fourth edition of Webster's dictionary and speller. He wanted to use the book to tutor his nieces. Frederick Douglass wrote that the men and women he taught all carried spellers. Charity Bowers also mentioned that slaves carried spellers. Similarly, the African American Civil War troops were observed to have spent much of their free time using the spellers to learn to read and spell. Other references to the link between readers examined here and Webster's spellers suggest that this was a widely popular and accessible text familiar to African Americans. His book appears again in a letter written to Sally Chase and her sister Lucy: "I am learning quite fast I study 3rd Geography, 3d Reader 2 Arithmetic Websters Dictionary Elementary Spelling Book" (see Swint, 1966, p. 230).

The number of topics in Webster's spellers and the amount and type of material that had to be mastered explains why the spellers were mentioned as a constant companion of many slave and free emergent readers. The spellers contained, in addition to history lessons, geography and many other kinds of facts.

The Bible is the most mentioned book in literacy histories. Other books mentioned in the testimonies of nineteenth-century African Americans include novels, biographies, sermons, first-aid books, and popular health books. Among those mentioned are: *Pilgrim's Progress*, *City Cousin*, *The Life of Reverend John Newton Doddridge*, *Life of Solomon*, *History of Christianity the First Three Centuries*, *Plymouth Hymn Book*, *Sabbath School Collection*, and *A New Guide to Health.*

Based on the family literacy histories presented thus far, reading materials other than books were available to slaves and freemen. Sella Martin read mainstream newspapers widely distributed to the homes and businesses of people outside the African American community. Ida B. Wells, it should be recalled, wrote of reading newspapers aloud to her family and friends, as did Isaiah Montgomery. Explicit references were made to the following periodicals: the *Religious Herald*, *African Repository*, *Independent*, *New York*, *New England Puritan*, *Boston*, *Liberia Herald*, *African Luminary*, *Congregational Quarterly*, and *Freedom's Journal.*

Many types of textbooks and reference books have been mentioned so far, including dictionaries, history, chemistry, geography, arithmetic, and literature. The literacy histories examined record specific titles of books such as the *McGuffy Readers*, *Smith's Geography*, *Smith's Arithmetic*, *Smith's Grammar*, *Historia Sacrae*, *History of Europe from the Commencement of the French Revolution in 1789 to the Restoration of the Bourbons in 1815*, and *Webster's Dictionary Volumes 1–4.* The nineteenth-century African American literacy histories examined suggest that gaining access to a variety of reading materials was difficult but not impossible.

Through informal education, a literacy tradition was indeed emerging by the nineteenth century, but further strides made by African Americans to develop formal schools were met with so many social obstacles it is a wonder that the schools managed to educate as many as they did. As seen earlier, paths toward the formal education of African Americans were blocked many times with the ever-present threat of school closings in the nineteenth century. Somehow, though, through perseverance and strong will, the increasing presence of formal African American schools in the North and the South stood as proclamations that formal education, especially publicly supported education for all children, was soon to be an indisputable American reality.

People like Daniel Payne were invaluable to the building of an African American literacy tradition. Payne received his early education in an African American school, Minor's Moralist Society School in Charleston, South Carolina. After the death of his parents, his great-aunt took care of him and sent him to Minor's School, operated by free African Americans. Payne, who lived to be over seventy years old, had a long and distinguished career as an educator and clergyman. In his youth, he was an avid reader who often read until late at night. He was an excellent communicator of ideas and was talented in languages, being literate in Greek, Latin, and French. In 1828, he opened his own school. His love of literature and learning, especially biology, attracted a large number of students, and he soon expanded his course of studies to include the sciences and erected a school building. He had learned a great deal about animal science and spent long hours dissecting animals to study. However, the South Carolina legislature passed laws that made the teaching of advanced courses to African American students illegal. The penalty that would be imposed for continuing his school at the standard he knew was desperately needed in his community was a stiff fine and a brutal flogging. So after six productive years, Payne closed his first school. He was reportedly so disturbed by this turn of events that he refused to return to South Carolina until slavery was abolished (Blassingame, 1977; Payne, 1888, 1891; Woodson, 1921).

Brothers Milton and William Holland, born in the 1840s in Texas, were sent to school in Ohio. They both graduated from Albany Enterprise Academy, which was one of the oldest schools fully owned and financed by free blacks. Afterward, William along with other men from Ohio, enlisted as a solider in the 16th U.S. Colored Troops out of Nashville, Tennessee. When peace was restored, William studied at Oberlin and returned to Texas to teach. Milton served as a Republican representative from Waller County, and, while in the Texas legislature, he spearheaded a bill, passed April 5, 1887, which was aimed at the founding of a school for handicapped African American children. William was appointed by Governor L. S. Ross to be the school's superintendent in August of the same year. He served as head administrator for the next eleven years, then moved on to pursue other interests. After the death of the superintendent who filled his place when William resigned, he returned to head the institute until his death in 1907. He was praised in his obituary as an excellent administrator and educator who was admired by all who knew him. The school, which was located on about one hundred acres of land near Austin, Texas, served African American children who were either hearing or visually impaired (Blassingame, 1977).

Madame Bernard Couvent, a free woman and former slave, founded a school in New Orleans that still exists at the time of this writing. Her husband Gabriel Bernard Couvent was a wealthy man, and after his death she used their wealth, including property, to establish a school for orphaned African American children called the Catholic Indigent Orphans' School. The school, which has also been known as the Bernard Couvent School, was officially recognized in 1852. Buildings belonging to the Couvents located on Union and Great Men Streets were renovated to house the school. While Couvent was well respected and admired in the New Orleans community, European Americans were initially wary about a school for African American children, but did not contest it officially, since the school was wisely to be affiliated with the Catholic Church at the request of Madame Couvent. The Couvent Bernard School, perceived to be one of the best schools in the city, served boys and girls of African heritage, especially those who lived in the Third District of New Orleans where it was located. Five African American teachers hired: Felicie Cailloux, Armand Lanuse, Paul Trevigne, Samuel Snader, and Joanni Questy. Lanuse was the principal. The teachers were all recognized for excellence; therefore, the school enjoyed high attendance and received generous endowments, all of which helped keep its doors open. The school received donations from African Americans leaders around the nation including Thomy Lafon, Armand Lanuse, Rodolphe L. Desdunes, Aristide Mary, and Paul Trevigne. The school, which today is called the Holy Redeemer School, is located on Dauphine Street in New Orleans. Its major contribution to American culture has been the number of talented African Americans in the arts and all fields who have graduated from the school (Blassingame, 1977).

An African American, Catherine Ferguson opened a school for unwed mothers that lasted from 1779 to 1854. Ferguson operated her school in a church basement. The mission of her school was to educate young mothers. The school also saw to the education of unwanted and homeless children and worked to place them in homes within the community (Mabee, 1979).

Francis Lewis Cardozo, born a free person in Charleston, South Carolina in the late 1830s, was graduated from the University of Glasgow, Scotland, then studied at seminaries in Edinburgh and London. He became pastor of a church in Connecticut in 1864. In 1865, Cardozo founded the Avery Normal Institute in Charleston and became its principal. He had served as secretary of state under Governor Daniel H. Chamberline from 1872 to 1874 and was later elected state treasurer. He also served as a representative in the South Carolina House of Representatives. As chairperson of the Committee for Education during the constitutional convention of 1868, he worked to lay the groundwork for the establishment of a public school system in that state. Meanwhile his work in his own local community resulted in two highly academic, well-operated schools for African American children: the Colored Preparatory High (1884–1891) and the M Street High School (1891–1896) (Blassingame, 1977).

Union Seminary, which operated in Washington, D.C., on the corner of 14th and H streets from 1822 to 1867, had an interesting history. The building was constructed by Henry Smothers in 1822, and the school it housed was financed by students' tuition. At one point the school became a free school, but this arrangement did not last long, and the board of trustees appointed John W. Proust to head the school. The school was renamed the Colombian Institute and it operated for about three years, again relying on students' tuition. By 1862, Congress, however, had passed a law requiring that African American schools receive operating funds from the property taxes of African Americans. The money allotted, however, could not meet the needs of these schools, so more money was allowed to fund public education of African American children. John Francis Cook Sr. was named the new director by the board and again the school was renamed. This time it was called Union Seminary (Blassingame, 1977).

By all standards, the school under Cook was successful. It soon came to the attention of those who opposed having tax money set aside for African American schools alongside money for the operation of European American schools. The competition of other African American educational enterprises was also openly protested. Therefore, in 1835, during what became known as the Snow Riot, the Union Seminary along with African American businesses, churches, and homes were targeted for destruction by angry mobs. Many African Americans left the area. The school building, destroyed by mob violence, remained abandoned for about two years. Meanwhile, Cook and his family had moved to Pennsylvania where he taught again, returning in 1837 to re-open the school under the same name. He continued as the head administrator of that school until 1855. Following his death that year, his sons George Cook and John Francis Cook Jr. codirected the school, which closed in 1867 for practical reasons. African American schools were to receive adequate provisions for public schooling in that community; therefore, African Americans shifted their support from private African American schools to the promise of local public schools for their children. A board of education for black schools was set up separately from the board for European American schools and George Cook was appointed superintendent for the African American schools (Blassingame, 1977)

Though few in number, African American informal and formal schools were established and supported by African Americans at the end of the 1700s through the 1800s. Learning to read and write for most literate African Americans, whether formally or informally, was a long, complex process, which they endured. Paths to literacy learning were diverse for most literate nineteenth-century African Americans such that most were to take many upexpected twists and turns, and suffer stops and delays. Nevertheless, literate African Americans in the nineteenth century, in doing all they knew how to do in order to obtain systematic instruction, laid the much-needed foundation for the establishment of African American public school systems.

Chapter 4

Community

This chapter examines African American group efforts in the nineteenth century to promote literacy in their communities. Like the already-examined roles played by individuals and their families, the role played by African Americans as a group to advance community literacy had a significant impact on the development of their reading and writing traditions. As true of their other efforts with regard to their reading and writing development in the nineteenth century, their group efforts also took various forms. This chapter emphasizes the roles of such forms, including African American literary and benevolent societies, national conventions, and the African American press in the development of their community literacy traditions.

An important African American group effort was the establishment of community literary societies. Literary societies, sometimes referred to as either reading room societies or debating societies, appeared in large urban African American communities early into the nineteenth century, especially in the 1830s and the 1840s, and remained important elements in African American literacy traditions into the next century. For example, in Philadelphia between the years of 1828 and 1841, African Americans established nine different literary societies: the Reading Room Society, formed in 1828; the Female Literary Society, formed in 1831; the Library Company of Colored Persons, formed in 1833; the Philadelphia Association for Moral and

Mental Improvement of the People of Color, formed in 1835; the Rush Library and Debating Society, both began in 1836; the Demosthenian Institute and the Edgeworth Society, formed in 1837; and the Gilbert Lyceum, formed in 1841. In Pittsburgh during the decade of the 1830s, more societies formed, the Theban Literary Society in 1831 and the Young Men's Literary and the Moral Reform Society of Pittsburgh and Vicinity, formed in 1837 (Porter, 1936).

By the mid-1800s, reading room societies had appeared in the state of New York in Albany, Buffalo, New York City, Poughkeepsie, Rochester, Schenectady, and Troy. In New York City, the New York African Clarkson Society was founded in 1829. It was followed by the New York Philomathean Society in 1830 and the Phoenix Society in 1833. Named after abolitionist William Lloyd Garrison, the New York Garrison Literary Association began in 1834, and in the same year, the Ladies Literary Society also appeared. While the exact date of the formation of the Female Literary Society is not known, it has been said to have been formed in about 1836 (Porter, 1936). Two literary societies began sometime before 1843 in Albany. In Buffalo, the Young Ladies Literary Society and the Debating Society each began in about 1837. Prior to 1845, a debating society was founded in Rochester, New York. Two other groups, the Ladies Literary Society and the Dorcas Society, were also established in Rochester about this time. The Debating Society, the Literary Society, and the Mental and Moral Improvement Society all appeared in Troy, New York, around 1837 (Porter, 1936, 1945).

In Massachusetts, Boston became the center of literary activity beginning in 1832 with the Afric-American Female Intelligence Society. In 1835, the Thompson Literary and Debating Society emerged, and in 1836 two reading rooms, the Adelphic Union for the Promotion of Literature and Science and the Boston Philomathean Society, were founded. Around 1845, the Young Men's Literary Society was formed in Boston. Debating societies were founded in New Bedford, cities in Rhode Island, and in the city of Detroit. A branch of the Phoenix Society appeared in Baltimore, Maryland, and the Young Men's Mental Improvement Society for the Discussion of Moral and Philosophical Questions of all Kinds also emerged in that city. In Washington, D.C., records show that the three societies were formed before 1837: the Debating Society, the Literary Society, and the Washington Conventional Society. Reading room societies were known to exist in Cincinnati and Columbus, Ohio (Porter, 1936; Wesley, 1939; Woodson, 1968).

About the time literary societies were popular in African American communities, they were also popular in Liberia. The societies known to be active in Liberia are as follows: the Maryland Academy of Philosophy, located in Cape Palmas; the Dr. Blyden's Literary Union, located in Monrovia; and the Ladies' Mutual Relief Society, also located in Cape Palmas. A debating society that began around 1845 met every two weeks. Members listened to speeches and lectures from distinguished colonists and printed them to distribute. The Cape Palmas Lyceum, the Hall Palmas Reading Club, and the Cape Palmas Reading Room and Library Association were also active organizations established by African American immigrants to Liberia (Johnson, 1906). Toward the end of the nineteenth century, many other notable organizations appeared. One important society, the Bethel Literary and Historical Association, was organized by Bishop Daniel Payne. Members of this group included Frederick Douglass, Alexander Crummell, and Henry McNeal Turner (Woodson, 1969).

The goals, objectives, and activities of each organization varied from group to group. However, the overall purposes typically stated by drafters of literary society constitutions were to encourage reading among African American people as an activity in itself, to disseminate knowledge among African American people, to provide avenues for their involvement in scholarly pursuits, to improve reading and writing skills, and to foster the development of positive reading attitudes and interests. These objectives were meant to be accomplished through group effort in a variety of ways (Porter, 1936).

Traditionally, reading room societies required members to volunteer time to a number of task committees. Members of the society were expected to work in committees to arrange special educational events for community residents that included formal debates, speeches, lectures, and the reading of literary works. These events were widely advertised in their newspapers, enthusiastically anticipated, and well-attended. Lectures, especially those delivered by distinguished guests, engaged as many as 400–500 people from a broad base of the community. Those in attendance included mostly skilled and unskilled laborers alongside the core members of the societies who were, most likely, professional, property-owning blacks. Copies of lectures presented at events were printed and distributed to residents. Weekly periodicals were also issued through some literary societies (Porter, 1945). The newspaper *Demosthenian Shield* was a project of the Demosthenian Institute (Dann, 1971; Porter, 1936). According to Porter

(1936) and Blackett (1986), other literary societies also issued their own newspapers as mouthpieces to make known their activities and accomplishments, to inform members of the organization's needs, and as a forum to speak out on issues of concern to slaves and free persons (Dann, 1971; Porter, 1936). These periodicals were widely circulated among and supported by African American readers.

Neighborhood lending libraries were at the very heart of literary societies' activities. Donations of books, globes, maps, dictionaries, magazines, and documents, as well as donations of money to purchase reading materials, helped toward the building of adequate collections to meet the reading, research, and intellectual needs of the community (Porter, 1936).

In addition to books, manuscripts, and magazines, African American newspapers were available through reading rooms. Church magazines, such as the *African Christian Herald*, the *Christian Recorder*, and the *A.M.E. Church Review* also were widely supported by African Americans. Other publications of general interest and with issues of concern to African Americans included *Colored American*, the *National Reformer*, the *Elevator*, and other periodicals, such as magazines written for women and children. Antislavery newspapers—for example, the *Liberator*—were common to reading room collections. Historical papers generated by members of various societies were available at the society libraries as well as at other social and religious organizations, including Sunday schools. Public addresses and open letters to the American public, such as David Walker's "Appeal," appeared in the newspapers. Members who had private libraries were generous with some of their own books, lending them to the societies to be circulated and returned after a specified time. Members serving as volunteer librarians managed the circulation process, and individuals could borrow periodicals, books, and other reading materials for a designated period (Porter, 1936, 1945, 1950).

In New York City, the Phoenix Literary Society organized a ward committee in order to bring a lending library to people in their community. The community was divided into wards or neighborhoods, and a volunteer would go from house to house to establish relationships and to either drop off or pick up reading materials. This outreach program was, thereby, unique in the manner in which members attempted to have a significant impact on family literacy. They not only made unusual efforts to supply families with reading materials, but they also kept parents informed about school activities and literary society activities and events, and encouraged faithful school attendance. Members of the ward committee kept records of the number of children enrolled and actually attending regular day schools and Sunday schools in order to document the numbers of public schools that were needed in their communities (Mabee, 1979; Porter, 1936; Rury, 1983; Woodson, 1969).

Literary societies, particularly women's groups that grew from these organizations, also served other functions. For example, when winter school attendance of African American children in New York City began to decline because of a lack of warm clothing among some, members of the Phoenix Society donated money, solicited donations, sewed garments, and organized a community clothing drive. In some wards, transportation for young children who lived too far from their schools to walk in the cold was also arranged. The collective efforts had a measurable effect on the number of children able to attend schools, and attendance consequently increased. School attendance reports suggest that during the periods the Phoenix Society was most active the number of African American children in New York who attended schools was greater than it had been before organized self-help efforts were extended. Committees of other societies, following the New York Phoenix Society model, also organized to aid families in times of need, especially during cold winters (Hirsch, 1931; Litwack, 1961; Mabee, 1979; Porter, 1936; Wesley, 1939).

Literary societies also promoted community literacy by providing institutional support for adult members of the community who wanted to learn to read and write. Members attended weekly, biweekly, or monthly meetings during which they took turns reading papers they had written. Some members wrote creative works while others wrote expository papers. Poetry writing inspired by the successes of African American poets Phyllis Wheatley Peters and Jupiter Hammon was popular at that time (Porter, 1936, 1945, 1950).

In some societies, peer evaluation was a common practice. That is, written work was critiqued by fellow members and volunteer teachers from the African American community. For example, one activity enjoyed by members of the Female Literary Society of Philadelphia was the random selection of a member's composition to be read in front of peers. Later, members provided critical oral and written feedback. The names of the authors were not written on their papers. Impressive works produced by members appeared in nationally known publications and community publications (Porter, 1936).

In addition to writing sessions, the group also developed a list of books to read and as a group decided the schedule for discussion of the books. Book talks in some reading rooms were referred to as "mental feasts" (Porter, 1936; Wesley, 1939).

Some societies provided an outlet for those interested in learning the art of public speaking. At literary meetings, members wrote speeches and practiced oratory skills, delivering their speeches to a group of their peers who challenged their thinking and delivery in the group discussions that followed each speech. In fact, some groups were organized mainly to ensure a pool of informed, gifted, and talented speakers from the community who would later emerge as leaders (Porter, 1936, 1945). The public debates were held to inform the community about health, education, and political issues.

Members of literary societies generally met in buildings rented or owned by the society, a friend of the society, or a member of the society. Whenever possible, rooms in the buildings were furnished as classrooms, sitting rooms for group discussions, and libraries. Private homes were also used as meeting places. Large meeting places, such as auditoriums, were secured for special events that involved crowds of participants.

Members, who were able, paid a fee that helped with the cost of the upkeep of the building, to enlarge lending collections, and to cover the expenses of invited lecturers brought in for special events. Well-known speakers, especially those who held leadership positions in the community, spoke at other community functions and therefore reached those who had not yet joined reading room societies (Porter, 1936).

The New York Garrison Literary Association was an interesting organization. The members of the society were young children recruited from area schools. The 150 children ranged in age from five years old to fourteen years old. Drafters of the society's constitution, which included men like Henry Highland Garnet, emphasized good moral behavior, leadership, and intellectual attainment (Blackett, 1986; Porter, 1936). William Howard Day, who later on in his life was to become a leading nineteenth-century African American educator, was a precocious nine-year-old when he served a term as the Garrison Association's librarian. As head of the lending library room and its collection, he reportedly took his appointment very seriously and was recognized by Garnet and his fellow Garrisonians as having done an excellent job fulfilling his role. The Garrison Literary Association children, aided by educator Garnet, wrote and presented papers at their meetings, which were held on Saturday afternoons. The Philomathean Society allowed the Garrisonians to use their offices for their weekly meetings (Blackett, 1986; Porter, 1936).

Abudantly aware of their influence, reading room societies in Pennsylvania used formal public debates as a means of gathering informed support from the community to attack problems regarding the hiring of teachers, the building of schools, and the achievement of educational equality for their children (Porter, 1936).

The Banneker Institute, founded in 1853 in Philadelphia, was regarded by its members and the Literary Congress in Pennsylvania as an exemplary scholarly reading room society. The members were especially proud of their organization and the principles upon which it had been founded. The drafters of their constitution stated that the independent organization was founded for the educational and intellectual improvement of its members by means of lectures, debates, and other scholarly activities and was committed to "the diffusion of knowledge among all who came within the pale of its influence" (Blackett, 1986, p. 148).

The Afro-American Historical Society was a project of the Institute. Its main purpose was to collect and preserve papers and documents generated by and about African Americans. William Carl Bolivar became a bibliophile whose collection of historical records of the lives and times of nineteenth-century African Americans made an important contribution to American history (Blackett, 1986; Spady, 1974). Proud of their society and wanting to expand their range of experiences, members sought recognition and affiliation with the parent Literary Congress in Harrisburg. Following the submission of a written request, members of the Literary Congress were sent to evaluate the society for membership consideration. The membership committee observed meetings, interviewed members, and found that this well-organized, intelligent group of young men should be recognized and included in the parent organization. However, one influential group of the Literary Congress' membership organizations, the Franklin Institute, refused their application (Blackett, 1986; Porter, 1936).

The lack of publicly supported schools for their children in many areas led many to use their literary societies to finance and support schools. Regular day schools and Sunday schools were conducted in communities and made possible through funds and other types of support from the literary societies. The schools operated in a number of locations using existing structures. In some cases, land was purchased and schoolhouses were erected by these societies (Porter, 1936; Woodson, 1916).

One school was operated by the Phoenix Literary Society in a building on the corner of Canal and Mercer Streets in New York City in the 1830s. Classes reportedly were held on Mondays, Wednesdays, and Fridays from 4:00 P.M. to 9:00 P.M. Each class was one to two hours in duration. The first class started at four o'clock, the second at six o'clock, and the last class of the evening began at eight o'clock. There were about twenty-five to thirty-five students in each class. Members decided as a group on topics that would be investigated, then developed a course of study and selected books. The reading selection was divided among all of the readers, with each assigned a section of a book to read aloud. This arrangement most likely was made because of a lack of multiple copies of reading materials (Porter, 1936).

The record does not show whether the book to be read was placed on reserve in the society's library. It is likely that the books were shared. One person from each class was assigned to be a reader for the first full hour. After the reading, the group reviewed the major ideas in the reading selection. The group then convened to meet for the second hour in another room to discuss the meaning of what was read and to relate major ideas from the selection to their daily lives. The stated objective of the discussion groups was to "cultivate the mind and improve the heart" (Porter, 1936, p. 567). Following the first hour, members could spend an equal amount of time listening to lectures planned to extend their reading, which included the topics "morals, economy, and the arts and sciences" (Porter, 1936, p. 567).

It is important to the study of African American literacy traditions to understand the usefulness and popularity of literary societies. These organizations, according to Porter (1936), served as early learning institutions, enabling African Americans, especially those of little means, to educate themselves and their children, to receive reading instruction, to practice speaking, reading, and writing skills, and ultimately build roads toward the development of their own community public school systems. According to Porter (1936), reading room societies also provided for the grooming of educational leaders and community activists chosen from a wide base of community members during a time when there existed either few or no other opportunities for blacks to assemble regularly and participate fully and publicly in such activities. Reading rooms were indeed one of the few places where blacks could borrow from a collection of reading materials or discuss literary ideas. With the exception of African American churches, which did not always welcome controversial speakers, reading rooms were one of the few places well-known African American leaders could be heard by the masses of African Americans.

While individual organizations may have existed for brief periods before dying out, their work would be carried on by newer societies (Porter, 1936). Reading room societies were organized, most likely around the ebbs and flows of new friendships, business ties, personal relationships, gender concerns, reading interests, and religious or political views of their members. Members from disbanded groups joined other literary organizations. And these too flourished for a number of years and either dissolved or saw their membership undergo change. As with any organization with an evolving membership, newer members may have prompted old organizations to meet the group's changing social, intellectual, reading, speaking, and writing needs. Whatever the fate of individual societies, according to Porter (1936), the societies were a strong presence in many urban communities and remained strong throughout the nineteenth and into the twentieth century.

A letter, for example, appeared in the December 12, 1857, issue of the *Mirror of the Times*. Its message was common. People wanted to establish more reading rooms: "[There should be more] . . . debating and other literary societies . . . by which information and intelligence would be diffused amongst those of us who are too far advanced in years to commence our education by ordinary means of schools" (Dann, 1971, p. 334).

Ida Wells, a former slave who became an educator, a newspaper person, and an aggressive spokesperson in the community from the late 1870s through the early 1900s, was an active member of a lyceum in Memphis. According to Royster (1997), the group met to listen to music, recite and discuss literary works, read their own writings, and debate what were current issues. Wells became the editor of the lyceum's newspaper, the *Evening Star*.

It will be seen that nineteenth-century African Americans saw literacy attainment primarily as a means of intellectual development.

And while they regarded literacy education as an individual and family responsibility, their collective behaviors early on suggest strongly that they also saw wide African American literacy attainment to be their community's responsibility. The evidence presented in this section suggests that in urban areas property-owning African Americans paid the obligatory taxes that went toward the support of public schools in their cities; however, they were denied the right to send their children to these schools. African Americans were forced to take collective action. Their communities, therefore, whenever possible, supported their own schools. Groups of families organized to do all they could, within their means, to maintain private educational institutions. Teachers, therefore, were given free room and board in African American homes, and their salaries were independently funded by the residents or privately supplemented by wealthy members of the African American community. African American parents and other members of the community freely supplied the building materials and physical work needed to erect and maintain schools. The community also donated books and other instructional materials, wood or coal to heat classrooms, and many other basic items and services that helped make teaching and learning possible (Woodson, 1968).

Prince Hall, a leading African American community organizer and the founder of the African Free Masonry Societies, systematically petitioned authorities on behalf of African American children who were denied access to Boston public schools. After much effort by Hall and many others, African American families did receive a share of public educational funds, but they were severely restricted with regard to how they were allowed to use their tax money for African American grammar and high school education. The community could use public funds neither to build schoolhouses nor to furnish and equip schools. Shortly after receiving school tax money, however, African American parents in Boston established a school that operated in the home of Primus Hall, another member of the community who worked to better educational opportunities for African American children. After meeting in Hall's home for a number of months, the African Free Masonry Society built a schoolhouse for the children (Woodson, 1968).

Community solidarity, such as that discussed earlier, made it possible for clandestine African American schools to exist for years in private homes despite laws prohibiting the teaching of reading and writing to their children. In Fredericksburg, Virginia, the DeBaptises, the Cooks, the Lees, and the Richardses were able to secretly keep a home school in operation for several years, following the passage of a Virginian law that prohibited reading and, especially, writing education to African American children (Hartgrove, 1916). A teacher was hired by the families, and classes were held daily in the home of the DeBaptise family.

The risk of detection and the threat of prosecution for educating their children were unbearable for most families. There were fourteen children in the Richards family and all of them attended the DeBaptise home school. Unsatisfied with the circumstances of their situation, the Richards family, along with other similarly affected families, looked for solutions. One solution was to send their children to schools outside the state. This was an unwelcome alternative, but one that some parents felt compelled to take. To further complicate parents' fears of sending children away for educational purposes, the new Virginian law specifically stated that any African Americans who left Virginia for the purpose of receiving an education in another state would not be allowed to take up residence in or even to reenter Virginia. Under such pressures, some continued to risk educating their children at home and others risked losing their children and all they had earned by sending their children to be educated in nearby states (Berry & Blassingame, 1982; Hartgrove, 1916).

In Fredericksburg, meanwhile, some took collective action to stand their ground on the issue of free public education for their children. The African American community as a whole petitioned the court requesting that their children be allowed to return to Virginia upon completion of their studies in a neighboring state (Berry & Blassingame, 1982; Hartgrove, 1916). Finally, after meeting with little success, prominent families, led by the example of the Richardses, sold their family homes and land, dissolved their businesses, and left Virginia. The Richards family, among the first of the group to leave Virginia, resettled in Detroit where the family grew even more prosperous and the children were educated in African American schools in that community. Most of the Fredericksburg group who had unsuccessfully worked together to bring about change reestablished themselves elsewhere, became prosperous once again, and had a significant impact on the lives of others. Fannie M. Richards, for example, became an educator. Throughout her career, she helped to initiate African American group efforts to successfully fight for educational equality for African American children (Hartgrove, 1916).

Community solidarity could also make it possible for an individual to rely on his good name and standing in the community as currency to promote his or her own interests. Robert Purvis, a wealthy homeowner, lived at 270 Lombard Street, Philadelphia. His children attended the neighborhood public school; however, when the Philadelphia public school district began to refuse African American children admission, Purvis, the second largest taxpayer in the city refused to pay his tax bill.

Outraged, Purvis wrote the following letter to a Philadelphian school official, Mr. Joseph J. Butcher:

> Dear Sir: You called yesterday for the tax on my property in this Township, which I will pay, excepting the 'School Tax.' I object to the payment of this tax, on the ground that my rights as a citizen, and my feelings as a man and a parent, have been grossly outraged in depriving me, in violation of law and injustice, of the benefits of the school system which this tax was designed to sustain. I am perfectly aware that all that makes up the character and worth of the citizens of this township look upon the proscription and exclusion of my children from Public School as illegal, and an unjustifiable usurpation of my right. I have borne this outrage ever since the innovation upon the usual practice of admitting all the children of the Township into the Public Schools, and at considerable expense, have been obliged to obtain the services of private teachers to instruct my children, while my school tax is greater, with a single exception, than that of any other citizen of the township . . . I shall resist this tax. (Letter from Robert Purvis to Jos. J. Butcher, 1853; see Woodson, 1969, pp. 178–179)

A successful businessman in his own right, Purvis had married into a prominent African American family. His father-in-law, Forten was revered by a great many of Philadelphia's citizens as a "venerable, distinguished" gentleman who "by his skill, prudence . . . [had] arisen to affluence . . . mainly on account of his gentlemanly qualities, shining virtues, and intellectual and moral characteristics" (Woodson, 1969, pp. 174–175). Forten was also considered a war hero who had "suffered many hardships in the revolutionary war, and was [even] captured by the British while endeavoring to save his country from a foreign yoke" (Woodson, 1969, p. 175).

Philadelphia's African American elite, according to Winch (1988), and Philadelphia's European American leadership depended greatly on each other in order to control the politics of both communities. That Purvis was a son-in-law of Forten, a well-known sailmaker and a leader in the African American community, probably added weight to his demands. It might have been understood that Purvis would get strong support from the Fortens and others. Recognizing the possible problems that could emerge from a backlash to their decision, the school board acquiesced and the Purvis children were enrolled in the public school nearest Lombard Street. Community solidarity, therefore, was brought to bear on unjust policies in order to meet immediate group and individual needs and to formally address long-term community educational needs as well.

In addition to literary societies, debating societies, and community solidarity, group efforts such as African American mutual aid societies, benevolent societies, and fraternal organizations also had an impact on African American reading and writing traditions. Benevolent and mutual aid societies played a necessary role in communities by providing material, moral, and social support for reading and writing development projects. As such, they strengthened and made more meaningful other African American group efforts to improve their condition during the nineteenth century. Like the New York Phoenix Society, the benevolent organization the African Dorcas Society also helped provide adequate school clothing to those African American children most in need. As a beneficial society and not a literary one, however, it was formed as an organization solely dedicated to clothing needy African American school children (Birnie, 1927; Dann, 1971; Foner, 1975; Franklin, 1980; Frazier, 1988; Levine, 1979; Raboteau, 1988; Woodson, 1969).

These social organizations drew the community together through parades, cultural programs featuring school children, Emancipation Day celebrations, Crispus Attucks Day celebrations, ceremonies in honor of distinguished residents, musical programs, family outings, socials, family ice-skating outings, and other rituals that made the nineteenth-century African American community alive and rich in heritage (Bethel, 1981; Blackwell, 1975; Foner, 1975; Woodson, 1969).

African Americans through such societies also reached out to other African Americans across the nation. For example, the San Francisco Afro-American League sent aid to slaves, free persons, and Civil War soldiers (Daniels, 1980; Foner, 1975, Franklin, 1980; Frazier, 1988; Woodson, 1969).

One of the earliest and most effective African American benevolent societies to be organized was the Free African Society (FAS). Founded in 1787 in Philadelphia by Richard Allen and Absalom Jones. The FAS worked to accomplish a variety of goals that had either a direct or an indirect impact on the quality of education among blacks in that area. While some early societies tended to meet the social and business needs of the African American elite exclusively, core members of the FAS from the very beginning were concerned with the needs among the poor and uneducated slaves and free persons. The FAS, therefore, stood as a standard for the benevolent and mutual aid societies that followed. African American institutionalized benevolence was defined clearly by the ethics of the society's founder. According to Raboteau (1988), Allen's brand of charity emphasized group effort over individual effort in order to do the most good for the greatest number of people. Allen saw eradicating illiteracy among African Americans, especially among their young and poor, as a means to improve the future condition of all African Americans. Allen's ethics influenced the direction of other organizations' missions, and his form of organized self-help was repeated in Philadelphia and other cities as well. More chapters of the FAS were established in many large Northern cities that had substantial African American populations (Bond, 1969; Boylan, 1988; Brown, 1972; Bullock, 1970; Raboteau, 1988).

Allen developed other organizations in Philadelphia, such as the Bethel Benevolent Society and the African Society for the Education of Youth, which had a direct impact on schooling in the African American community. The following organizations were also formed: the Brooklyn Woolman Benevolent Society, in 1818; the African Society for Mutual Relief, in 1810; the Wilberforce Philanthropic Society of New York, in 1812; the Brown Fellowship Society, in 1790; and the Society of Free Blacks, in 1791 (Raboteau, 1988).

The Brown Fellowship Society School adopted articles that guided its practices. Its constitution stated that members were to be upright citizens, and temperate, orderly people. Money, a shilling of silver, was collected every month and dues were used to help those who were in need of assistance. A deceased member's family became wards of the society and were able to receive death benefits that could be used for education. The society supported a school, placed surviving children as apprentices in the community, and offered aid until the children had reached maturity.

The African Society of Boston (ASB) was organized ten years after the founding of the FAS. According to this organization's list of rules published in 1802, the society was formed as a mutual aid society that was open only to those of "high moral standards." Those who had broken any laws of the Commonwealth or the country were not allowed membership. Members were introduced to the ASB by three members of good standing, and a letter of application from the candidate was required a month in advance of the presentation. The rules were read and approved of by the candidate before acceptance in the organization. Monthly dues were twenty-five cents. The ASB invested interest accrued on money raised and dues collected. Reserving the right to invest members' funds in African American businesses was important to the development of their community. Members were able to borrow funds from the organization for a variety of reasons and receive sick benefits as well (Frazier, 1988).

In addition to paying monthly dues, a member was required to file a copy of his will with the society. If the member took an extended trip, the society protected the member's property and family. In the event of a member's death the society pledged financial assistance to the member's "lawful widow and children" (Frazier, 1988, p. 41). The constitution stated that "the Society shall consider themselves bound to relieve [the widow's] necessities, so long as she behaves herself decently, and remains a widow; and that the Society do the best in their power to place the children so that they may in time be capable of getting an honest living" (Frazier, 1988, p. 41). The ASB also took care of the deceased member's funeral expenses. The rules of this society were typical of the rules of many groups that developed throughout the nineteenth century in African American communities. Refused aid from either mainstream civic organizations or charities, African Americans took great pride in their membership in their societies as insurance for themselves and their families during times of sickness, death, natural disaster, or any other crisis (Frazier, 1988).

One example of the importance of the mutual aid societies is shown in the experiences of Ida B. Wells, who was born a slave in Holly Springs, Mississippi, in 1862. An epidemic of yellow fever took her parents and three of her siblings, leaving Wells as the head of the family before her seventeenth birthday. She and her five brothers and sisters relied on money left to them from their father who was a member of the African American Free Masons and aid from relatives; as wards of the African American Free Masons, the children received additional financial assistance. With such support, following Wells's teacher training program, she was able to take charge of the family. The American Free Mason Society helped an already capable, responsible, and talented young woman receive an education that ultimately benefited her siblings and hundreds of others (Royster, 1997).

The American Freedmen's Friend Society, formed in 1863 in New York, concerned itself with African American education among free persons. Politically, the society advocated slave resistance to slavery. This society, under the leadership of William Howard Day, worked to recruit and retain African American educators for New York grammar schools (Blackett, 1986).

Unable to enroll their children in District of Columbia schools, three freemen from that community, George Bell, Nicholas Franklin, and Moses Liverpool, came together to build a school for a population of about 500 children. All three men were, at the time they conceived the school project, illiterate. The men did not come from privileged backgrounds and in fact had spent a good part of their lives as slaves. From the onset the project appeared to have been hampered by their lack of money and administrative experience. However, the men persevered, and with the help of the community and money the men had worked to accumulate, the school was built. The Bell School existed for a short period of time before it was forced to close because of a lack of funding, among other problems. The building that was deeded to Bell remained in his hands and was to be used years later as a schoolhouse for adult education (Logan & Winston, 1982).

In the aftermath of their first failed attempt, the men became better organized to face their second challenge. Their second attempt to establish a school was buttressed by a benevolent society they had founded, the Resolute Beneficial Society. The new school was housed in the society's building. Public notice of the society's new day school opening was advertised in a newspaper as follows:

> Opening of new school for the reception of free people of color, and that ladies and gentlemen think proper to send, to be instructed in reading, writing, arithmetic, English grammar or other branches of education, applicable to their capacities. (Logan & Winston, 1982, p. 38)

Another example of how African American benevolent societies made education possible for their children can be seen in the history of African American public education. Public education was opened to African American children in Brooklyn, New York beginning in 1816. A school-within-a-school concept was used, meaning that African American children attended the same school as their European American counterparts but were taught in separate classrooms. Although housed in the same building, the two schools also had different names with the African American children's rooms being called the African District School (Mabee, 1979). Later, the African American children were removed from the building.

Ostensibly, a shortage of space in 1827 for children attending the regular district school led to the removal of the African District School and its students from the building. The Brooklyn Woolman Benevolent Society quickly moved to keep the promise of black public education in Brooklyn alive (Mabee, 1979). The organization built a school house for the displaced children and public funding continued, even though the building was privately owned and maintained. Control over the school's operation was given to the community. The school, later known as the African Public School, was operated by a board of trustees from the African American community appointed by the Brooklyn Common Council. Included on the board was a former member of the Brooklyn Woolman Benevolent Society, a former teacher at the school, a farmer, laborers, a manufacturer, and a parent. The board raised funds for the school to supplement money allotted to them from public funds. The community, through its board of trustees, took pride in the upkeep of the building and strongly influenced, perhaps for the first time in New York history, the type of education their children were to receive. They had a voice in the quality of teachers employed. African American teachers wrote the school's curriculum and instructional materials, including textbooks. The conceptional framework of the curriculum placed emphasis on African American culture and traditional, classical education. African American and European residents, each group for their own purposes, threw their support behind the efforts. According to Mabee (1979), the school received community donations and more students were enrolled over time.

The Pennsylvania Augustine Society for Education of People of Colour was developed in 1822. The belief that African American education was a community duty is made clear in its charter:

> It is our unquestionable duty which we owe ourselves, to our prosperity, and our God, who has endowed us with intellectual powers, to use the best energies of our minds and hearts in devising and adapting the most effectual means to procure for our children a more extensive and useful education than we heretofore had the power to effect. (see Woodson, 1969, p. 145)

The foregoing discussion suggests strongly that while African Americans saw literacy attainment as a means of intellectual development and regarded literacy education to be an individual and family responsibility, early on they saw literacy attainment as a community responsibility. The newspaper called the *Rights of All* effectively served as a forum for the African Free Society. The paper published African American views regarding their communities' responsibility for the fulfillment of their own educational needs. In one issue, among many the editor devoted to education and the community's responsibility, the paper proposed that free African Americans everywhere give according to that which:

> The Lord hath prospered them . . . [and that] the monies raised in this way [be used for] the establishment of libraries, reading rooms, [and] academies . . . [and to form] associations communicating with our people and the public generally, on all subjects of interest, . . . delivering stated lectures on industry, frugality, enterprise . . . thereby linking together, by one solid chain, the whole free population, so as to make them think, and feel, and act as one solid body, devoted to education and improvement. (*The Rights of All*, New York, September 18, 1829; see Dann, 1971, pp. 299–301)

African American churches in the nineteenth century developed as a strong force within both their own community and the larger community. Some African American ministers were accused of being conservative by nineteenth-century leaders, such as Frederick Douglass, because they would not permit the discussion of certain issues related to slavery and freed persons' rights to be voiced in their churches. The churches were nonetheless more than places of worship (*National Anti-Slavery Standard*, August 20, 1847; see Woodson, 1969, pp. 461–464). African American ministers such as Richard Allen aided slaves and fugitive slaves through their congregation's efforts and their own personal efforts (Raboteau, 1980).

The African American church was indeed the focal point of the community. The churches provided structure and identity to their communities while serving the practical as well as the religious needs of their members. African American congregations built places of worship and insisted that plans include classrooms for day and night schools, Sabbath schools, literary societies, temperance societies, and Bible study groups, all of which increased members' opportunities for secular reading and writing instruction and the pursuit of knowledge. Reverend Absalom Jones, who headed the St. Thomas Episcopal Church of Philadelphia, allowed the Philadelphia Library Company of Colored Persons to meet weekly in the church's basement. Among other reading, writing, and speaking activities, the literary group met to listen to lectures by fellow "members of the society and others from the first week in October to the following May of each year" (Porter, 1936, p. 526). Churches were also places where members could freely assemble to discuss issues of concern to their community and to hear antislavery speeches (Johnson, 1968).

Beginning in 1835, Philadelphia's African American churches, along with literary societies, mutual beneficial societies, and other groups, held annual conferences to report on the status of African American education in Philadelphia and other cities. They organized under the name of the Council of Philadelphia Association for the Moral and Mental Improvement of People of Color. Survey reports on the impact of their organizations on African American life were read and discussed, and plans were devised to increase their effectiveness. The numbers attending various public, private, or church-operated schools were noted in the council's reports. This coordination of efforts between churches and other social and cultural groups demonstrates how deeply seeded the group efforts were in the nineteenth century with regard to the advancement of literacy among African American people (Porter, 1936).

The African Methodist Episcopal (A.M.E.) church appointed educated and administratively talented African American clergymen such as Bishop Daniel Payne to set up community schools in their churches in the North and the South. Payne worked to maintain a high standard of education for African American children in the 1850s through church-sponsored elementary schools. Efforts to educate African American adults were also made. Many African American youth and adults, in fact, were certainly indebted to the A.M.E. Church for their first formal educational experiences (Woodson, 1968).

Through the church, home schooling was made available to poor, young African American mothers who had either little or no opportunity to receive reading and writing instruction. Teachers were sent to the neighborhoods to tutor the women in basic reading, writing, and arithmetic. Parenting and homemaking information was also emphasized in the A.M.E. church's home schooling program (Woodson, 1969).

The African American Baptist churches also organized elementary schools and Bible study groups. The Joy Street African Baptist Church of Boston, as an example, sponsored systematic schooling in its community. Ministers such as J. W. C. Pennington spent most of their careers responding to the educational needs of youths by establishing and supporting reading room societies, teaching, and lecturing. Wherever Pennington worked and preached, his churches became agents for literacy development through his weekly sermons, writings, and speeches (Blackett, 1986).

Individuals such as Alexander T. Augusta and Fannie M. J. Choppin Jackson were aided by the A.M.E. church. Under the leadership of Payne, money was raised to provide academic scholarships. Augusta learned to read and write with the help of Payne and later earned a medical degree in Toronto. After graduation, Augusta was placed in charge of that city's hospital. Following his work there, he earned a medical commission to serve in the U.S. Army. Jackson was awarded an annual scholarship of nine dollars by the church to finance part of her education. She was educated at the Rhode Island Normal School and also graduated from Oberlin College (Woodson, 1969).

Benevolent societies sponsored by churches gave funds to support the education of African Americans who emigrated to Africa in the nineteenth century. The members of the Mobile Colored Missionary Society, sponsored by the Government Street Church in Mobile, in November 1854 sent seventy-five dollars to the "cause of the Mission on Coast of Africa." The letter is signed: "S. A. Turner, Philip Wilson, James Somerville, Simon Ashe, A. Saxon, F. H. Smith, Elijah Vaughon, Godfrey Taylor, David Wilson, And 100 others" (Letters received by the American Colonization Society, July to September 1854; see Woodson, 1969, p.157).

Schools were strongly supported by the African American community in Cincinnati in the 1800s. According to Woodson (1916), African American children attended African American–owned and –supported schools by the 1820s; and by 1834, a considerable number of the 2,255 African American children and adults were regularly attending day and night schools and writing schools. Benevolent societies in mid-nineteenth-century Cincinnati raised money to aid slaves in other states and to pay teachers' salaries in their own schools. Six schools were established before the Civil War, and two additional public schools were maintained. Methodist churches and one Baptist church supported four Sabbath schools with attendance of over 300 children. A "Sabbath School or Youth's Society" was established (Woodson, 1916, p. 11). According to Woodson (1916), the following African American churches and clergymen were instrumental in the development of a literacy tradition among blacks in Cincinnati prior to the Civil War: the Baker Street Baptist Church, the Third Street Baptist Church, the Colored Christian Church, the New Street Methodist Church, and the African Methodist Church. Among the preachers then promoting this cause were John Warren, Rufus Conrad, Henry Simpson, and Wallace Shelton. Church-organized activities such as temperance and Bible-study groups were also fertile soil for the growth of literacy among African Americans.

The African American church by virtue of its dual mission to attend to both the liberation and the spiritual needs of its people, fostered the use of reading and writing as tools of liberation. The theology of liberation launched by Henry Highland Garnet, Absalom Jones, David Walker, Henry Neal Turner, and Richard Allen in the eighteenth and nineteenth centuries laid the groundwork for the role of the African American church in the liberation of African Americans. The third article in David Walker's *Appeal, in Four Articles*, entitled "The White Church's Oppression of the Black Man: Our Wretchedness in Consequence of the Preachers of the Religion of Jesus Christ," shocked many. The work attacked the oppressive nature of mainstream churches and took a radical stance on slavery that supported the right of African Americans to revolt (Aptheker, 1965; Payne, 1969).

Walker's widely read work printed in African American newspapers was followed in 1843 by Garnet's "An Address to the Slaves of the United States of America" (Frazier, 1988). Garnet, a well-known, out-spoken African American minister, headed a European American church in Troy, New York. His address, delivered at the 1843 African American Convention held in Buffalo, was entitled "The Slave Must Throw Off the Slaveholder" (Frazier, 1988). The speech called for violent slave insurrections as a means of putting an end to slavery. Both Walker's and Garnet's works were "published together in a special edition in 1848" (Frazier, 1988, p. 103). The literature that gave rise to an African American theology of liberation espoused by eighteenth- and nineteenth-century African American clergymen like Allen and Payne was well read by many African Americans. Such literature and its creators played an important role in the history of African American literacy traditions. Liberation theology included views on intellectual as well as personal freedom.

Very early in the development of the African American Methodist and Baptist churches, congregations were regularly exposed to religious literature, resulting in those who "picked up" reading through observation of daily or weekly church activities, rituals, and services. Ministers also dedicated themselves to the promotion of reading and writing through religious activities. George Liele, a minister responsible for setting up the first African American Baptist Church in Georgia, found reading to be an important way to reach members of his congregation. On this matter, an eyewitness stated "that he [George Liele] began to discover his love [for] other[s] . . . on the same plantation with himself, by reading hymns among them, encouraging them to sing, and sometimes by explaining the most striking parts of them" (Liele, 1790–1793, *Baptist Annual Register*, pp. 332–337; see Woodson, 1916, pp. 70–71).

Liele organized a free school for slave and free children. In a letter requesting reading materials for his congregation he stated that he already had:

> a few books, some good old authors and sermons, an one large bible; a good many of our members can read, and all are desirous to learn; they will be thankful for a few books to read

on Sundays and other days. (Liele, 1790–1793, *Baptist Annual Register*, pp. 332–337; see Woodson, 1916, p. 73)

All the members of Liele's church were either poor free persons or slaves, and from Liele it can be inferred that they enjoyed reading as a leisure activity on Sundays, their only day of rest (Woodson, 1916). Clearly, their reading behavior was linked to both the joy of reading and the encouragement to read by their church leaders.

Andrew Byran, head of the African Baptist Church in Savannah, wrote that fifty members of his congregation could read. The congregation was made of about 350 slaves, "many of whom have not permission from their owners to be baptized. The whole number is judged to be about five hundred and seventy-five, from the towns being taken to this present day" (see Woodson, 1916, p. 79). One church official observed that the Byran congregation was in "need of a few Bibles, the *Baptist Confession of Faith*, and *Catechism*; *Wilson on Baptism*, some of Bunyan's works, or any other that your wisdom may think useful to an [illiterate] people" (Letter from Jonathan Clarke, *Baptist Annual Register*, January 20, 1788; see Woodson, 1916, p. 79). Byran said he observed that reading religious literature to members would be useful to strengthen them religiously and therefore he advocated a practice of a regular reading aloud of church doctrine to the church body as a part of regular services.

Prior to the founding of independent African American churches, they attended European American churches where they were not allowed to fully participate in church affairs and services. They listened to sermons from assigned pews and they had little opportunity to engage in church-related reading and writing activities, especially in the way of record keeping. However, along with their full participation in the affairs of their own churches came new administrative and clerical experiences.

From the very start of the African Methodist Church, literacy was important in their struggle to achieve autonomy in their religious affairs. After Richard Allen's congregation won the right to form a black congregation in 1796, as a member of the General Methodist Conference, the Bethel Church still was subject to its rules. That meant that the Bethel Methodist Church had to sign their property over to the General Methodist Conference and have their sermons delivered or monitored weekly by a clergyman appointed by officials of the Conference. Members of the Bethel Church nevertheless held on to the keys of their church, kept their own records, controlled their own pulpit, and, for the most part, operated autonomously from the strong arm of the Methodist Conference (Raboteau, 1988).

However, in 1806, a European American clergyman, James Smith, seeking complete authority over the Bethel Church, "demanded the church keys and books and forbade meetings not called by him" (Raboteau, 1988, p. 9). After several serious confrontations, the matter was ultimately decided by the Pennsylvania Supreme Court. As a result of the court's decision, the Bethel Church became the first of many African American Methodist churches able to legally exist free of domination. The churches created their own governing body, the African Methodist Church, and formulated their own rules. Slaveholders were excluded from membership and "the office of the presiding elder was abolished" (Raboteau, 1988, p. 10). The *Methodist Discipline* served as a model for the *A.M.E Discipline*, or bylaws with some notable differences (Raboteau, 1988, p. 10). Even today, the following historical statement appears in weekly A.M.E. church bulletins to remind members that their ancestors had:

> deemed it expedient to have a form of Discipline, whereby we may guide our people in the fear of God, in the unity of the Spirit, and in the bonds of peace, and preserve us from that spiritual despotism which we have so recently experienced—remembering, that we are not to Lord it over God's heritage, . . . but with long suffering, and bowels of compassion, to bear each other's burdens, and so fulfill the law of Christ. (Raboteau, 1988, p. 10)

Other African American churches began to free themselves from outside domination, resulting in their complete control over the church records. The Williamsburg, Virginia African Baptist Church, as one of many examples, kept a church book to keep track of its members. The Williamsburg church book reported vital manuscript information on five hundred members. They kept data on members' ages, births, deaths, marriages, baptisms, and petitions for admission to church (Fichett, 1941).

The *Marriage Book of St. Phillip's Church* of Charleston, South Carolina, contains a list of marriages of free persons married by the church prior to emancipation. The earliest date recorded was 1823. The record shows eighty-four marriages listing the man, the woman (with her unmarried name), and the minister who married them. The *Book of Baptisms of St. Phillip's Church* of Charleston lists the names, dates, and names of parents of forty-three free African American children baptized there between 1824 and 1857 (Fichett, 1941).

Along with the development of their independent Methodist churches came the recording of African American spirituals and gospel songs by African American clergymen and songwriters. *The New Hymn and Tune Book for the Use of the African M. E. Zion Church,* for example, was first published in 1878 (Fisher, 1953). Richard Allen's (1801) book, *A Collection of Hymns & Spiritual Songs from Various Authors,* was also widely used in A.M.E. churches. According to Fisher (1953), Allen "kept his house open for fugitive slaves . . . [and] it was significant and important that he collected familiar hymns and spiritual songs into a book that gave evidence of what fugitive [African Americans] were singing about" (p. 37). Fisher wrote that song lyrics such as those of "Free Grace," "Weary Travelers," "Canaan, "Farewell," and "Yonder" that expressed African Americans' need to escape their conditions and other themes were typical of their songs of the time (pp. 37–38).

Indeed, Fisher writes that it was African Americans who were:

> either actual or hopeful colonists, [who] emerged as leading makers of spirituals with their themes of 'home,' 'Jacob's ladder,' and 'roll, Jordan, roll,' and with their words 'no mo' rainfall to wet you'or 'no mo'peck of corn for me,' 'I can't stay behind [away],' and 'swing lo, sweet chariot,' as well as songs about the ship of Zion. (Fisher, 1953, p. 181)

The song makers were not always ministers but often laypeople who wrote and customarily "lined songs" and made them available to the rest of the congregation. Songs or chants that were composed of words taken verbatim from the various books in the New Testament and the Old Testament became a part of meeting songs that spread from congregation to congregation. Hymnbooks that reflected the innermost thoughts of nineteenth-century African Americans were commonly found in their churches. Equally important is the fact that African American churches were being established by the thousands, involving as many as a half-million African Americans, who would be exposed to African American–composed hymns and hymnbooks (Fisher, 1953). The spread of independent African American churches hastened during the Civil War as African American churches sent missionaries into the South to minister to the spiritual needs of black troops. African American

> Baptists received permission to go within the Union lines from President Lincoln on August 21, 1863. Secretary Stanton gave approval to the African Methodist Episcopal Zion Church in 1864 and the African Methodist Episcopal Church in 1865 to follow the Union Army. (Fisher, 1953, p. 167)

Thousands of African American churches were established in southern states during this time (Fisher, 1953).

The influence of the African Baptist Church and the African Methodist Church on their congregation's exposure to and uses for print can be seen in the literacy experiences of Civil War soldiers. In the evening, the men built shelters of palm leaves and sang African Methodist hymns or just read the hymns to themselves. The following is an example: "[An] old [army] cook . . . with enormous spectacles [was] perusing a hymnbook by the light of a pine splinter, in his deserted cook booth of palmetto leaves" (Higginson, 1971, p. 24).

The following literacy event took place during a funeral for a African American soldier. To better understand the nature of the experience and how it relates to reading and oral language, it is important to understand the term *deaconing out.* One way of sharing the words from a written text was through deaconing out the lines to members of the group. That is, the song leader or chorister would read or sing the words of a hymn or a passage of the Bible line by line pausing a the end of each line to allow the group to repeat or echo what was sung. This call–response pattern of singing is very much a part of the West African heritage and became integral to services in the African American church tradition. The call–response style of singing has lasted to the present (Fisher, 1953; Herskovits, 1941; Higginson, 1971; Levine, 1971, 1979; Raboteau, 1978). The event, presided over by an African American army chaplin, provides another example of how African Americans' written traditions became entwined with their oral traditions:

> [T]he chaplin deaconing out the hymn in their favorite way. This ended, he announced his text,— 'This poor man cried, and the Lord heard him, and delivered him out of his trouble'

> . . . Instantly the cracked voice of the [lead singer] was uplifted, intoning the text, as if it were the first verse of another hymn. (Higginson, 1971, p. 26)

Literacy events such as this suggest that the African American church was indeed important to the development of literacy traditions of African Americans in the nineteenth century.

Plantation ministries organized sermons and lectures, attended by slaves and slaveholders. Although the religious instruction received was handed down to them from the slaveholders' perspectives, African Americans found ways to adapt the slaveholders' teachings, which emphasized obedience to the slaveholder, to their own worldviews, creating new meanings for the sermons for themselves. They searched the Bible for passages that could support their emancipation rather than justify their perpetual enslavement. Slaveholders encouraged religious instruction "without letters" to avoid teaching slaves to write (Cornelius, 1983, 1991). Salvation, it was believed, could be reached only by those who could read God's word themselves. Reading instruction for the purpose of enabling the slave to read the Bible was not considered to be as dangerous a threat to the slave–master relationship as was writing instruction. Without the ability to write, they believed, slaves would have been limited in their struggles for emancipation. An oral method was preferred in order to teach religion to slaves (Cornelius, 1991). This lack of understanding of how literacy develops, on the part of slaveholders, led to a number of literate slaves.

Various forms of literature for family prayers were printed and distributed to slaveholders by Bishop William Meade, William Capers, Charles C. Jones, and other founders of plantation ministries. Meade, Capers, and Jones encouraged slaveholders to teach Christianity to slaves. The *Catechism of Jones* was widely used and contained sections on the " Duty of Masters," the "Duty of Servants," and the Ten Commandments (Fisher, 1953, p. 136). According to Fisher, some plantation evangelists used "Apostles Creed and the Lord's Prayer as lesson material" (p. 136). A sacred time was set aside in either the early morning or the evening for family prayers. Popular during the antebellum period were the following religious instructional guides: *A Short Catechism for the Use of Colored Members on Trial of Methodist Episcopal Church of South Carolina*, *A Catechism for Colored Persons*, and *Sermons, Dialogues and Narratives for*

Servants, To Be Read To Them in Families (Raboteau, 1980). Also available for prayers were "audiovisual aids, such as hymns and scripture cards, illustrations of Bible stories with texts, questions, and answers printed on the back" (Raboteau, 1980, p. 162).

Although slaveholders were encouraged by their church leaders to lead the morning or evening prayers, the duty was often handed over to a literate slave, as in the case of Lucy Skipwith on the Hopewell Plantation. However, Skipwith's discussion of the attitude of the slave families in regard to portions of family prayers confirms Fisher's (1953) argument that slaves resisted the teachings of slaveholders. Skipwith wrote that although she tried to conduct family prayers in the manner she was instructed to, presumably according to one of the above guides, the slave families rejected parts of the service in favor of, in her own words, "their own prayers" (Letter from Lucy Skipwith to John Cocke, Hopewell Plantation, August 17, 1854; see Miller, 1978, p. 196).

Much in the same way that Cocke placed Skipwith in charge of family prayers, other plantation owners, according to Raboteau (1980), assigned servants to lead the prayers. Sometimes prayers were held at midnight or just before sunrise. An older servant on some plantations was assigned to teach little children their prayers and catechisms. Family prayers, which included singing hymns, reading the Bible, reciting prayers, and other reading-related activities, were a normal part of some African Americans' daily lives.

The emergence of African American owned–newspapers in the nineteenth century was as important to the development of African American reading and writing traditions as any group effort discussed thus far. Equally important was the development of mass authentic literature through the African American newspapers' widespread publication of works written by slaves and free persons (Bontemps, 1969; Davis & Gates, 1985; Foner, 1975). The printed word was a weapon against slavery and social injustice that African Americans mastered and exploited beyond the scope that slaveholders and their supporters feared they would or could. The newspapers were, in some places, available in abundance, relatively cheap to produce, and accessible on either a daily or weekly basis. The newspapers influenced their thinking, fostered the building of loyalties and consensus on issues. The newspapers brought African Americans together as a national community (Dann, 1971; Foner, 1975; Gross, 1947; Porter, 1936). Newspapers were read not only in urban areas, but in rural areas as well (Dann, 1971; Woodson, 1969). Newspaper agents traveled to increase circulation of the papers in remote areas. Traveling lecturers employed by various organizations also increased the worldliness of rural people through the circulation of African American newspapers. These lecturers delivered copies of African American newspapers and collected subscriptions as well. This enabled families who did not live in or near large urban areas to have access to reading materials. On this, the *Colored American* published its following mission statement that reads in part:

> This paper is designed to be the organ of the Colored Americans—to be looked on as their own, and devoted to their interests—through which they can make known their views to the public—can communicate with each other and their friends with them. (see Dann, 1971, p. 45)

The statement continues with a call for lecturers and agents to promote the newspaper among African Americans in over 5,000 towns in the nation. Each subscription cost $1.50 per year, so the aim was to keep the weekly publication within the means of most people. The goal of the *Alienated American* as stated in its mission statement was to provide "aid to [African American] educational development" (Dann, 1971, p. 51). The newspaper promised to have a "considerable amount of reading material at a low price" (Dann, 1971, pp. 51–52). The paper also boasted the writing talents of well-known African American journalists including "Samuel R. Ward, J. W. C. Pennington, Amos G. Beman, Dr. Martin R. Delany, and Charles Howard Day" (Dann, 1971, p. 52). Each journalist was located in a major American city, in Canada, or in Europe.

William Wells Brown wrote that as a traveling lecturer employed by the Association of Education and Industry, he traveled to many places to provide educational lectures in African American communities in New England, Ohio, New York, and elsewhere. In Wyoming County, New York, Brown visited people in the communities of Warsaw, Weathersfield, and Castile all of which are located at the western end of the state. Upon entering Wyoming County, he was greeted by members of the community, John W. Paney and Rodolphus W. Hewitt, who traveled about 30 miles by wagon to meet Brown and welcome his arrival. The men, whom Brown described as "noble-hearted," were accompanied by their wives and children (Letter from

William Wells Brown to Mr. Gay, *National Anti-Slavery Standard*, November 12, 1846; see Woodson, 1969, p. 353).

While visiting the small communities in Wyoming County where he was well received, Brown gave lectures, made available to residents copies of the *National Standard*, an antislavery publication, and took orders for subscriptions. Brown traveled to Stueben County, New York, and visited people in the towns of Bath, Avoca, Mud Creek, Corning, and Hammondsport, as well as the city of Rochester. In Yates County, Brown visited Penn Yan, Geneva, and Canoga. His later travels took him to the state of Ohio. He spoke in churches, such as the African Baptist Church on Baker Street in Cincinnati, and met with African American educators and clergymen. He was welcomed into Salem, Ohio, and described it as a "centre of radical anti-slavery in the Buckeye State," which indeed it was in the 1800s (see Woodson, 1969, p. 368). Also he traveled to lecture and further promote the *National Standard* in Springfield, Pittsfield, and Cleveland (*Correspondence of The Anti-Slavery Standard*, March 31, 1855; see Woodson, 1969, pp. 367–369). In Cleveland, he was met by William Howard Day who was then the editor of the *Alienated American*, published in that city. Again, Brown, as would many other lecturers and newspaper agents, left copies of African American and antislavery papers not only to inform them about events happening in communities around the nation, but also to encourage reading among African Americans living in the most remote areas (Woodson, 1969).

Crucial to the survival of churches, schools, benevolent and literary societies, and other organizations, the African American newspaper was in itself a community. Newspapers linked together many African Americans and others who shared common interests in ways not available to them before the 1820s (Dann, 1971). The first African American newspaper to be founded was *Freedom's Journal*. It was founded in 1827 following the emancipation of African Americans in New York State. Later, the paper became *Colored American* followed by many others. Newspapers developed on the East Coast and the West Coast linked regional concerns of blacks and broadened the definition of the black community, giving it a national identity. Without the African American newspaper, a black national community may have never truly developed when and as it did (Dann, 1971).

Without the courage and talents of black journalists and the proliferation of reading material they produced during this period, less would known about the thoughts of ordinary blacks with regard to literacy and schooling. African American thought regarding literacy education as a means of social advancement, a patriotic duty, and a divine moral duty entrusted to blacks became an important theme to appear again and again in African American newspapers at the close of the Civil War, as the following letter to the editors of *The Black Republication* illustrates:

> The Duty of Colored Men In Louisiana
> The people who have just thrown off their chains, have now a high duty before them. God has surely broken the bonds that bound us, and man was made the instrument -his blood the price. We have privileges now. Let us enjoy them rationally, and like men. We have been outraged. Our intellects have been chained as well as our bodies. Indeed, our very souls were not our own. It was a crime to teach us. We dar[ed] not hold a book in our hands. . . . Better times have come . . . [we as a people can succeed] . . . not by the sword, . . . but by our life, our conduct, our honesty, industry, temperance, religion, education, truthfulness-these will be the virtues that will make us strong. . . . Above all, our devotion to our flag, and our manly conduct must be our loud appeal and the ground of our hope. (*The Black Republican*, New Orleans, April 15, 1865; see Dann, 1971, pp. 338–339)

It is through weekly or monthly periodicals that informational reports were disseminated, ideas were given a national platform, and national movements that affected blacks' lives were for the first time openly debated by the masses of African Americans. This alone gave impetus to reading and writing traditions as reading periodicals became a weekly ritual and a pastime. On the important role played by African American journalists, Ida Wells, as a columnist for the *Living Way*, wrote:

> I had an instinctive feeling that people who had little or no school training should have something coming into their homes weekly which dealt with their problems in a simple, helpful way. So in weekly letters to the Living Way, I wrote in a plain, common-sense way on the things which concerned

> our people. Knowing that their education was limited, I never used a word of two syllables where one would serve the purpose. (see Royster, 1997, p. 16)

A commentary on Wells's contribution to journalism and to African American community literacy traditions in general is noteworthy. It was well-known that Wells was one who had the ability to reach all readers, including the young, old, male, and female. Additionally, Wells was known to have inspired other young African American people to write and publish because she spoke out on issues of importance to freemen and slaves. She "believ[ed] that there is no agency so potent as the press in reaching and elevating people" (Dann, 1971, p. 63). The term *elevation* in nineteenth-century African American journalism most often referred to social improvement through education and, especially, mass literacy. Wells also wrote for African American women's and children's publications, including the *Ivy* and *Our Women and Children Magazine.* Poet and educator Francis Watkins Harper was also a regular contributor to the two magazines (Dann, 1971).

Other African American female journalists wrote specifically for children and women. Lucretia Newman Coleman wrote poetry for *Our Women and Children Magazine.* W. E. Matthews, under the pen name Victoria Earle, wrote stories for the *New York Weekly and Family Paper.* Coleman wrote history textbooks for African American children. Amelia Johnson's children's magazine, *Ivy,* contained eight pages of stories, poems, and essays of interest to African American children. Her interest in children and reading led her to write a story book that she hoped would be used by children in Sunday schools. Another important contributor to *Our Women and Children Magazine* and *Ivy* was Mary E. Britton who wrote under the pen name of Meb. Britton was also editor of the Women's column of the *Lexington Herald* (see Dann, 1971; Woodson, 1969).

One of the most valuable contributions the newspapers made to the development of African American literacy traditions was the publication of slave narratives. Davis and Gates (1985) point out that the most widely known slave narratives, such as those written by Frederick Douglass, Booker T. Washington, and George Washington Carver, were published as single volumes; however excerpts from these and many others often appeared in black newspapers. Narratives in their entirety also appeared in newspapers.

Like many Americans in the nineteenth century, African Americans read the narratives and other literature with great interest. Additionally, African Americans faithfully subscribed to African American papers. The *North Star*, edited by Frederick Douglass, had a circulation of about 3,000, and Thomas Fortune's paper, the *Freeman*, had about 5,000 regular subscribers (Dann, 1971). In San Francisco, the *Elevator* had a circulation of about 1,000, which, according to Dann (1971), was significant because of the size of the black population at the time the paper was printed. According to Dann, newspapers printed between 1827 and 1890 were passed along, such that one paper was often read by as many as one hundred people. William Lloyd Garrison, a European American abolitionist and the founder of the *Liberator*, wrote that African American subscribers as a group bought the most newspapers and were the most prompt with paying their subscription bills of all groups in the country (Cain, 1995). Therefore, it can be argued that African American newspapers were instrumental in bringing reading materials into the homes of many African Americans in the nineteenth century.

However useful African American journalists, male and female, were to their community, they paid a high price for their devotion and contribution. They were not always able to freely express their ideas without repercussions. One writer, John Hill, discussed the problem of being able to write and literacy freedom. As a runaway slave, Hill settled in an African American community in Canada and spoke of his feelings regarding his desire to be able to enjoy the freedom of expression. Hill wrote:

> I'm in America, but not under Such a Government that I cannot express myself, speak, think, or write so as I am able, and if my master had allowed me to have an education I would make them American slave-holders . . . tremble when I spoke, and when I take my Pen in hand their knees smote together . . . I say give me freedom . . . or death. (see Woodson, 1969, p. 582)

Wells wrote about her experiences as a journalist in the eighteenth and nineteenth centuries. Her autobiography, *To Speak the Truth Freely*, was written when she was sixty-nine years old. After her death, her youngest daughter published the work in 1970. The work speaks of Wells's frustration, throughout her long career, with being unable, without fear of reprisal, to truly document social and moral crimes and to record the African American community's reaction to them (Henderson, 1993; Royster, 1997). As a journalist she wrote a column that appeared in newspapers across the nation, and her name thus became familiar to American readers. This was to be a bittersweet accomplishment. When she later took over ownership of a newspaper in Memphis, *Free Speech*, greater name recognition was followed by a greater number of hostile readers. Wells's condemnation of the lynching of African American males, both young and old, in the South aroused the anger of Southern hate groups who responded, often violently, to Wells's writing. While she was away from Memphis at a speaking engagement at an African Methodist Church in Philadelphia, her newspaper's building was destroyed by an angry mob (Franklin, 1995; Royster, 1997). Worse still, Wells's life was threatened; and thus, she moved to New York where she worked as a journalist for *New York Age*. It was during this time that she wrote her autobiography in which she said, "Having lost my paper, and a price put on my life, and been made exile from home for hinting at the truth, I felt I owed it to myself and to my race to tell the whole truth now that I was where I could do so freely" (see Royster, 1977, p. 18). Journalists like Wells were instrumental to the success of nineteenth-century newspapers and this in turn fostered and hastened the development of African American family and community traditions.

From the newspapers generated by African Americans, much can be learned about their national and regional efforts to promote literacy among their people. Principally, the National Black Convention Movement in the nineteenth century stands as a forerunner for the African American national organizations of today that have had a crucial impact on civil rights movements in the twentieth century, including the struggle for educational equality.

National African American conventions began in the 1800s, and were especially influential in the 1820s, 1830s, and 1840s. These times were marked by acts of extreme violence toward African Americans. African American churches, schools, businesses, newspaper offices, bookstores, and homes were destroyed by European American mob violence. African Americans were physically attacked and lynched, and free African Americans were subjected to enslavement if they could not prove their legal status or pay fines imposed on them to maintain their status. Legal restrictions were increasingly imposed on African Americans to regulate their mobility and to prohibit their learning to read and write and their use of public funds to educate their children. They were also prohibited from the use of public transportation. In places where they had a right to vote, they were suddenly and abruptly disenfranchised. In response to laws barring them from full participation in American society, African Americans organized at the national level (Gross, 1947; Woodson, 1969).

Additionally, the movement by leaders in the American government to remove free African Americans from America and to resettle them on the coast of West Africa was alarming to many African Americans. The formation of the ACS by members of the government and slaveholders for these purposes was considered to be a means to eliminate free persons' opposition to slavery, reduce labor competition between groups, and accomplish many other equally disturbing aims (Beyan, 1991; Gross, 1947).

For much of the 1800s, the call for unity among African American benevolent societies, literary societies, churches, mutual aid societies, temperance societies, and other organizations resulted in the holding of large conventions. State conventions were held to discuss regional issues and to determine representatives to national conventions. Notable state conventions were held in New York State. California African Americans organized to send delegates to conventions on the East Coast. State conventions were held in San Francisco during the years 1855 to 1857 and then again in 1865, 1873, 1880, and 1882. African American churches opened their doors and gave over their pulpits to black and white abolitionists. Boarding arrangements for speakers and attendants who traveled long distances were made with the members of the congregations and friends of African American people (Gross, 1947; Woodson, 1969).

African American clergy, representative of many different denominations, met in Philadelphia at Bethel Methodist Church on August 10, 1817. The president of the conference was James Forten. Russell Parrot was the secretary and others such as Absalom Jones, Richard Allen and John Gloucester, the heads of the three largest African American churches, were leading participants (Gross, 1947). All were devoted to the advancement of African American literacy. Proceedings of the convention were published in the *Freedom's Journal* (Gross, 1947).

The first National Negro Convention was formally held in 1830 in Philadelphia at the Bethel Baptist Church. The conference convened with sessions open to leaders from September 15 to September 20 and continued from September 20 to September 24 with sessions open to all delegates. The president of the 1830 conference was Richard Allen. The Second National Convention was held in Philadelphia from June 6, 1831 to June 11, 1831. A conference was held every year after that until 1836. Following a temporary halt in national conventions, they gained support once again in the later years of the nineteenth century. Besides Philadelphia, national conventions were held in New York City, Syracuse, and Albany. Regional meetings were held in New York in Syracuse, Rochester, Troy, Buffalo, and Utica (Gross, 1947, Raboteau, 1980; Woodson, 1969).

Overall, the state, regional, and national conventions accomplished a great deal with respect to African Americans' ability to cope with the major problems facing them during this period, especially in the area of education where there were legal restrictions to their access to education. Committees were formed at conferences to meet the practical educational needs. The committees worked to establish community-based Phoenix Literary societies in large urban areas and to support schools, orphanages, and the individuals who bravely maintained schools that enrolled African American children. Reports of social and educational progress and plans for the regular collection of data related to the educational status of African Americans were made.

David Ruggles, a leader of the American Reform Society, asked committee members who attended the meeting of the Convention of the American Reform Board held in New York City in September 1841, to come prepared "to report to the Convention," the following:

> The statistics of our people in the place in which you reside; the number of children in schools, and the state of education; the number of mechanics, their different trades, and how employed; the number of people in chain gangs in the south; the number of churches, church members, and clergymen, designating their denomination; and the condition of our people generally, in relation to the "pursuit of happiness." (see Woodson, 1969, p. 252)

Petitions to the American government were formulated by national conventions with regard to the education of African American children. A black college was organized in 1831 in New Haven, Connecticut, by the Second National Negro Convention. Addresses to the American people were made and published as pamphlets to give the uniform political positions of African Americans as a people.

The conventions represent the largest, most widespread, organized effort of African Americans in the nineteenth century to promote literacy among their people. This legacy carried over into the next century as black organizations such as the National Association for the Advancement of Colored People (NAACP) hired African American lawyers like Thurgood Marshall, who later was appointed to the Supreme Court, to use the courts to fight for equal education for African American children.

The impact of various African American unified efforts to promote literacy among their people was indeed significant to the development of nineteenth-century African American reading and writing traditions. Churches, benevolent societies, literary societies, newspapers, and national conventions played significant roles in the development of African American family and community literacy traditions.

Chapter 5

Conclusions

This study examined the influence of the nineteenth-century African American family and community on the development of their literacy traditions from their own perspectives based on the cultural meanings they attached to their reading, writing, speaking, listening, and viewing behaviors. This study investigated three research questions about nineteenth century, literate African Americans: (1) What were the family and community literacy motivations, functions, perceptions, interests, and attitudes that determined their traditions; (2) In what concrete ways did the family and community support literacy development; and (3) What was the formative nature of their family and community literacy traditions?

African Americans used the language arts as follows: (1) to protect their family and community ways of life; (2) as a means of group and individual expression; (3) as a means of intellectual growth and stimulation; and (4) to secure their rightful place in society.

Literate and emergent literate families pursued diverse forms of formal and informal educational opportunities. Literacy learning was a family responsibility and a community responsibility. The nature of daily family rituals provided rich contexts for the development of literacy knowledge, attitudes, values, and interests. Community solidarity and collective resistance to social and legal barriers to formal education resulted in the formation of separate African American social and cultural organizations and the development of African American educational leaders. The latent and manifest functions of community rituals that grew out of the activities of church and other social and cultural organizations provided meaning for literacy development.

What was the formative nature of their family and community literacy traditions? The processes of learning to read and write for nineteenth-century African Americans did not differ from those of contemporary readers and writers. Literacy learning was a collaborative effort. Spelling development progressed in stages from early phonemic, transitional, and conventional spelling. Decoding and understanding environmental print was valued. Reading comprehension was emphasized in Bible and secular reading. Emphasis was placed on reading and writing to effect social change.

A variety of informal learning strategies were detailed in African American literacy histories including modeling of reading and writing processes, making connections between written traditions and oral traditions, and repeated readings to develop fluency and sight vocabulary. Formal reading instruction reflected then-current thought about how reading, writing, and spelling should be taught and reinforced. African Americans developed diverse reading and writing interests and functions.

Of the three questions investigated, the first is indeed the most complex. There are multiple explanations of the underlying motivations for nineteenth-century African American literacy behaviors borne out of African American thought and experience. African American conceptualizations of freedom, literacy, the universal rights of all humans, and the responsibilities of family and community to educate their young offer the best explanations of why they acquired the tools of literacy and why they developed literacy traditions.

The themes or categories of meanings directly related to the question of literacy—attitudes, interests, perceptions, function, and motivations—that emanated from the examined oral and written testimonies are discussed. Expressions of these categories of meanings are used in this analysis to organize and highlight the empirical evidence already presented in the previous chapters.

Categories of Cultural Meanings and Expressions of Themes

Before I'd Be a Slave, I'd Be Buried in My Grave

Freedom, regardless of the cost, is a dominant theme of the African American experience, which has developed complex configurations.

The words in this category come from the song "O Freedom" sung by African American Union soldiers during the Civil War. This song represents their resolve to sacrifice all in their struggle for freedom.

For the many African American men, young, old, slave and free, who joined the Union Army, and their families who traveled along with the troops in the back of the lines, the word *freedom* undoubtedly had multiple and yet common shades of meanings. African Americans regardless of their legal status generally spoke of freedom in innumerable ways.

For example, the word *freedom* was at times synonymous with the terms social or legal status and at other times it meant a state of mind. Freedom also meant mobility for free men and women as well as enslaved men and women whose parents, spouses, siblings, and friends lived away from them. Freedom, as it has been mentioned earlier in this work, to move around freely from one plantation to another or from one state to another state to see family was an important liberty that most could not enjoy (Levine, 1971, 1979). Freedom as a construct appears in African American literacy speech. It is also found in African American art forms, including dance, humor, folk sayings, stories, song, music, literature, paintings, sculpture, film, and photographs (Bontemps, 1969; Daniels, 1980; Davis & Gates, 1985; Fisher, 1953; Franklin, 1995; Gates, 1989; Herskovits, 1941; Levine, 1971, 1979). Abolitionists were sometimes referred to as friends of freedom, sons and daughters of freedom, or brothers and sisters of freedom. It is likely that the word *freedom* appears in nineteenth-century African American speech and writings more so than any other single word. Freedom at any cost is a recurrent theme in African American life histories and it has come to mean many complex and different ideas in the African American community. Lyrics from the song, "O Freedom," demonstrate this:

> O freedom, O freedom,
> O freedom after a while
> And before I'd be a slave, I'd be buried in my grave,
> And go home to my Lord and be free. (see Lomax, 1947)

Expressions

Freedom, for nineteenth-century African Americans, meant intellectual sovereignty, control over one's inner self or deepest soul

(Andrews, 1986; Bontemps, 1969; Davis & Gates, 1985). Evidence from the literacy histories examined in this study suggests that this is true. In fact, the concept of freedom of the inner self appeared in their literacy talk more often than any other form of freedom. For many of the people examined in the previous chapters, being a reader and a writer, figuratively, was to be a free man or a free woman, and, conversely, being a slave meant being unable to read and write regardless of legal status (Bontemps, 1969; Davis & Gates, 1985; Genovese, 1976; Levine, 1979). The latter concept of freedom was the foremost underlying motivation for reading and writing.

This study showed that both literate and emergent literate African Americans associated freedom with reading and writing. Life for the nineteenth-century African American was a continuous struggle for the freedom to obtain the type of intellectual stimulation and development that can be had from reading and writing. Inner self refers to the intellectual development that comes with reflection upon ideas and the generation and production of ideas through written and oral language. As evident in the literacy histories of the families examined, most of the authors explicitly and implicitly wrote that they would have preferred death to a life devoid of intellectual growth and stimulation for themselves and their children. Some wrote that life before learning to read and write was a cramped, musty prison, a social death. On the other hand, learning to read was commonly likened to a rebirth or awakening, or a feeling of independence.

An example of literacy awareness is presented in Chapter 2 and can be seen in the poem, "Learning to Read" by Frances Watkins Harper. This poem was written before the Civil War (Davis, Redding & Joyce, 1991). The former slave woman, Chole, characterized in the poem, learned to read after the age of sixty. Like many slaves and former slaves, Chole read and reread Bible passages she had heard along the way and memorized them verbatim. She read them until she was able to recognize certain words in other contexts. Chole practiced her reading in the face of ridicule from others who wanted to know why at her late age she would even want to trouble herself to learn to read. Chole's becoming a reader was likened to her finally acquiring a "place to call [her] own and [feeling] independent as a queen upon her throne" (see Davis, Redding, & Joyce, 1991, pp. 206–207).

That place Chole found, or her inner self where she alone reigned, was a place from which she knew she could never be separated. Others, such as the Evans family, Josiah Henson, and Frederick Douglass's students equated learning to read, regardless of how late in life they acquired their reading and writing skills, either to gaining a sense of independence or having their minds unshackled. Literacy as freedom from ignorance and the development of an inner self was indeed an important theme in the reading and writing histories examined in this work.

Another common shade of meaning of this theme, literacy as freedom from ignorance and the freedom to develop an inner self, speaks to the problem of literate African Americans' lack of freedom of to express their thoughts openly. Freedom of written expression was indeed important. Literacy histories discussed previously demonstrated the frustration of nineteenth-century African Americans in being unable to use writing as a tool of self-expression and intellectual growth. This was evident in the histories of Ida B. Wells, John Hill, Father Josiah Henson, Frederick Douglass, and many others. In years following the Civil War, for the so-called freed African American, the label *free* was bittersweet. Unable to tell their stories without harm and the threat of harm was for them indeed social imprisonment.

In slightly different terms, the analogy of the lack of literacy freedom to a social death can be seen in Jennie Hill's account. Hill, introduced in Chapter 2, found being literate meant that she could proudly claim her place in a long, collective memory. She did not emphasize what literacy meant to her in terms of her legal status. Instead, she told with pride that she was more fortunate than most because she had a literate mother who was able to record the dates of her own and Hill's birth. Hill implied that this gave her a valuable written record of her own existence or history: to whom, when, and where she was born and her family name (Woodson, 1969). A written record of her existence written by her mother's hand, not the slaveholder's whose entry of every slave born on his plantation might have been recorded in the same manner as the birth of his cattle, was her proof that she was far more than a slave. It meant that she was first and foremost a human being. She also linked the value she placed on literacy to her marriage bonds. She told of her wedding ceremony, performed by a literate slave preacher who used the Bible. Many other women examined in this study were not as fortunate as Hill; Susan Boggs for example, implied that being unable to enter their own names and their children's names into the record of human history on their own and to tell their stories in their own hand was indeed a cruel social death.

Another commonly expressed variation on the theme of literacy as freedom evidenced in the family and community literacy histories examined in this study is African Americans' definition of literacy freedom as a means to protect their family and their family way of life. For the families studied, the Purvis family, the Richardses, the Braddocks, and others, the freedom of reading and writing meant being able to have a measure of control over their spouses', children's, and their aging relatives' lives and futures. Like all parents, African American parents, literate and emergent literate, free and enslaved, felt the need to protect, nurture, and influence the lives of their children. The universal role of parents is to pass along the knowledge of their culture or traditions to their children so that their children will have the necessary information and skills to successfully mature into functional, self-reliant, and productive adults, capable of continuing the cycle and perpetuating the culture and their family ways of life.

With respect to the preceding idea about the universal role of parents and the use of literacy, African Americans wrote to protect their children's present and future well-being and to create short-term and long-range educational opportunities for them. Families examined in this study wrote and received letters and telegraph messages as a means of communicating with antislavery organizations such as the Underground Railroad. They also wrote to slaveholders on behalf of their children; as taxpayers they demanded in letters to public school officials that their children receive a public education; they filed petitions to the courts to allow their children to be educated in their home states; they submitted editorials to newspapers; and they wrote public addresses, all of which were done to protect their children's well-being and their family way of life.

It was discovered in this work that families left written documents that provide detailed evidence of their long-range planning for the education of their children. After a long illness, John Miller, as noted in Chapter 2, made arrangements in the event of his death for the education of his youngest daughter Philena. The arrangement for his daughter's education was made between Miller and a Quaker teacher who lived in town. It was agreed that after learning to read, write, and sew, his daughter Philena would be returned to her natural mother in a better position to care for her mother and be a source of security and comfort for her as she aged (Woodson, 1969). Thomas Braddock, whose family was also referred to earlier, left a will much more formal than the letter Miller wrote. In this document, he gave his library to his children, and he also gave specific instructions regarding the regular academic education he wanted for his children and the type of trade apprenticeships he had planned for them when they had finished formal schooling (Schweninger, 1990).

Literacy freedom in order to protect their families and their family life as a literacy history theme was manifested in the ways that African Americans kept family bonds strong through letter writing. As was demonstrated in this work, the realities of American society for African Americans left most families little choice but to maintain, at a high emotional cost, long distance relationships between siblings and spouses, between parents and their children, and between one's family and extended family members (Gutman, 1976).

It has been concluded from the evidence gathered and evaluated in this study that African American family life and literacy are historically linked. The links between the concept of literacy as freedom to grow intellectually for children and adults, literacy as freedom from ignorance, literacy as freedom to express ideas openly, literacy as freedom to record family history and add one's own history to the record of human literacy, and literacy as freedom to protect family members and family life, and to strengthen family bonds were indeed commonly expressed in the literacy histories of the families examined.

It has also been concluded that families' desire for literacy freedom was not solely for survival nor reserved for times of crisis, but also for simpler, less complex reasons. Families in this study, it may be remembered, sometimes wrote to share a bit of news or family gossip. It has been discovered that family reading and writing activities were integral to family life. Ceremonies that marked key events in the life course such as birth, marriage, the burial of deceased family members, along with daily rituals such as reading aloud from the Bible, reading family documents, reciting family prayers, and singing hymns, and many other religious and secular family traditions that enriched and gave meaning to African American family life also gave purpose to reading, writing, and speaking activities. As evidenced by the literacy histories studied in this work, men, women, and children read a variety of fiction and nonfiction popular in the wider culture, including stories, novels, poems, newspaper and magazine articles, narratives, autobiographies, biographies, humorous anecdotes, and religious books. It has been discovered in this study that textbooks in all disciplines were read, including geography, arithmetic, grammar, spelling, and philosophy. Specialized books such as family health books and authoritative first aid books were read as were health books popularized by lay people.

African American families also engaged in a variety of other literacy experiences that were integral to their family and community life. For example, in addition to the religious literature noted in Chapter 4 in the discussion of the relationships between literacy tradition and the African American church, slaves were very familiar with and contributed to religious literature published and distributed by the American Tract Society, which was founded in 1825 (Swint, 1966).

It has been discovered in this work that African American family literacy talk revealed their multiple perceptions of literacy as a form of freedom. Literacy freedom was associated with the development of an inner self, freedom from ignorance, and freedom to contribute to the record of human experience. Moreover, literacy freedom as it was associated with literacy acquisition, literacy attitudes, values, and literacy functions commonly focused on reading- and writing-related activities that were embedded in family life. Literacy was an integral enrichment of family life, a means of intellectual growth and stimulation, a leisure activity, and it enabled family members to protect each other and their family life.

So That I Can Enjoy the Right of Man

The name of this category comes from a letter written by a former slave, Peter Butler, who was introduced in the beginning of the study. Butler wrote about his wish to live in a place where he could "educate [his] children and enjoy the right of man" (see Woodson, 1969, p. 93). The fulfillment of human needs and the exercise of basic human rights is a pervasive theme in African American studies. Expressions of this category of literacy motivations are discussed below.

Expressions

Closely related to the theme of literacy as a freedom is the theme of literacy as a universal right. The perception of literacy defined in universal terms like literacy as a basic human right suggests its importance to the culture. Defined as such, literacy becomes sacred; also sacred would be the rituals and artifacts associated with reading and learning to read. This would include reading and writing materials such as books, writing slates, chalkboard, quills, paper, ink, and the like. African Americans' deification of reading and writing supported the development of their literacy traditions. Behaviors that do not take on a higher meaning beyond ensuring basic survival could not survive the test of time and space.

It was discovered in this study that in order to keep their family and community literacy traditions robust, African Americans who could not provide an education for their children where they lived uprooted their families, sent children to places where they would be allowed to learn freely, educated their children in secret, or taught them to read at home. African Americans, including those who were preliterate, struggled to educate their children, and thus acted on their belief that literacy was a sacred and fundamental human right that they would seize for themselves and their children if they were not granted the opportunity to exercise this right openly. This belief was indeed central to the families' transmission of African American literacy traditions.

Specific Ways Families Promoted Literacy

Keep Your Hand on the Plow

This section addresses the diverse ways in which African Americans were committed to family literacy development. The theme of family literacy achievement as a long and difficult struggle was persistent in African American family literacy histories. Thus the title of this section, "Keep Your Hand on the Plow," is an attempt to make clear the relationship between African American family life and literacy development.

The song "Keep Your Hand on the Plow" is a synthesis of different versions of African American and European American folk songs. Sometimes known by the title "Hold On," "Keep Your Hand on the Plow" was not a hymn, but a work song sung by field slaves to make their long hours of labor bearable. The song served to advise a people who were locked in a seemingly endless struggle to hold on to faith that they would succeed in the end. The lyrics reflect a belief that they as a people could win any battle if they fought it cleverly enough and long enough. The theme of patient, tireless struggle is common in African American songs. For example, among the most widely recognized words of this century's Civil Rights movement are "we shall overcome" from the African American song sung by marching protesters.

The same theme finds a place in not only other African American songs, but also, as discussed in Chapter 2, in African American folk literature. For example, the African American folk tales of the adventures of Brother Rabbit told by slaves in the South are rooted in West African tales of Anansi the Spider. The names of the characters changed after the Africans' forced migration to America; however, the basic stories and characters remained intact. Again, as with his West African brother, Anansi, Brother Rabbit came to represent the common man who, although small, was able to outwit his enemy, Brother Fox, time and time again. The slaves identified with their Brothers Anansi and Fox as they told and retold humorous anecdotes of the countless ways they had managed to outwit slaveholders and other foes.

The belief, therefore, that "we shall overcome some day," or the need to "keep your hand on the plow," was manifest in almost all aspects of nineteenth-century African American life. Attitudes and perceptions, as with all human behaviors, are informed by one's system of meaning. If nineteenth-century African American adults viewed life as a continuous struggle during which they could expect arbitrary, unreasonable, and irrational obstacles and delays in the achievement of key life goals, then this was most likely the knowledge that they were compelled to pass along to their children. They would need to pass along the knowledge that success comes with long struggle and requires patience and wit. Consequently, children as well as adults were expected to be resourceful and ever watchful for opportunities to meet any of their life's goals. Lyrics from "Keep Your Hand on the Plow" include:

Got my hands on the gospel plow,
Wouldn't take nothin' for my journey now,
Keep your hand on the plow,
Hold on. . . .

Freedom's name is mighty sweet,
All the world's gonna meet,
Keep your hand on the plow,
Hold on. (see Goss, 1989)

Expressions

The behaviors of the families studied in Chapter 2 suggest that they were indeed guided by the belief that along with struggle came success. Three examples suggest that this was the case for the families studied. In most cases African Americans in the 1800s devoted their entire lives to acquiring the basic tools of literacy. Like most parents, those studied would have preferred that their children learn to read and write at a young age, but they expected that because of the objective reality of their circumstances learning to read and write may not begin for their children until late childhood, early adulthood, or even late adulthood.

Many, as has been demonstrated, acted on the beliefs that their success and their children's success was inevitable and that the good always win in the end. This, they believed, was true as long as a family could maneuver around the many obstacles in their path. Many parents expressed the belief that even if they did not learn to read and write themselves, they would have considered themselves successful if their children did. The same can be said about their siblings. Many implied that they worked to help a brother or sister learn to read and write because they believed that achievement was not an individual accomplishment but a shared experience. Learning to read was indeed affected by the family's life course.

For many of the families examined, educational activities, strategies for gaining access to reading and writing instruction and materials, and routines for learning and practicing reading changed suddenly, profoundly, and often. This left families with few choices but to adapt quickly to the change, formulate new strategies, establish new routines, and continue on until the next crisis. Thus siblings in any given family in the African American community were commonly guided or forced along widely different paths of literacy learning, depending on where and when they were born. To whom they were born was most certainly a factor of their success;

however, as discovered in Chapter 3 on African American informal and formal schools, regardless of parents' financial resources, they did not always have control over where and how their children would be educated.

Additionally, families could not assume that the legal, social, and historical circumstances under which one child in the family was schooled would be available in the immediate future for their other children in the family. Children were expected to keep plans about learning to read or write secret. The same was true with regard to a community's expectations. Parents developed community-wide networks and strategies for promoting literacy that were often profoundly and suddenly affected by changes in social and historical circumstances. Different cohorts, therefore, had widely different schooling histories. Like the family, the community as a whole kept its strategies for schooling its children from becoming general knowledge as well as possible.

Educational opportunities for African American children varied across time and geography. When, how, or if children were able to reach certain milestones in their life courses, such as learning to read and write, was affected by their parents' resourcefulness, social and historical circumstances, their individual life courses, and their families' life courses. The educational experiences of most African Americans in the 1800s were characterized by a number of different kinds of attempts, obstacles, and delays. Their belief systems led them to invent strategies to cope with the objective realities of American society. The goal of parenting for nineteenth-century African Americans was to teach their children to prepare for and adapt to change.

In some cases, families affected their environment to the benefit of themselves and their children. As observed in this study, some slaves were capable of positioning themselves in ways that led to educational opportunities for their children and the children of the community as well. Educational opportunities could lead to a generation of literate adults or at least a small cohort of literate people in a given area. This could be said, for example, about the Skipwith family and the other families on the Hopewell plantation. Lucy Skipwith's children and grandchildren, and those of other parents, learned to read and write under difficult circumstances.

The plantation school was operated at cross-purposes since both the teacher and the school children held slave status. They were, as noted by Miller (1978) and Wiley (1980), laborers first and scholars second as far as slaveholder John Cocke was concerned. Nonetheless, Lucy expected parents to send their children to evening school regularly and the children to participate fully. She was demanding of herself in running the infant, Sabbath, and evening schools. Moreover, she demanded the cooperation of her students and their parents, the overseer Mike Smith, and Cocke in the running of the schools.

Lucy successfully negotiated for the best teachers she could get to help the children and herself, and for supplies and reading materials. She rode out threats of assault when she did not disband her students and close her schools only to begin again when she felt it was safe to do so. She developed teaching and learning strategies and rewrote texts so that they would be appropriate for the children she taught. Lucy also managed to educate the oldest children during harvest and planting times and withstood periods of low enrollment caused by poor health, work schedules, and deaths among her students. Through all her problems, Lucy remained optimistic. Some battles she won; others she lost.

Educators in African American formal and informal schools in urban areas commonly faced similar battles, but, like Lucy, continued to educate as best they could. The idea that reading and writing were obtainable skills, provided one was clever and worked long enough, removed as many obstacles as humanly possible, and learned to expect and plan for irrational delays, characterized the family literacy histories examined in this study.

Specific Ways the Community Promoted Literacy

The evidence presented suggests that African American communities promoted literacy among their people through formal and informal means. Community activities and cohesiveness led to collective action; community solidarity, camp meetings, and collaborative literacy events were among the many informal ways the African American community promoted literacy. Organized, formal efforts to promote literacy were also evident in the literacy histories discussed. The following categories address the research question of the specific ways the African American community promoted mass literacy among its people.

Many Thousand Go

"Many Thousand Go" is a farewell song written spontaneously by a former slave "as he was on the gangplank of a ship bound for Liberia" (Fisher, 1953, p. 125). Although nearly two centuries have passed since the song first appeared, it is still sung by African American choirs today. The song appeared around 1832 along with hundreds of other farewell songs written and sung by thousands of African Americans who left their homes to live in new lands. Farewell songs were written to tell of the harshness of slavery and to encourage family and friends to leave for the Promised Land. The theme of escape from the hardships of life is so common to the African American experience of the past centuries that it would be impossible to imagine that the theme would not be a part of the African American literary histories.

An estimated 18,000 African Americans left America as settlers in new lands like Liberia. Most left in deep despair, intending not to become a new people, but to reestablish their African American social and cultural institutions in a new land where they could be free to live out the American ideal.

Most African Americans, alarmed by the many thousands who had gone, banded together, fully aware that the organized, institutional efforts of European Americans to enslave them, legally or otherwise, would have to be countered with organized efforts of their own. This awareness, once acted upon, resulted in collective resistance through the rapid proliferation of African American organizations such as reading rooms and benevolent societies, neighborhood lending libraries, debating societies, church groups, national conventions, and the African American press, all of which hastened the development of a national and international African American community. Following are the words of the song "Many Thousand Go":

No more peck o'corn for me,
No more, no more
No more peck o'corn for me,
Many thousand go.
No more driver's lash for me,
No more, no more,
No more driver's lash for me,
Many thousand go.

No more pint o'salt for me,
No more, no more,
No more pint o'salt for me,
Many thousand go.
No more hundred lash for me,
No more, no more,
No more hundred lash for me,
Many thousand go. (see Fisher, 1953, p. 125)

Expressions

Collective resistance to slavery and harsh social conditions for African Americans was a characteristic strategy used by this group during the nineteenth century. African American religious and secular organizations took the responsibility of educating their people. The strong force of independent African American churches and other social organizations provided material support for educating the masses of African American slave and free families. While nineteenth-century African Americans developed separate institutions in response to immediate social circumstances, they have had a long history of social and cultural institutions that functioned as means to assemble, to educate, to govern, and to provide for the spiritual and materials needs of members of their society. As mentioned in the body of this work, African Americans' social institutions were influenced by their retention of the West African secret society. African Americans who transmitted, reproduced, and modified this institution to meet the institutional needs of their community developed strong organizations that had a lasting and profound effect on the development of their literacy traditions. In America the secret society took the form of the camp meeting that was, it is argued in this work, a setting for informal literacy learning. African American's early collective efforts to formally and informally educate their people eventually laid the foundation of public education in the South for African Americans and poor European Americans, the latter being included because they were often similarly voiceless (Franklin, 1980; Woodson, 1968).

African American newspapers and other publications that functioned as organs of these organizations provided literature for the masses of African Americans who for the first time had an opportunity to express their ideas in print and to see the ideas of many of their leaders and ordinary people like themselves in print. Literature was relatively accessible and affordable to the many who heretofore had little opportunity to own or borrow a variety of reading materials. Agents for newspapers traveled to large cities, small towns, and remote rural areas in order to increase circulation of their publications and to encourage growth in readership among their people.

The role of the nineteenth-century African American church in the promotion of mass literacy in the African American community has been examined in Chapter 4 of this study. It can be concluded from the empirical evidence that the African American church had a profound impact on the development of African American literacy traditions. The church had a dual mission to provide spiritual guidance and to liberate its people. Church leaders saw the promotion of mass literacy among their people as a form of liberation and therefore provided material support for the education of thousands of their own people.

Moreover, the literacy activities that were a natural outgrowth of church services and church- or community-related activities also gave material, social, and cultural support for the development of a written tradition or an invisible curriculum for literacy learning. African American hymnals, church record books and publications, along with church-sponsored schools and neighborhood educational programs were a part of the church's invisible curriculum for literacy learning. All these were indeed important to the development of the African American written tradition.

Steal Away

Steal away, steal away,
Steal away to Jesus,
Steal away, steal away home,
I hain't long to stay here. (see Fisher, 1953)

It was noted in Chapter 3 that the song "Steal Away" is believed to have been written by a literate slave, Nat Turner, who led a bloody rebellion against slaveholders and their families in Virginia in 1831. The long-held fear that a literate slave was dangerous was reinforced by slaveholders' association of literacy with slave rebellions. There were serious repercussions from the Nat Turner rebellion and other such rebellions throughout the African American community for decades. Restrictions and bans were placed on teaching of African Americans to read and write or on slaves' freedom to engage in any reading- and writing-related activities. This and other events had a direct impact on the life histories of slaves and freemen. Regarding this analysis, Chapter 3 presents the thoughts of former slave Charity Bowery whose testimony about the known risks and dangers to African Americans for learning to read and write at camp meetings is important to recall. Bowery and Frederick Douglass both talked about lashings and lynchings that were known to have happened when African Americans were found secretly learning to read and write.

The lyrics of "Steal Away" are forever reminders of the ways in which nineteenth-century slave culture developed at times unobserved or unnoticed by the slaveholder. The lyrics are also reminders of the degree to which the slaveholders' ignorance of the slaves' culture was one of the slaves' greatest strengths. According to Blassingame (1972), slaveholders who were ignorant of slave culture overestimated their control over the slave community. This song, along with many others such as "Follow the Drinking Gourd," "O Run, Mary, Run," and "Swing Lo, Sweet Chariot," was a signal song (Fisher, 1953). Signal songs can be thought of as cultural signs, words, or behaviors that signify different levels of meanings depending on the context in which they are embedded. Cultural signs are signals for those who understand them to act in specific ways. One can have tacit and explicit knowledge of signs in one's culture while those outside the culture may not notice the subtle meanings and changes of meaning when the signs are contextualized in unfamiliar ways. Signal songs, for example, were used to call people together for a secret meeting, commonly referred to as a camp meeting. Oral tradition precedes all written traditions. It is clear why songs and meetings were major to African American literacy development.

It was found in this study that camp meetings were not only a means to meet with family and friends without the knowledge of slaveholders to plan escapes or insurrections, or for prayers or singing, but were also rich opportunities for slaves to learn from each other. Informal learning experiences for nineteenth-century African American adults and children were critical to the passing on of cultural knowledge, especially literacy knowledge that favors studies of learning in formal classrooms. It is assumed in this study that cultural knowledge in the African American community was passed along through the ritual of the community camp meeting and the family meeting. Learning as a collaborative family or community act is an important theme to understanding the role of the family and community in the development of a literacy tradition.

Expressions

Group meetings had common characteristics. Meetings were called together using signal songs or cultural signs that were as central to the ritual of the camp meeting as the ringing of a school bell. There were participation structures that were well rehearsed and followed in a predictable manner. In order to participate one had to share a song, or tell of, read, or dramatize an actual or imagined event. Other common characteristics were prescribed ways of calling a group together and ending a meeting, a purpose or focus to the meeting, a sacred object in the form of a respected and knowledgeable person, rituals of songs and speeches, and often a recitation or reading. Messages espoused by storytellers and other speakers were sacred truths, meaning that the group shared beliefs that were affirmed in their stories, songs, and other forms of expression. The meetings were usually held beyond the observation of outsiders and members of the group had a definite sense of belonging to a group almost as important as the family.

Fisher (1953) found that camp meetings also usually included reading from a sacred book, most often the Bible. Raboteau (1980), however, found that religious ceremonies led by illiterate exhorters or preachers were more common and were characterized by the leader of the services being capable of reciting whole chapters of the Bible from memory. Some, according to Raboteau, held the Bible open to the appropriate section while speaking rather than actually reading while others claimed that they had no need to look at the words for the words were written in their hearts. From a developmental perspective, this type of emergent literacy behavior has long been recognized by reading scholars as a prerequisite for mature reading behaviors. To any of these events, written text was sacred and as much a part of the ritual as any other element.

Similar informal learning participation structures were indeed evident in the nineteenth-century church services described by William Wells Brown, Frederick Douglass, and others. Those described in the literature resemble the camp meeting participation structures and included similar rituals. The same can be said about the participation of family and neighbors in the collaborative reading of family documents witnessed by interviewer Lydia Child (see Blassingame, 1977). The gathering of families in the slave community kitchen after sundown to dictate messages to Martin Sella and to listen to the young boy read them letters, newspapers, documents, stories, and other items of importance to the community is another example of informal learning in the African American community.

Understanding literacy learning as an integral part of family and community life is important to understanding the development of nineteenth-century African American literacy traditions. Informal learning through family meetings and variations of the camp meeting was as important to the early African American as any of the learning that took place in formal educational settings. It was through the camp, family, and community meetings that the range of language activities and rituals common to any classroom were learned, practiced, evaluated, and given group sanction and meaning. The range of language activities included preaching (a form lecturing), making speeches, storytelling, acting out stories and events, listening to stories and responding appropriately, letter writing, informational and recreational reading, discussing life skills, the relating of autobiographical and biographical accounts, reciting the alphabet, and spelling words, among other activities that enriched the development of a written tradition.

Somebody's Calling My Name

Hush, hush, somebody's calling my name,
Hush, hush somebody's calling my name,
O my Lord, O my Lord,
What can I do?

The spiritual "Somebody's Calling My Name," written during the antebellum period, was most likely used as a signal song or a call to meeting song. However, the words of this particular song appear to demand that the singer answer a somewhat more important call. Answering the call of one's divine duty to his fellow man is very much a theme in African American thought. According to Sweet (1976), "throughout the nineteenth century, African Americans leaders such as Frederick Douglass, Booker T. Washington, William Wells Brown, Henry Highland Garnet, Martin Delany, and Robert Purvis shared a common belief system" (p. 1). Sweet argues that the African American nineteenth-century leadership acted on the belief that they as a people were entrusted with a divine duty to hold Americans to the promise of the ideas fought for in the American Revolution. Further, Sweet argues that nineteenth-century African American thought among the most articulate regarded the struggle against slavery and the Civil War as a continuation of the American Revolution. The writings and actions of nineteenth-century African Americans reflect the theme that all Americans, especially America's oppressed, had a "high, moral, duty" to fight for the equality of all (see Woodson, 1969, p. 339).

African American leaders in the 1800s, like many reform-minded leaders of the time, spoke often of social and moral reform, social elevation, and moral uplift when referring to social problems. The leaders typically preached sermons, wrote articles, and made speeches advising people to be a law-abiding, sober, and educated people. In the speaking and writing style of the times, African American community leaders told their people that only "by their conduct, honesty, industry, temperance, religion, education, and truthfulness . . . and their devotion to the flag" could they hope to overcome racial prejudice and discrimination (Dann, 1971, pp. 338–339). The belief that their community and their institutions should reflect the highest moral standards was expressed by nineteenth-century African American leaders and the founders of African American nationalism. Words of reform were part of the written constitutions of their many benevolent and mutual-aid societies. African American church youth groups and adult temperance groups proliferated in the nineteenth century as did ladies' auxiliary clubs, such as the African Dorcas Society, which was dedicated to the welfare and education of African American youth.

According to Sweet (1976), from the very beginnings of the African American nationalist movement, they for the most part were dedicated to the idea of maintaining their identity and African heritage while at the same time committed to the idea of inclusion in American society. His argument is confirmed in the names of the African American community organizations discussed in Chapter 4, the African Free Society, the African Methodist Episcopalian Church, the African Baptist Church, the New York African Clarkson Society, among an extensive list of other organizations in which the word

African was central to the organization's purpose. Maintaining African identity and working for inclusion were typical institutional responses to social issues. Their responses can be characterized as a unity of opposites. While the two ideas, inclusion and African American nationalism, seem to be at odds, Sweet argues that the synthesis of the two guided the ways in which African Americans responded to the objective realities of American society. Nineteenth-century African American thought supported community efforts to advance their people.

Expressions

Mass literacy as a means of social uplift or elevation was a common theme associated with nineteenth-century African American community efforts to promote literacy among their people. The role of the African American community in the development of reading and writing traditions has been discussed. African American thought regarding literacy suggests the belief that everyone had a divine moral duty to learn to read and write and teach others as well. Mass literacy as social reform, moral uplift, or social elevation was also associated with patriotic duty as African American leaders came to the defense all America's poor as well as their own people, accusing the American system of ignoring the powerless and voiceless. The efforts of African Americans in the years immediately following the Civil War led to the development of public schools in the South, not only for African American children but also for poor European American children (Bullock, 1970; Franklin, 1980; Woodson, 1969). The role of the community in providing material, instructional, and financial support for literacy development was guided by the belief that education for all African American people was necessary for full inclusion into American society.

Plenty O' Room

The words of the song "Plenty O' Room" represented an important contradiction of the idea that American society had been expansive enough to comfortably house all. The word *room* as a cultural symbol did not refer to heavenly accommodations, but to earthly ones. Fisher (1953) argues that the symbolism of African American folk music lyrics, such as "I'm going home to my Lord" and "I am bound for Canaan land," were references to this world and not the world beyond. One fugitive slave, discouraged by events in America, wrote of his feelings and encouraged other fugitives to come to Canada. He wrote that he "believe[d] that there is Rome enough for the coloreds and the whites of United States" (see Woodson, 1969, p. 582). The words *room enough*, along with related words and phrases, appear frequently in African American life and literacy histories.

Although Christian doctrine espoused by plantation ministries was used as a means to encourage slaves to wait for freedom in the hereafter, slaves wrote and sang songs about finding heaven and freedom on earth (Fisher, 1953; Herskovists, 1941; Levine, 1971, 1979; Stuckey, 1987). Their references were rooted in the here and now. The meanings nineteenth-century African Americans attached to their separate institutions suggest that they were created as a means to accommodate their people in the present, not some distant future. Further, their words and actions suggest that African American institutions functioned not only to meet immediate needs but also to work toward the expansion of the American ideal. The lyrics from one version of the song "Plenty O' Room" are:

> [Chorus:]
> God got plenty o'room, got plenty o'room,
> 'Way in [the] kingdom. (see Fisher, 1953)

Expressions

The formation of separate African American educational institutions in the nineteenth century was an effort by the African American community and parents to meet the immediate needs of their people while at the same time work for educational equality. African Americans expressed the belief that there was plenty of room for all in America's public schools. This is manifested by the aims of some African American educators and their early educational institutions to emphasize high academic standards and basic literacy, and at the same time foster the development of African American community leaders dedicated to promoting literacy and fighting for equality. Literary societies, the educational arm of the A.M.E. Church and the African Baptist Church, benevolent societies, and other organizations, promoted literacy while at the same time taking collective steps through national, regional, state and local conferences to prepare their community and the larger American community for the support for public educational African Americans.

The Nature of African American Literacy Traditions

Having answered this study's most complex questions of how and especially why nineteenth-century African Americans developed their literacy traditions, conclusions can now be drawn regarding the nature of the traditions themselves. References to the nature of the literacy traditions have been made already since it is not possible to discuss either one or both of the first two research questions without some discussion of the types of reading and writing traditions in which the people under examination engaged. This section, therefore, directly addresses the third research question: What was the formative nature of nineteenth-century African American literacy traditions? The emphasis, at this point, is on descriptions of the types of reading and writing knowledge that members of this group learned, practiced, held on to, and passed along to their children and others. It was decided that because of the descriptive quality of this third research question, a departure from the themes or categories of meanings established earlier would be pragmatic. This is not to imply that the categories of meanings and expressions of these are no longer relevant, for, though they are pushed to the background for the purpose of this section, they are not forgotten. Taken as a whole the categories of meaning that emanated from the data collected regarding nineteenth-century African Americans' underlying motives for the making of their literacy traditions and the specific ways they promoted literacy among their people stand as a necessary backdrop for the following description of the nature of their literacy traditions. Without the understanding established from the previous analysis, such descriptions would be groundless.

This description of literacy traditions is also grounded in the definition of tradition formulated earlier in this work that asserts that traditions are acquired ways of thinking, believing, and behaving that are dynamic, mutable, and resilient. By this definition, traditions, including literacy traditions, are recurring behaviors that are integral and meaningful components of group interactions and function to actively and purposely engage the group in rituals intended for the maintenance, well-being, and continuation of a social group. Social and cultural groups, then, by this definition, reproduce their ways of life through their traditions, as can be seen in their values, interests, attitudes, and practices. The evidence presented in Chapters 2, 3, and 4 suggests that there were many different African American family and community literacy traditions shaped by the objective realities of a range of social and historical circumstances and the unique ways that African Americans, as a group, responded to those difficult circumstances. Conclusions based on the findings of this study about what constituted nineteenth-century African American literacy traditions, the diversity of nineteenth-century African American literacy traditions, and the universal qualities of those traditions are again highlighted in this section.

With regard to what constituted nineteenth-century African American literacy, the readers and writers examined demonstrated emergent and mature reading and writing behaviors. Their oral and written testimonies along with other artifacts produced in their communities provided evidence throughout this study that a wide range of literacy knowledge was acquired, practiced, and transmitted from one generation to the next.

As might be expected, environmental print was discovered to be commonly mentioned in the literacy history studied. Simple recognition of the names of towns, streets, and ships, and family names, members of the slaveholding community, and the prices of goods and services enabled African Americans some measure of control over their circumstances. During the Civil War, people read public notices regarding where, how, and with which unit to enlist. One may recall that Susie King Taylor's grandmother read Confederate propaganda signs and explained their political meanings to Susie. One might also recall that in order to continue to elude patrollers, fugitive slaves read wanted posters written by slaveholders and distributed by local authorities. Slaves read newspaper headlines to gain knowledge regarding changes to laws or local ordinances that could affect plans for a general emancipation and the quality of their lives. News regarding antislavery efforts and progress often spread quickly through slave communities via newspapers.

The evidence gleaned from the literacy histories examined suggests that readers mastered rudimentary reading skills by reading and rereading Bible chapters until they could do so with fluency and understanding. Some people read for traditional religious reasons while others read the Bible solely for the purpose of learning to read, as the Bible and other religious materials were the most accessible sources of print available in their community. Words were copied over in the sand or on slates until readers were able to recognize them in new contexts. It was discovered in the evidence presented that emergent and mature readers fashioned writing tools such as quills. They made ink and paper out of natural elements in order to practice handwriting and preserve their thoughts. African American families expected and received books and writing materials as rewards from missionaries and other teachers for their conversion to Christianity or for secular learning and spent their days of rest reading and writing or learning to read and write. They carried spellers, public notices, and newspapers with them in order to read them whenever they had time.

Analysis of the texts produced by many of the writers in this study suggests that they learned in a manner that was characteristic of most writers. Writers ranged in development from early phonemic through phonemic and transitional, to conventional spellers (Clay, 1982a). Their writings were powerful statements of their understanding of relationships between written and oral language. They wrote to inform, to entertain, to inquire about, and to persuade their readers. Letters took on a characteristic format and style. That is, letters typically were dated, had a greeting, a body, and predictable closing statements, and were signed. Penmanship in the original writings was in keeping with nineteenth-century style. Handwriting, therefore, tended to be flowery and ornate.

Knowledge of the alphabet, letter sounds, and the sounds of chunks and clusters of letters were stressed in their literacy histories which would be very much in line with nineteenth-century literacy traditions in America. Many remembered, therefore, that their earliest experiences with print involved learning how to recognize and write the alphabet and using primers. Those who began their education within a formal tradition generally recalled that after they learned the alphabet, they were allowed to progress to one-syllable words, then to those with two, three, and so forth. It appeared that those who learned entirely from an informal tradition generally learned more holistically. In some rural settings, it should be recalled, African Americans learned from listening to others read, observing others write, and practicing what they learned alone or with a multiage group of family and kin from their community. Urban dwellers developed traditions that involved formal reading room societies, debating societies, and lyceums. Reading and writing traditions studied emphasized the power of the written word to effect change and the use of literacy to better understand their social and historical conditions, characterized the types of reading and writing activities practiced and promoted in urban centers. Those who experienced a mixture of formal and informal traditions, which included most, relied on textbook lessons as well as practical lessons in which there was an emphasis on reading at the letter and word level.

African American literacy histories also emphasized reading comprehension. Interpreting religious and secular literature in ways that were meaningful to their lives was mentioned often as was their need to express their personal and political ideas as a means of resistance to their circumstances. Relating whole Bible chapters, such as Exodus, to the African American experience and the use of symbolic language in letter writing and song making was characteristic. Slave narratives, newspaper articles, speeches, and many other forms of African American written expression developed as genres that were moving and powerful.

Number recognition, the understanding of mathematical concepts, and the use of mathematical symbols daily were life skills discussed by cooks, carpenters, dressmakers, wheelwrights, printers, farmworkers, blacksmiths, storekeepers, stonemasons, clergy, teachers, and many others. Some families kept books to record their purchases, the selling or trading of goods, bank savings, and earnings from overwork and the hiring out of their labor. Dates and numbers of births, marriages, baptisms, deaths, and other such records were important to those examined. Many made references to their gaining a heavenly reward in the afterlife as "being included that number." Presumably, they meant being among the few righteous chosen by God to enter heaven. Calendars, thermometers, weights, scales, and other measuring tools were used. The evidence presented suggests that both mature and emergent readers were familiar with reading, interpreting numbers, writing numerals, and the application of mathematical processes.

African Americans in the nineteenth century learned, practiced, held on to, and passed along literacy knowledge that was characteristically diverse and universal. They made use of the print and other materials in their environments to read and produce written materials. They followed traditional routes to or formal practices for learning to read and when necessary created their own informal paths toward literacy. They found unique ways to practice their literacy knowledge, they valued what they learned and they transmitted a tradition of literacy learning to their children.

Summary

This study has illustrated the specific ways in which the nineteenth-century African American family and community influenced the development of their literacy traditions. African American motivations for reading and writing during this period have also been examined, and an analysis of the developmental stage nature of their literacy traditions has been presented. The developmental stages of nineteenth-century African American literacy traditions can be seen as (1) literacy as an outgrowth of family and community development; (2) family and community literacy development and the defining of America during the American Revolution; (3) family and community literacy and intellectual and legal freedom during the American Civil War; and (4) literacy and the creation of a new America, following the American Civil War through to the present. The nature of these developments has been illustrated in a variety of contexts.

Despite the many obstacles faced by those studied, literacy was an integral part of the nineteenth-century African American community. Motivated to read and write by intellectual, social, and cultural forces, African Americans found diverse paths to literacy development as they originated or shaped traditions that grew out of their worldviews and social and historical circumstances. African American literacy traditions were, therefore, characteristically unique and universal. Literacy traditions that originated in the African American community were reinforced by the examined African American families, individuals, formal schools, informal schools, reading room societies, benevolent societies, newspapers, and other African American social and cultural institutions. It was the African American family, however, that played the major role in the development and transmission of literacy traditions. The implications of the foregoing findings are many. Implications for reading and writing research are considered first.

Implications for Reading and Writing Research

This study contributes to what is already known regarding the role of the family in reading and writing development by demonstrating the universal and historical role the examined families have played in the development of their literacy traditions. African American literacy traditions discussed in this study were primarily promoted by the family and secondarily by other social cultural institutions. Current literacy studies that focus on literacy failure concentrate on factors such as poverty, crime, and underfunded school systems that evidently have undermined reading efforts in today's African American community need to refocus their efforts (Ogbu, 1984). Current research should focus on family and community efforts toward literacy development that have historically been successful. Since this study has shown that African American literacy traditions are dynamic, mutable, and resilient, it makes sense to examine current African American family and community literacy behaviors that are successful. The collection of African American literacy histories can be part of an ongoing research agenda aimed toward better understandings of how families and communities can continue to sustain literacy traditions.

Research on literacy learning focuses mainly on reading and writing instruction that takes place in classrooms. The findings of this study suggest that research on reading and writing learning that takes place outside classrooms would also be beneficial. Successful informal reading and writing experiences that are a natural extension of family and community life are powerful learning models. The types of literacy learning valued, practiced, and passed along from one generation to the next in the African American community are indeed important information. How parents, significant adults in the community, and community-sponsored programs use literacy needs to be examined by educators (Cooper, 1979; Dillard, 1972; Labov, 1972). Community- and family-centered research would be revealing as it would help teachers develop and apply multiple perspectives on how to best incorporate culturally responsive ways of learning into community-based literacy programs.

Implications for Literacy Instructional Practices

Family-centered and community-based research could do much to inform instructional practices as educational researchers seek ways to incorporate what is learned about literacy learning outside schools into classroom reading programs. For example, successful informal literacy traditions observed in homes, churches, recreational centers, and the like can be examined for their common elements, incorporated into formal classroom instruction, and evaluated. Community input as to whether such instructional practices would be desirable would be encouraged.

The revival of reading rooms, literary societies, and debating societies should indeed be considered. It was discovered in this study that community-sponsored reading and writing centers and locally owned and operated libraries were enthusiastically supported and had a great impact on school attendance and the numbers of families involved on a regular basis in reading- and writing-related activities and the publication of community literature. Interaction between community reading and writing centers and public school programs would enhance the meaningfulness and effectiveness of each institution.

Educational research that can inform institutional practices in the manner described can shift the focus of African American literacy research away from an emphasis on failure toward a better understanding of the universal role of the family and community in the development of reading and writing traditions.

References

African Luminary. (1836–1846). Monrovia, Liberia.

African Repository. Washington, DC: Library of Congress.

American Colonization Society Papers (Microfilm ed.) Washington, DC: Library of Congress Manuscript Division.

Anderson, R. C., Hiebert, E. H., Scott, J. A., & Wilkinson, I. A. G. (1985). *Becoming a nation of readers: A report of the Commission on Reading*. Washington, DC: National Institute of Education.

Andrews, C. C. (1969). *The history of the African free schools*. New York: Negro University Press.

Andrews, W. L. (1986). *To tell a free story: First century of African-American autobiography, 1760–1865*. Urbana: University of Illinois Press.

Andrews, W. L. (1996). *The Oxford Frederick Douglass reader*. New York: Oxford University Press.

Aptheker, H. (1939). *Negro slave revolts in the United States, 1526–1860*. New York: International.

Aptheker, H. (1946). *The Negro people in America*. New York: International.

Aptheker, H. (Ed.). (1951). *A documentary history of Negro people in the United States* (Vols. 1–2). New York: Columbia University Press.

Aptheker, H. (1965). *One continual cry*. New York: Humanities Press.

Aptheker, H., & Wesley, C. H. (Eds.). (1973). *A documentary history of the Negro people in the United States: From colonial times through the Civil War* (Vol. 1). New York: Citadel Press.

Barnett, E. (1951). Educational activities by and in behalf of the Negroes in New York, 1800–1830. *Negro History Bulletin, 14,* 102–121.

Berger, P. L. (1963). *Invitation to sociology: A humanistic perspective*. New York: Doubleday.

Berger, P. L., & Luckmann, T. (1967). *The social construction of reality: A treatise in the sociology of knowledge*. New York: Doubleday.

Berk, L. E. (1994). Vygotsky's theory: The importance of make-believe play. *Young Children, 50,* 30–39.

Berlin, I. (1974). *Slaves without masters: The free Negro in the antebellum South*. New York: Vintage.

Berlin, I. (1980). Time, space, and evolution of Afro-American society on the British mainland in North America. *American Historical Review, 85*(1), 44–78.

Berlin, I., & Hoffman, R. (1986). *Slavery and freedom in the age of the American Revolution*. Urbana: University of Illinois Press.

Berry, M. F., & Blassingame, J. W. (1982). *Long memory: The black experience in America*. New York: Oxford University Press.

Bertaux, D. (1981). From the life-history approach to the transformation of sociological practice. In D. Bertaux (Ed.), *Biography and society* (pp. 61–76). Beverly Hills, CA: Sage.

Bethel, E. R. (1981). *Promise land: A century of life in a black community*. Philadelphia: Temple University Press.

Beyan, A. J. (1991). *The American Colonization Society and the creation of the Liberian state: A historical perspective, 1822–1900*. Lanham, MD: University Press of America.

Billingsley, A. (1968). *Black families in white America*. Englewood Cliffs, NJ: Prentice-Hall.

Birnie, C. W. (1927). Education of the Negro in Charleston, South Carolina, prior to the Civil War. *Journal of Negro History, 12*(1), 13–21.

Blackett, R. J. M. (1986). *Beating against the barriers: The lives of six nineteenth-century Afro-Americans*. Ithaca, NY: Cornell University Press.

Blackwell, J. E. (1975). *Black community: Diversity and unity*. New York: Dodd, Mead.

Blassingame, J. W. (1972). *The slave community: Plantation life in the antebellum South*. New York: Oxford University Press.

Blassingame, J. W. (1977). *Slave testimony: Two centuries of letters, speeches, interviews, and autobiographies*. Baton Rouge: Louisiana State University Press.

Bloome, D. (1980). *An ethnographic approach to the study of reading among black junior high school students*. Unpublished doctoral dissertation, Kent State University, Ohio.

Bloome, D., Harris, O. L., & Ludlum, D. (1991). Reading as sociocultural activities: Politics and pedagogy in the classroom. *Topics in Language Disorders, 11*(3), 14–27.

Blumer, H. (1969). *Symbolic interactionism*. Englewood Cliffs, NJ: Prentice-Hall.

Bohannan, P., & Glazer, N. (Eds.). (1988). *Highpoints in anthropology*. New York: Harper and Row.

Bond, H. M. (1969). *Negro education in Alabama: A study in cotton and steel*. New York: Octagon Books.

Bontemps, A. (Ed.). (1963). *American Negro poetry*. New York: Hill and Wang.

Bontemps, A. (1969). *Great slave narratives*. Boston: Beacon Press.

Borchert, J. (1982). *Alley life in Washington: Family, community, religion, and folk life in the city, 1850–1970*. Urbana: University of Illinois Press.

Boylan, A. M. (1988). *Sunday school: The formation of an American institution*. New Haven, CT: Yale University Press.

Brameld, T. (1957). *Cultural foundations of culture: An interdisciplinjary exploration*. New York: Harper.

Brown, L. W. (1972). *Free Negroes in the District of Columbia, 1846–1970*. New York: Oxford University Press.

Bullock, H. A. (1970). *A history of Negro education in the South from 1619 to the present*. New York: Praeger.

Cade, J. B. (1935). Out of the mouths of ex-slaves. *Journal of Negro History, 20*(3), 294–337.

Cain, W. E. (Ed.). (1995). *William Lloyd Garrison and the fight against slavery: Selections from the Liberator*. Boston: Bedford Books for St. Martin's Press.

Cambourne, B. (1988). *The whole story: Natural learning and the acquisition of literacy in the classroom*. Auckland, New Zealand: Aston Scholastic.

Cambourne, B. (2000/2001). Conditions for literacty learning: Turning learning theory into classroom instruction: A mini case study. *Reading Teacher, 54*, 414–417.

Carr, E. H. (1972). *What is history?* New York: Knopf.

Chartier, R. (1988). Figures of the other: Peasant reading in the age of Enlightenment. In L. G. Cochrane (Ed.), *Cultural history: Between practices and representations* (pp. 151–171). Ithaca, NY: Cornell University Press.

Child, L. M. (1977). Interview with Charity Bowery, 1847–1848. In J. W. Blassingame, *Slave testimony: Two centuries of letters, speeches, interviews, and autobiographies* (pp. 261–266). Baton Rouge: Louisiana State University Press.

Child, L. M. (1996). *An appeal in favor of that class of Americans called slaves*. Amherst: University of Massachusetts Press.

Christian, M. B. (1945). The theory of the poisoning of Oscar J. Dunn. *Phylon, 6*, 254–266.

Christie, J. F. (1995). The importance of play. In J. F. Christie, K. A. Roskos, B. J. Enz, C. Vukelich, & S. Neuman (Eds.), *Readings for linking literacy and play* (pp. 1–7). Newark, DE: International Reading Association.

Christie, J. F., Roskos, K. A., Enz, B. J., Vukelich, C., & Neuman, S. (Eds.). (1995). *Readings for linking litercy and play*. Newark, DE: International Reading Association.

Clark Hine, D., Barkley Brown, E., & Terborg-Penn, R. (Eds.). (1993). *Black women in America: An historical encyclopedia* (Vol. 1). Bloomington: Indiana University Press.

Clay, M. M. (1966). *Children who read early*. New York: Teachers College Press, Columbia University.

Clay, M. M. (1982a). *Observing young readers: Selected papers*. Portsmouth, NH: Heinemann.

Clay, M. M. (1982b). *What did I write?: Beginning literacy behavior*. Exeter, NH: Heinemann.

Clay, M. M. (1991). *Becoming literate: The construction of inner control*. Auckland, New Zealand: Heinemann.

Coles, G. (2000). "Direct, explicit, and systematic"—bad readng science. *Language Arts, 77*, 443–545.

Collins, R. (1988). *Theoretical sociology*. San Diego, CA: Harcourt, Brace, Jovanovich.

Colored American. (1837–1841). New York.

Cone, J. H. (1970). *Liberation: A black theology of liberation*. Philadelphia: Lippincott.

Cook-Gumprez, J. (Ed.). (1986). *The social construction of literacy*. Cambridge: Cambridge University Press.

Cooley, C. H. (1902). *Human nature and the social order*. New York: Scribner.

Cooper, H. M. (1979). Pygmalion grows up: A model for teacher expectation, communication, and performance influence. *Review of Educational Research, 49*(3), 39–140.

Cornelius, J. D. (1983). We slipped and learned to read: Slave accounts of the literacy process, 1830–1865. *Phylon, 44*, 171–186.

Cornelius, J. D. (1991). *When I can read my title clear: Literacy, slavery, and religion in the antebellum South*. Columbia: University of South Carolina.

Cullen, C. (1963). Yet do I marvel. In A. Bontemps (Ed.), *American Negro poetry* (p. 8). New York: Hill and Wang.

Daniels, D. H. (1980). *Pioneer urbanites: A social and cultural history of black San Francisco*. Philadelphia: Temple University Press.

Dann, M. E. (1971). *The black press, 1827–1890: The quest for national identity*. New York: Putnam's.

Davis, A. P., Redding, S. J., & Joyce, A. J. (Eds.). (1991). *Selected African American writing from 1760 to 1910*. New York: Bantam.

Davis, C. T., & Gates, H. L. (Eds.). (1985). *The slave's narrative.* New York: Oxford University Press.

Davis, D. B. (1975). *The problem of slavery in the age of revolution, 1770–1823.* Ithaca, NY: Cornell University Press.

De Castle, S., & Walker, T. (1991). Identity, metamorphosis, and ethnographic research: What kind of story is ways with words? *Anthropology and Education Quarterly, 22*(1) 3–10.

Dew, C. B. (1974). Disciplining slave ironworkers in the antebellum South: Coercion, conciliation, and accommodation. *American Historical Review, 79*(2), 393–418.

Dew, C. B. (1994). *Bond of iron: Master and slave at Buffalo Forge.* New York: Norton.

Dillard, J. L. (1972). *Black English: Its history and usage in the United States.* New York: Random House.

Dollard, J. (1971). *Criteria for the life history: With analysis of six notable documents.* Freeport, NY: Books for Library Press. (Original work published 1935)

Douglass, F. (1993). *Narrative of the life of Frederick Douglass, an American slave, written by himself* (D. Blight, Ed.). Boston: Bedford Books.

Drew, B. (1856). *A north-side view of slavery: The refugee: or the narratives of fugitive slaves in Canada related by themselves.* Boston: Jewett.

DuBois, W. E. B. (1903). *The Negro church.* Atlanta, GA: Atlanta University Press.

DuBois, W. E. B. (1968). *The Negro family.* Atlanta, GA: Atlanta University Press. (Original work published 1908)

Dunn, E. D., Beyan, A. J., & Burrows, C. P. (Eds.). (2001). *Historical dictionary of Liberia* (2nd ed.). Lanham, MD: Scarecrow.

Durkheim, E. (1951). *Suicide.* Glencoe, IL: Free Press. (Original work published 1918)

Durkin, D. (1966). *Children who read early.* New York: Teachers College Press.

Earp, C. A. (1941). The role of education in the Maryland Colonization movement. *Journal of Negro History, 26,* 10–25.

Ehri, L. C., & Sweet, J. (1991). Finger point reading of memorized text: What enables beginners to process the print? *Reading Research Quarterly, 26*(4), 442–462.

Elder, G. H., Jr. (1981). History and the life course. In D. Bertaux (Ed.), *Biography and society: The life history approach in social sciences* (pp. 61–76). Beverly Hills, CA: Sage.

Elder, G. H., Jr. (1985). Perspectives on the life course. In G. H. Elder, Jr. (Ed.), *Life course trajectories and transitions, 1968–1980* (pp. 52–71). Ithaca, NY: Cornell University Press.

Elder, G. H., Jr., & Clipp, E. C. (1988). War experience and social ties: Influences across 40 years of men's lives. In M. W. Riley (Ed.), *Social change and life course* (Vol. 1, pp. 306–327). Newbury Park, CA: Sage.

Elder, G. H., Jr., Pavalko, E. K., & Clipp, E. C. (Eds.). (1993). *Working with archival data: Studying lives series, Quantitative Applications in the social sciences*. Newbury Park, CA: Sage.

Elkins, S. M. (1959). *Slavery: A problem in American institutional and intellectual life*. Chicago: University of Chicago Press.

English, R. H. (1974). Beyond pathology: Research and theoretical perspectives on Black families. In L. E. Gary (Ed.), *Social research and the black community: Selected issues and priorities* (pp. 53–65). Washington, DC: Howard University, Institute for Urban Affairs and Research.

Ernst, R. (1949). The economic status of New York City Negroes, 1850–1863. *Negro History Bulletin, 12*(6), 131–143.

Featherman, D. L., & Lerner, R. M. (1985). Ontogenesis and sociogenius. *American Sociological Review, 50*(5), 659–676.

Fichett, H. E. (1941). The origin and growth of the free Negro population of Charleston, South Carolina. *Journal of Negro History, 23*(3), 421–437.

Fisher, M. M. (1953). *Negro slave songs in the United States*. New York: Citadel Press.

Foner, E. (1993). *Freedom's lawmakers: A directory of black officeholders during Reconstruction*. New York: Oxford University Press.

Foner, P. S. (1975). *History of black Americans: From Africa to the emergence of the cotton kingdom*. Westport, CT: Greenwood Press.

Foner, P. S., & Lewis, R. L. (1989). *Black workers: A documentary history from the Colonial time to the present*. Philadelphia: Temple University Press.

Foner, P. S., & Walker, G. E. (Eds.). (1979). *Proceedings of the black state conventions, 1840–1865* (Vol. 1). Philadelphia: Temple University Press.

Franklin, J. H. (1980a). *From slavery to freedom: A history of Negro Americans* (5th ed.). New York: Knopf.

Franklin, J. H. (1980b). Mirror for Americans: A century of Reconstruction history. *American Historical Review, 85*(1), 1–14.

Franklin, J. H., & Schweninger, L. (1999). *Runaway slaves: Rebels on the plantation*. New York: Oxford University Press.

Franklin, V. P. (1995). *Living our stories, telling our truths: Autobiography and the making of the African-American intellectual tradition*. New York: Oxford University Press.

Franklin, V. P., & Anderson, J. D. (Eds.). (1978). *New perspectives on black educational history*. Boston: Hall.

Frazier, F. E. (1930). The Negro family. *Journal of Negro History, 15*, 198–259.

Frazier, F. E. (1948). *The Negro family in the United States*. New York: Citadel Press.

Frazier, F. E. (1963). *The Negro church*. New York: Schocken Books.

Frazier, T. R. (1988). *Afro-American history: Primary sources*. Chicago: Dorsey Press.

Fred, L. (1920). The Negro migration to Canada after the passing of the Fugitive Slave Act. *Journal of Negro History, 5*, 22–36.

Freedom's Journal. (1827–1829). New York.

Gans, H. J. (1965). The Negro family: Reflections on the Moynihan Report. *Commonwealth, 83*, 47–51.

Gates, L. H. (1989). *Words, signs, and "the racial self."* New York: Oxford University Press.

Geertz, C. (1973). Thick description: Toward an interpretive theory of culture. In P. Bohannan & M. Glazer (Eds.), *Highpoints in anthropology* (pp. 531–552). New York: Knopf.

Genovese, E. D. (1971). *The world the slaveholders made*. New York: Vintage Books.

Genovese, E. D. (1976). *Roll, Jordan, roll: The world the slaves made*. New York: Vintage Books.

Giglioli, P. P. (Ed.) (1972). *Language and social context: Selected readings*. New York: Penguin Books.

Glazer, N., & Moynihan, D. P. (1963). *Beyond the melting pot: The Negroes, Puerto Ricans, Jews, Italians, and Irish of New York City*. Cambridge, MA: Harvard University Press.

Goffman, E. (1959). *The presentation of self in everyday life*. Garden City, NY: Doubleday.

Goffman, E. (1967). *Interaction ritual*. New York: Anchor/Doubleday.

Goffman, E. (1974). *Frame analysis*. New York: Basic Books.

Goodenough, W. (1971). *Culture, language, and society*. Reading, MA: Addison-Wesley.

Goodman, K. (1967). Reading: A psycholinguistic guessing game. *Journal of the Reading Specialist, 6*, 126–135.

Goody, J., & Watt, I. (1968). The consequences of literacy. In J. Goody (Ed.), *Literacy in traditional society* (pp. 27–68). Cambridge, England: Cambridge University Press.

Goody, J., & Watt, I. (1972). The consequences of literacy: Excerpts from J. Goody and I. Watt, "The consequences of literacy." In P. P. Giglioli (Ed.), *Languages in social context: Selected readings* (pp. 311–357). New York: Penguin Books.

Goss, L., & Barnes, M. E. (Eds.). (1989). *Talk that talk*. New York: Simon and Schuster.

Graff, H. (1978). Literacy past and present: Critical approaches in the literacy-society relationship. *Interchange, 9*, 1–29.

Graff, H. (1979). *The literacy myth: Literacy and social structure in nineteenth century*. New York: Academic Press.

Graves, D. (1983). *Writing: Teachers and children at work*. Portsmouth, NH: Heinemann.

Green, J. L. (1992). Multiple perspectives: Issues and directions. In R. Beach, J. L. Green, M. L. Kamil, & T. Shannon (Eds.), *Multidisciplinary perspectives on literacy research* (pp. 19–34). Urbana, IL: National Conference on Research in English.

Green, L. (1942). *The Negro in Colonial New England*. New York: Columbia Univesity Press.

Greenberg, K. S. (Ed.). (1996). *The confessions of Nat Turner and related documents*. New York: Bedford Books for St. Martin's Press.

Gross, B. (1932). *Freedom's Journal* and the *Rights of All*. *Journal of Negro History, 17*(3), 241–286.

Gross, B. (1947). *Clarion call: The history and development of the Negro people's convention movement in the United States from 1817 to 1840*. New York: Atwater Press.

Guthrie, L. F., & Hall, W. S. (1985). Ethnographic approaches to research. In D. P. Pearson, R. Barr, & M. I. Mosenthal (Eds.), *Handbook of reading research* (pp. 91–110). New York: Longman.

Gutman, H. G. (1976). *The black family in slavery and freedom, 1750–1925*. New York: Vintage Books.

Handlin, O., & Handlin, M. (1950). Origins of the southern labor system. *William and Mary Quarterly*, 3rd ser., 7, 199–222.

Hannon, M. T. (1988). Social change, organizational diversity, and individual change. In M. W. Riley (Ed.), *Social change and the life course* (Vol. 1, pp. 161–174). Newbury Park, CA: Sage.

Harding, V. (1969). Religion and resistance among antebellum Negroes, 1800–1860. In A. Meier & E. Rudwick (Eds.), *The making of black America* (pp. 179–197). New York: Athenaeum.

Hareven, T. (Ed.). (1978). *Transitions: The family and life course in historical perspective*. New York: Academic Press.

Hareven, T. (1982). *Family time and industrial time*. Cambridge, England: Cambridge University Press.

Hartgrove, W. B. (1916). The story of Maria Louise Moore and Fannie M. Richards. *Journal of Negro History, 1*(1), 23–33.

Heath, S. B. (1983). *Ways with words: Language, life, and work in communities and classrooms*. Cambridge, England: Cambridge University Press.

Hermann, J. S. (1981). *The pursuit of a dream*. New York: Oxford University Press.

Hermann, J. S. (1988). Isaiah T. Montgomery's balancing act. In L. Litwack & A. Meier (Eds.), *Black leaders in the nineteenth century* (pp. 291–304). Urbana: University of Illinois Press.

Herskovits, M. (1939). Some recent developments in the study of West African life. *Journal of Negro History, 14*(1), 65–103.

Herskovits, M. (1941). *The myth of the Negro past.* Boston: Beacon Press.

Higginson, T. W. (1971). *Army life in a black regiment by Thomas Wentworth Higginson, late Colonel 1st South Carolina Volunteers.* Williamstown, MA: Corner House.

Hill, R. B. (1972). *The strength of black families.* New York: Emerson Hall.

Hirsch, L. H. (1931). New York and the Negro from 1783 to 1865. *Journal of Negro History, 26*(3), 382–453.

Hite, R. W. (1974). Voice of a fugitive: Henry Bibb and antebellum black separatism. *Journal of Black Studies, 4,* 269–289.

Hodges, R. E. (1977). In Adam's fall: A brief history of spelling instruction in the United States. In H. A. Robinson (Ed.), *Reading and writing instruction in the United States: Historical trends* (pp. 1–16). Urbana: University of Illinois Press.

Hofstadter, R. (1944). U. B. Phillips and the plantation legend. *Journal of Negro History, 29,* 109–124.

Holloway, J. E. (Ed.). (1991). *Africanisms in American culture.* Bloomington: Indiana University Press.

Holt, T. (1977). *Black over white: Negro political leadership in South Carolina during Reconstruction.* Urbana: University of Illinois Press.

Horton, J. O., & Horton, L. E. (1979). *Black Bostonians: Family life and community struggle in the antebellum North.* New York: Holmes and Meier.

Huggins, N. I. (1971) Afro-American history: Myths, heroes, reality. In N. I. Huggins, M. Kilson, & D. M. Fox (Eds.), *Key issues in the Afro-American experience* (pp. 5–20). New York: Harcourt Brace.

Huggins, N. I. (1977). *Black odyssey: The Afro-American ordeal in slavery.* New York: Pantheon.

Hymes, D. (1972). Toward ethnographies of communication: The analysis of communicative events. In P. P. Giglioli (Ed.), *Language and social context: Selected readings* (pp. 21–44). New York: Penguin Books.

Hymes, D. (1974). *Foundation in sociolinguistics: An ethnographic approach.* Philadelphia: University of Philadelphia Press.

Jackson, L. P. (1927). Free Negroes of Petersburg, Virginia. *Journal of Negro History, 12,* 365–388.

Jacobs, H. (1987). *Incidents in the life of a slave girl: Written by herself.* Cambridge, MA: Harvard University Press.

Johnson, H. (1906). *Liberia.* New York: Dodd, Mead.

Johnson, J. W. (1968). *Black Manhattan.* New York: Athenaeum.

Johnson, M. P., & Roark, J. (Eds.). (1984). *No chariot let down: Charleston's free people of color on the eve of the Civil War.* New York: Norton.

Joyner, C. W. (1983). The South as a folk culture: David Potter and the southern enigma. In W. J. Frazier & W. B. Moore (Eds.), *The southern enigma: Essays on race, class, and folk culture.* Westport, CT: Greenwood Press.

Joyner, C. W. (1984). *Down by the Riverside: A South Carolina community*. Urbana: University of Illinois Press.

Knight, E. (1953). *A documentary history of education in the South before 1800* (Vol. 5). Chapel Hill: University of North Carolina.

Kornfeld, E. (2001). *Creating an American culture, 1775–1800: A brief history with documents*. Boston: Bedford Books for St. Martin's Press.

Labov, W. (1972). Excerpts from The logic of nonstandard English. In P. P. Giglioli (Ed.), *Language in social context: Selected readings* (pp. 179–215). New York: Penguin Books.

Lange, W. J. (1983). W. E. B. DuBois and the first scientific study of Afro-America. *Pylon, 45*(2), 135–149.

Langness, L. L. (1965). *The life history in anthropological science*. New York: Holt, Rinehart, & Winston.

Letters showing the rise and progress of the early Negro churches of Georgia and the West Indies. (1916). *Journal of Negro History, 1*(1), 69–92.

Levine, L. (1971). Slave songs and consciousness. In T. Hareven (Ed.), *Anonymous Americans* (pp. 99–130). New York: Oxford University Press.

Levine, L. (1979). *Black culture and black consciousness: Afro-American folk thought from slavery to freedom*. New York: Oxford University Press.

Lewis, R. L. (1979). *Coal, iron, and slaves: Industrial slavery in Maryland and Virginia, 1715–1865*. Westport, CT: Greenwood Press.

Liberator. (1831–1865). Boston.

Liberia Bulletin. (1892–1909). Washington, DC.

Liberia Herald. (1826–1862). Washington, DC.

Litwack, L. F. (1961). *North of slavery: The Negro in the free states, 1790–1860*. Chicago: University of Chicago Press.

Litwack, L. W., & Meier, A. (Eds.). (1988). *Black leaders of the nineteenth century*. Urbana: University of Illinois Press.

Lockeridge, K. (1974). *Literacy in Colonial New England: An inquiry into the social context of literacy in early modern West*. New York: Norton.

Logan, R. W., & Winston, M. R. (Eds.). (1982). *Dictionary of American Negro biography*. New York: Norton.

Lomax, J. A., Lomax, A., Seeger, C., & Seeger, R. C. (Eds.). (1975). *Folk song U. S. A*. New York: New American Library.

Luckmann, F., & Berger, P. L. (1967). *The social construction of reality: A treatise in the sociology of knowledge*. New York: Doubleday.

Lynch, H. R. (1967). *Edward Wilmot Blyden: 1832–pan Negro patriot–1912*. New York: Oxford University Press.

Mabee, C. (1979). *Black education in New York state from colonial to modern times*. Syracuse, NY: Syracuse University Press.

Magdol, E., & Wakelyn, J. L. (1980). *The southern common people: Studies in nineteenth-century social history*. Westport, CT: Greenwood Press.

Malinowski, B. (1961). *Argonauts of the western Pacific*. New York: Dutton.

Martin, E. P., & Martin, J. M. (1978). *The black extended family*. Chicago: University of Chicago Press.

Maryland Colonization Papers. (Microfilm ed.). Washington, DC: Library of Congress Manuscript Division.

McAdoo, H. P. (1981). *Black families*. Beverly Hills, CA: Sage.

McDaniel, A. (1990). The power of culture: A review of the idea of Africa's influence on family structure in antebellum America. *Journal of Family History, 15*(2), 225–238.

Mead, G. H. (1934). *Mind, self, and society: From the standpoint of a social behaviorist*. Chicago: Chicago University Press.

Meyer, J. W. (1988). Levels of analysis: The life course as a cultural construction. In M. W. Riley (Ed.), *Social change and the life course* (Vol. 1, pp. 49–62). Beverly Hills, CA: Sage.

Miller, R. (Ed.). (1978). *Dear master: Letters of a slave family*. Ithaca, NY: Cornell University Press.

Mills, C. W. (1959). *The sociological imagination*. New York: Oxford University Press.

Mintz, S. W. (Ed.). (1993). *African American voices: The life cycle of slavery*. New York: Brandywine.

Mintz, S.W., & Price, R. (Eds.). (1976). *An anthropological approach to the Afro-American past*. Philadelphia: Institute for the Study of Human Issues.

Mintz, S. W., & Price, R. (1992). *The birth of African-American culture: An anthropological perspective*. Boston: Beacon Press.

Morrow, L. M., & Weinstein, C. (1985). Developing young voluntary readers: The home—the child—the school. *Reading Research Quarterly, 21*, 330–343.

Moses, W. J. (1989). *Alexander Crummell: A study of civilization and discontent*. New York: Oxford University Press.

Moynihan, D. P. (1965). *The Negro family: The case for national action*. Washington, DC: Office of Policy Planning and Research, U.S. Department of Labor.

Mullin, M. (1992). *Africa in America: Slave acculturation and resistance in the American South and the British Caribbean, 1736–1831*. Urbana: University of Illinois Press.

Myrdal, G. (1944). *An American dilemma: The Negro problem and modern democracy*. New York: Harper & Row.

Nash, G. B. (1986). Forging freedom: The emancipation experience in northern seaport cities, 1775–1820. In I. Berlin & R. Hoffman (Eds.), *Slavery and freedom in the age of the American Revolution* (pp. 3–48). Urbana: University of Illinois Press.

Nathan, G., & Moynihan, D. P. (1963). *Beyond the melting pot: The Negroes, Puerto Ricans, Jews, and Irish of New York City*. Cambridge, MA: MIT Press and Harvard University Press.

National Intelligencer. (1818). Washington, DC.

Nicholas, C. H. (1963). Many thousand gone: The ex-slaves account of their bondage and freedom. Luden, Netherlands: Brill.

Norton, M. B., Gutman, H. G., & Berlin, I. (1986). The family in the age of revolution. In I. Berlin & R. Hoffman (Eds.), *Slavery and freedom in the age of the American Revolution* (pp. 175–192). Urbana: University of Illinois Press.

Oates, S. (1975). *The fires of jubilee: Nat Turner's fierce rebellion*. New York: Harper & Row.

Ogbu, J. U. (1968). Black education: A cultural ecological perspective. In A. Gillingsley (Ed.), *Black families in white America* (pp. 139–154). Englewood Cliffs, NJ: Prentice-Hall.

Olney, E. (1941). Social aspects of the slave in New York. *Journal of Negro History, 26*(1), 66–67.

Olney, J. (1985). I was born: Slave narratives, their status as autobiography and literature. In C. T. Davis & H. L. Gates, Jr. (Eds.), *The slave narrative* (pp. 148–174). New York: Oxford University Press.

Osofsky, G. (Ed.). (1969). *Puttin' on ole massa: The slave narratives of Henry Bibb, William Wells Brown, and Solomon Northrup*. New York: Harper & Row.

Park, R. (1919). The conflict and fusion of culture. *Journal of Negro History, 4,* 111–113.

Patterson, O. (1982). *Slavery and social death: A comparative study*. Cambridge, MA: Harvard University Press.

Payne, D. A. (1968). *History of the African Methodist Episcopal Church*. New York: Johnson. (Original work published 1891)

Payne, D. A. (1969). *Recollections of seventy years*. New York: Arno Press. (Original work published 1888)

Pearson, D. P. (1984). *Handbook of reading research*. New York: Longman.

Perdue, C., Jr., Barton, T. E., & Phillips, R. K. (Eds.). (1975). *Weevils in the wheat: Interviews with ex-slaves*. Charlottesville: University Press of Virginia.

Perkins, A. E. (1943). Oscar James Dunn. *Phylon, 4,* 105–121.

Phillips, U. B. (1969). *American Negro slavery: A survey of supply, employment, and control of Negro labor as determined by the plantation regime*. Baton Rouge: Louisiana State University Press.

Piaget, J. (1962). *Play, dreams, and imitation in childhood*. New York: Norton.

Piaget, J. (1977). *The development of thought*. New York: Viking.

Porter, D. B. (1936). The organized educational activities of Negro literary societies, 1828–1846. *Journal of Negro Education,* 5(4), 555–576.

Porter, D. B. (1945). *Early American Negro writings: A bibliographical study*. New York: Bibliographical Society of New York.

Quarles, B. (1961). *The Negro in the American Revolution.* New York: Norton.

Quarles, B. (1964). *The Negro in the making of America.* New York: Simon & Schuster.

Raboteau, A. J. (1980) *Slave religion: The "invisible institution" in the antebellum South.* Oxford, England: Oxford University Press.

Raboteau, A. J. (1988). Richard Allen and the African church movement. In L. Litwack & A. Meier (Eds.), *Black leaders of the nineteenth century* (pp. 1–18). Urbana: University of Illinois Press.

Rachman, S. (1999–2001). *Shaping the values of youth: Sunday school in 19th century America.* East Lansing: Michigan State University Libraries.

Rainwater, L., & Yancey, W. (1967). *The Moynihan Report and the politics of controversy.* Cambridge, MA: MIT Press.

Randall, D. (Ed.). (1971). *Black poetry.* Detroit, MI: Broadside Press.

Rease, J. H., & Rease, W. H. (1974). *They who would be free: Blacks' search for freedom, 1830–1861.* New York: Athenaeum.

Recording Arts. (2001). *Dejavu Retro Gold Collection* (2 CD deluxe ed.). Twenty-page booklet with rare photographs (p.16): Billie Holiday.

Redding, S. (1982). Phillis Wheatley. In R. Logan & M. Winston (Eds.), *Dictionary of Negro biography.* New York: Norton.

Resnick, D. P., & Resnick, L. B. (1977). The nature of literacy: An historical exploration. *Harvard Educational Review, 3,* 372–381.

Ripley, P. (Ed.). (1991). Speech by Henry Highland Garnet delivered before the National Convention of Colored Citizens, Buffalo, New York, 16 August 1843. *The black abolitionists papers* (Vol. 3, pp. 403–412). Chapel Hill: University of North Carolina Press.

Robinson, H. A. (1977). *Reading and writing instruction in the United States: Historical trends.* Urbana, IL: International Reading Association.

Robinson, W. A. (1950, March). Thomas Day and his family. *Negro History Bulletin,* 123–126, 140.

Royster, J. J. (Ed.). (1997). *Southern horrors and other writings: The anti-lynching campaign of Ida B. Wells, 1892–1900.* Boston: Bedford Books for St. Martin's Press.

Rury, J. L. (1983). The New York African Free School, 1827–1836: Conflict over community control of black education. *Phylon 44*(3), 187–197.

Russell, J. H. (1913). *The free Negro in Virginia, 1619–1865.* Baltimore: John Hopkins University Press.

Samuels, S. J., & Kamil, M. L. (1984). Models of the reading process. In D. P. Pearson (Ed.), *Handbook of reading research* (pp. 186–208). New York: Longman.

Schor, J. (1977). *Henry Highland Garnet: A voice of radicalism in the nineteenth century.* Westport, CT: Greenwood Press.

Schweninger, L. (1990). *Black property owners in the South, 1790–1915.* Urbana: University of Illinois Press.

Sellers, J. B. (1950). *Slavery in Alabama.* University: University of Alabama Press.

Shick, T. M. (Ed.). (1971). *Emigrants to Liberia, 1820–1843: An alphabetical listing.* Newark: University of Delaware.

Shick, T. M. (1980). *Behold the promised land: A history of African-American settler society in nineteenth-century Liberia.* Baltimore: Johns Hopkins University Press.

Shields, J. C. (1993). Phillis Wheatley (Peters). In D. C. Hines, B. B. Brown, & R. Terborg-Penn (Eds.), *Black women in America: An historical encyclopedia* (Vol. 2, 1251–1255). Bloomington: Indiana University Press.

Simmons, W. J. (1968). *Men of mark: Eminent, progressive, and rising.* New York: Arno Press.

Simpson, G. E. (1978). *Black religions in the new world.* New York: Columbia University Press.

Singer, H., & Ruddell, R. B. (Eds.). (1969). *Theoretical models and processes of reading* (3rd ed.). Newark, DE: International Reading Association.

Soltow, L. S. (1981). *The rise of literacy and the common school in the United States: A socioeconomic analysis to 1870.* Chicago: University of Chicago Press.

Spady, J. H. (1974, June/July). The Afro-American society: The nucleus of black bibliophiles, 1897–1923. *Negro Historical Bulletin,* 255–256.

Stafford, A. O. (1916). The mind of the African Negro as reflected in his proverbs. *Journal of Negro History, 1*(1), 42–48.

Stampp, K. M. (1956). *The peculiar institution: Slavery in the antebellum South.* New York: Vintage Books.

Starobin, R. S. (Ed.). (1974). *Blacks in bondage: Letters of American slaves.* New York: New Viewpoints.

Still, W. (1872). *The Underground Railroad.* Philadelphia: Porter & Coates.

Stockwell, G. (1868). *The republic of Liberia: Its geography, climate, soil, and production with a history of its early settlements.* New York: Barnes.

Strange, D. C. (1967). Document: Bishop Daniel Alexander's protestation of American slavery. *Journal of Negro History, 52,* 63.

Strickland, D., & Morrow, L. M. (Eds.). (1989). *Emergent literacy: Young children learn to read and write.* Newark, DE: International Reading Association.

Stuckey, S. (Ed.). (1972). *The ideological origins of black nationalism.* Boston: Beacon Press.

Stuckey, S. (1987). *Slave culture: Nationalist theory and the foundations of black America.* New York: Oxford University Press.

Sweet, L. I. (1976). *Black images of America 1784–1870.* New York: Norton.

Swint, H. L. (Ed.). (1966). *Dear ones at home: Letters from contraband camps.* Nashville, TN: Vanderbilt University Press.

Syndor, C. B. (1933). *Slavery in Mississippi.* New York: Appleton.

Tallman, I. (1986). Social history and the life course perspective on the family: A view from the bridge. In J. F. Short, Jr. (Ed.), *The social fabric: Dimensions and issues* (pp. 255–281). Beverly Hills, CA: Sage.

Taylor, D. (1998). *Beginning to read and the spin doctors of science: The political campaign to change America's mind about how children learn to read.* Urbana, IL: National Council of Teachers of English.

Taylor, D., & Dorsey-Gaines, C. (1988). *Growing up literate: Learning from inner-city families.* Portsmouth, NH: Heinemann.

Taylor, S. K. (1995). *Susie King Taylor, reminiscences of my life in camp with the 33rd U.S. Colored Troops, Late 1st South Carolina Volunteers: A black woman's Civil War memoirs* (P. W. Romero & W. L. Rose, Eds.). Princeton, NJ: Markus Wiener. (Original work published 1902)

Teale, W. H., & Shulzby, E. (1986). *Emergent literacy: Writing and reading.* Norwood, NJ: Ablex.

Vinoskis, M. A. (1988). The historic and life course: Reflections on recent approaches to the study of American family life in the past. In P. B. Baltes, D. L. Featherman, & R. M Lerner (Eds.), *Life-span development and behavior* (Vol. 8, pp. 33–54). Hillsdale, NJ: Erlbaum.

Vygotsky, L. S. (1978). *Mind in society: The development of psychological processes.* Cambridge, MA: Harvard University Press.

Wade, R. C. (1954). the Negro in Cincinnati, 1800–1830. *Journal of Negro History 39,* 43–57.

Wade, R. C. (1964). *Slavery in the cities: The South, 1820–1860.* New York: Oxford University Press.

Walker, C. E. (1982). *A rock in a weary land: The African Methodist Episcopal Church during the Civil War and Reconstruction.* Baton Rouge: Louisiana State University Press.

Walker, D. (1830). *An appeal in four articles, together with a preamble, to the colored people of the world, but in particular and very expressively to those of the United States of America, written in Boston, State of Massachusetts, September 28, 1829.* Boston: Author.

Webber, T. L. (1978). *Deep like the rivers: Education in the slave community, 1831–1865.* New York: Norton.

Wells, I. B. (1997a). *Mob rule in New Orleans.* In J. J. Royster (Ed.), *Southern horrors and other writings: The anti-lynching campaign of Ida B. Wells, 1892–1900.* Boston: Bedford Books.

Wells, I. B. (1997b). *A red record.* In J. J. Royster (Ed.), *Southern horrors and other writings: The anti-lynching campaign of Ida B. Wells, 1892–1900.* Boston: Bedford Books.

Wells, I. B. (1997c). *Southern horrors: Lynch laws in all its phases.* In J. J. Royster (Ed.), *Southern horrors and other writings: The anti-lynching campaign of Ida B. Wells, 1892–1900.* Boston: Bedford Books.

Wesley, C. H. (1939). The Negroes of New York in the emancipation movement. *Journal of Negro History, 24*(1), 65–103.

White, D. G. (1985). *Ar'n't I a woman?: Female slaves in the plantation South.* New York: Norton.

Wiley, B. I. (Ed.). (1980). *Slaves no more: Letters from Liberia, 1833–1869.* Lexington: University of Kentucky Press.

Winch, J. (1988). *Philadelphia's black elite: Activism, accommodation, and the struggle for autonomy, 1987–1848.* Philadelphia: Temple University Press.

Winthrop, J. D. (1968). *White over black: American attitudes toward the Negro, 1550–1812.* Baltimore: Penguin Books.

Wood, P. H. (1988). Nat Turner: The unknown slave as a visionary leader. In L. Litwack & A. Meier (Eds.), *Black leaders of the nineteenth century* (pp. 21–40). Urbana: University of Illinois Press.

Woodson, C. G. (1916). The Negroes of Cincinnati prior to the Civil War. *Journal of Negro History, 1*(1), 1–22.

Woodson, C. G. (1921). *The history of the Negro church.* Washington, DC: Associated.

Woodson, C. G. (1968). *Education of the Negro prior to 1861.* Washington, DC: Arno Press.

Woodson, C. G. (Ed.). (1969). *The mind of the Negro as reflected in letters written during the crisis, 1800–1860.* New York: Greenwood Press.

Yetman, N. R. (Ed.). (1984). *Life under the peculiar institution: Selections from the slave narrative collection.* Huntington, NY: Krieger. (Original work published 1970).

Index

abolitionists, 21, 22, 79, 88, 92, 96, 116, 147
abolition movement, 21, 22, 23, 79, 89
  friends of freedom or sons and daughters of freedom, 155
African American fugitive slave songs and chants, themes of escape in, 139
African American independent churches
  African American–created hymnbooks published for services (*Collection of Hymns & Spiritual Songs from Various Authors, A*, 139; *New Hymn and Tune Book for the Use of the African American M.E. Zion Church, The*, 139. *See also* Allen, R.
  call-response patterns in services: "Canaan," 139; "Farewell," 139; "Free Grace," 139; "Weary Travelers," 139; "Yonder," 139
  creation of church documents for practical purposes, births, deaths, marriages, 138
  impact of African American–composed hymnbooks on literacy development, 139–140
  and liberation theology, 9
  literacy societies and church schools to build alliances among churches and community organizations, 133
  Old Testament and New Testament as sources for songs, 139; record keeping, 139; *Book of Baptisms of St. Phillip's Church of Charleston*, 139; literature distributed by slaveholders ("Apostles' Creed"; *A Catechism for Colored Persons*, and *Sermons, Dialogues, and Narratives for Servants, To Be Read to Them in Families*; *Catechism of Jones* [sections: "Duty of Masters" and "Duty of Servants"]; the Lord's Prayer; *Short Catechism for the Use of Colored Members on Trial of Methodist Episcopal Church of South Carolina*; the Ten Commandments), 141–142; nature of instructional guides for families, 141–142 (accompanying audiovisual aids [hymns], Bible story text with

African American independent churches (*continued*)
illustrations, question-and-answer) scripture cards, 142
relationships among multiple roles of churches, 133–138
set standards for schools, 134. *See also* benevolent societies; literary societies in America and Liberia; Payne, D.
use of deaconing out of songs and oral language development, 140
uses of literacy, 72, 80
African American national community development, 142–150
and national, state, and regional conventions, 148–150, 166
and newspapers, 142–148
African American newspapers, 21, 23, 66, 70, 71, 74, 109, 117–118, 123, 132, 144–148, 168, 177, 178. *See also* African American national community; individual newspapers
African American support for antislavery newspapers, 47. *See also Anti-Slavery Standard*; Child, L. M.; Douglass, F.; Garrison, W. L.; *Liberator*; Still, W.; Tappan, A.; Wells, I. B.
African Baptist Church, 137, 140
Baker Street in Cincinnati, Ohio, 144
in Boston, 134
in New York City, 172
in Savannah, Georgia, 137
in Williamsburg, Virginia, 138
See also benevolent societies; newspapers
African Christian Herald, 118. *See also* newspapers
African District School, 131–132
African Dorcas Society, 116, 127, 172. *See also* benevolent societies
African Free Masonry, 124. *See also* benevolent societies
African free schools, 89, 91
African Free Society (AFS), 173
African Luminary, 66, 109
African Methodist Episcopal Church (A.M.E.), 134, 137, 138, 139, 140, 148, 172. *See also* Allen, R.; Payne, D.
African Repository, 43, 70, 73, 74, 109. *See also* American Colonization Society
African Society of Boston (ASB), 129
African Society for the Education of Youth, 128
African Society of Mutual Relief, 128. *See also* benevolent societies
Alexander Classical High School, 62, 75
Alienated American, 143, 144. *See also* newspapers
Allen, R., 22, 128, 133, 135, 137, 139, 149, 150
A.M.E. Church Review, 118. *See also* African American independent churches; newspapers
American Civil War, 1, 3, 20, 23, 105
Bible scripture as source of text for speeches and songs, troops use of, 105
collaborative learning among troops as, informal literacy events, 23, 103–104, 105
contraband school attendance, 106–107, 169, 170
emergent African American literacy among soldiers and their families, 106–107
events, 23, 103–104, 105; building sight vocabulary, 105; critical literacy, political speech making, 104–105; examples of literacy learning as social and intellectual processes, 93, 103 (see also catechism cards); literacy learning as an affective process: literacy attitudes, functions, interests, motivations, perceptions, 93–107, perceptions of catechism cards as written passes to heaven, 106; literacy talk in sermons, shout

American Civil War (*continued*), prayers, songs, spirituals, 105; setting purposes for reading and monitoring reading strategies, 103; storytelling, extemporaneous speeches, lectures, songwriting, 103–105
  Union officers, 23; Higginson, T., 103–104
  Union troops, African American, 105; informal community literacy events, 103: storytelling, extemporaneous speeches, lectures, songwriting, 103–104, 105; and literacy, 23, 103–104
American Colonization Society (ACS), 2, 19, 42–46, 63, 73, 74, 75, 135, 149
  Reverend R. Gurley as long-serving secretary for, 43, 71, 72
American Spelling Book, The, 108–109
Anansi, 41, 162
Anti-Slavery Standard, 21, 78, 133, 144
Appeal, in Four Articles, 135
Aptheker, H., 25, 85, 136

balanced literacy approach, 29. *See also* Skipwith family
Baptist Annual Register, 13
Baptist Confession of Faith, 137
Bell, G., 130–131
  Bell school in Washington, D.C., 130, 131
Bells, N., 82
benevolent societies, 115, 127–132, 134, 144, 149, 151, 166, 172, 175, 179
Berger, P., 29
Berlin, I., 14, 90, 100
Bethel Benevolent Society, 124. *See also* benevolent societies
  conference of 1817, 149. *See also* African American national community development: national, state, and regional conventions
Bethel Literary and Historical Association, 117. *See also* literary societies in America and Liberia
Bethel Methodist Church, 137. *See also* African American independent churches
Bethel Methodist Church in Philadelphia, 137, 139; convention of 1817, 137, 149. *See also* conventions
Beyan, A. J., 2, 44, 97, 149
Bible
  church and community study groups, 133, 134, 135, 141, 142
  in community rituals, 133, 134, 135, 140; copies of in African American slave communities, 100, 108
  and family rituals, 140, 142, 156, 157, 159, 142, 156, 158: and critical reading behaviors, 141 and morning, daily, or evening prayers, 80, 91
  and oral language practice, 97: to compete academically in local school or community events, 54, and rote memorization and recitation of scripture, 80, 81, 54
  scripture used to write age-appropriate, didactic literature for children, 80, 81
  as source for extemporaneous speeches, 140;
  as text for reading instruction, 16, 49, 51, 54, 55, 57, 63, 64, 72, 78, 101–102, 109, 142, 177, 178
  uses of scripture for speech making and songwriting, 105. *See also* American Civil War: Union troops and literacy as source for spontaneous songwriting and singing, 140.
Billingsley, A., 15, 17, 18, 24, 36
Blackett, R. H., 102, 118, 120, 121, 130, 134, 145. *See also* newspapers
black national community. *See* African American national community; conventions
Black Republican, The, 145. *See also* newspapers

Blassingame, J.
conceptual frameworks for studies of African American community, 1, 18
definition of nineteenth-century African American community, 18–19
Slave Testimony: Two Centuries of Letters, Speeches, Interviews, and Autobiographies, 77, 79, 80, 81, 82, 83, 84, 100, 101, 111, 112, 113, 171
Bloome, D., 5
Blumer, H., 26
Blyden, E. W., 22, 66
Boggs, S.
and adult literacy, 22, 79, 158
Bolivar, W. C.
as a bibliophile, 121
Bond, H. M., 14, 128
Bontemps, A., 5, 22, 96, 155, 156
and conceptual and theoretical framework, 5
Book of Baptisms of St. Phillip's Church, 139
books. *See* literacy instructional materials
Bowery, C.
and adults as emergent readers, 22, 98, 101, 169
Brooklyn Woolman Benevolent Society, 128, 131. *See also* benevolent societies
Brother Bear. *See* Anansi
Brother Fox. *See* Anansi
Brown Fellowship Society, 128–129, 132. *See also* benevolent societies
Bruce, H., 80, 82, 94
Bryan, A.
and mail service between America and Liberia, 73
Bullock, H. A., 90, 91, 128, 173
Butler, P., 46, 160

Cain, W. E.
and Garrison's views on slavery and Liberian immigration, 147. *See also Liberator*
camp meetings
as literacy events, 105, 107, 165, 167, 171; African American Civil War soldiers' collaborative literacy learning (*see* American Civil War); call to meeting songwriter, N. Turner, 46, 98; oral and written language participation structures, 16, 170, 171; Turner, N., 46, 98
Cardozo, F. L., 112
Carr, E. H., 7
catechism cards, 106
Chase, L., 106, 122
Chase, S., 122
Child, L. M., 21. *See also Anti-Slavery Standard*
children, 20, 23, 41
child–adult teaching and learning behaviors (*See* Skipwith family); and child and labor and literacy learning, 52–54; death of schoolchildren and a teacher's concern, 53; homeschooling, 87, 88; intergenerational literacy, 41–51, 61, 62, 82; letter writing, 61, 65–69, 74–75; as literate immigrants to Liberia, 42; and literature for, 23, 51, 52, 54, 146; and parents, kin, and extended family efforts: hiring out labor to pay for tutors, 79, labor and child literacy education, 42, 48, 49, 91–92, providing for education in written wills or verbal agreements in the event of parents' death, 82, 88, 158–159; reading aloud in family settings, 51, 52, 62, 67, 68, 70, 77, 80, 81, 84; reading aloud to, 51, 52, 55, 62, 67, 68, 70, 72, 80, 84. (*See also* family literacy-related rituals); reading and writing interests and motivations, 66, 70, 74, 75, 77, 78, 80, 88; sending children away to be educated, 41, 42, 49, 90–91, 125; and Sunday school or Sabbath school literacy lessons, 64, 79, 80, 81; uprooting families to provide education for, 86, 89
Choppin, L., 94, 134
Cincinnati, Ohio, 116, 133, 135, 144

and African American religious and secular institutional literacy events, 135; churches: African Methodist, Baker Street Baptist, Colored Christian, New Street Methodist, Third Street Baptist, 135; school attendance, 135

Civil War. *See* American Civil War

Clay, M. M., 4, 102, 177

Cocke family, 47–67, 144, 165, 177. *See also* Skipwith family

Collection of Hymns & Spirituals Songs from Various Authors, 139. *See also* Allen, R.

Colored American, 118, 143, 144, 186, 198. *See also* newspapers

Colored Preparatory High School, 112

community literacy-related events, celebrations, debates, lectures, public speeches, 23, 104, 105, 115, 116, 117, 120, 127, 131, 134, 166, 170, 171, 172, 178, 181

community perceptions of literacy and literacy educational needs, 17, 124, 132, 153, 167

community resistance to oppression and literacy uses, 20, 178. *See also* newspapers; African American independent churches

community solidarity, 125–127

mutual aid, benefit, relief, or self-help societies, 18, 117, 118, 119, 124, 127, 128–130, 133, 149, 172

Purvis's refusal to pay school tax, 126–127. *See also* benevolent societies, literary societies in America and Liberia

and support for literacy learning, celebrations, spelling bees, lectures, literary events, 23, 27, 28, 104, 105, 115, 116, 117, 120, 126–127, 131, 133, 134, 166, 170, 171, 172, 178, 181

concept of word. *See* emergent literacy

conceptual and theoretical frameworks, 1–31

African American art and perspectives on literacy, 5–6

approaches to study of nineteenth-century African American family and community, 7, 18–19

Blassingame, J., 1, 18, 19, 24, 34, 35

Cullen, C. 5–6.

cultural, historical, and social foundations as contexts for study, 1–2, 7

definitions, 7–8, 15–18

Dorsey-Gaines, C., 1

Durkheim, E., 4, 8, 15, 27, 29

evolving dynamic nature of community and family literacy traditions, 1, 2

Goffman, H., 27

Gutman, H., 1, 18

Heath, S. B., 1, 8, 14

Holiday, B., 5–6

Huggins, N., 4, 8, 9, 14, 25, 52, 90

images, 2–4

life course perspective, 26, 28–31, 38; literacy and the life course or life cycle, 80, 81, 84, 85, 87, 163, 164

literacy heroes, heroines, and myths, 7–15

researcher's stance, 3–4

ritual theory, 27–28; and persistence of literacy traditions, 2

sources, 19–25

Stampp, K., 19

symbolic interactionism, 28–29

Taylor, D., 1

conclusions, emanating, recurrent themes, and expression of themes, 154–175

Cone, J. H., 1

Congregational Church in Greenville, Liberia, 71–72

contraband camps. *See* American Civil War

conventions: national, regional, state, 39, 115, 148–150, 166, 172

accomplishments of, 148–151

as movement, 148

Ruggles, 150

and school attendance, 119, 135, 181

conventions: national, regional, state, (*continued*)
  support for African American formal schools, 111
Cook, G., 112–113
Cook-Gumprez, J., 7
Cornelius, J. D., 14, 141
Council of Philosophy Association and the Moral and Mental Development of People of Color, 116, 133
Couvent family
  and the Bernard Couvent School, 111
Craney Island, 106–107
Cullen, C. *See* conceptual and theoretical frameworks

Dann, M. E.
  views on African American national development and African collection of newspapers, 21, 23, 88, 117, 118, 123, 127, 132, 142, 143, 144, 145, 146, 147
Davis, C. T., 24, 89, 117, 118, 142, 146, 155, 156. *See also* conceptual and theoretical frameworks
Davis and associates, 10, 97, 156
Dew, C. B., 100
Dollard, J., 24, 35
  qualitative research methods from *Criteria for the Life History: With Analysis of Six Notable Documents*, 24. *See also* conceptual and theoretical frameworks
Douglass, F., 10, 22, 23, 58, 77, 89, 92, 93, 108, 117, 133, 146, 147, 157, 169, 170, 172
Durkheim, E., 4, 8, 15, 26, 27, 28–29, 172

Elder, G. H., 30. *See also* conceptual and theoretical frameworks; life course perspective
Elevator, 118
Elkins, S., 33
  conceptual and theoretical frameworks, 33
emergent literacy, African American, 108
  concept of word, 12,
  environmental print, 12
  See also children; Taylor, S.; Wheatley, P.
English Postal Service
  and African American letter writing in Liberia, 73
environmental print, 16, 154, 176. *See also* emergent literacy; exposure to print
Evening Star. See Wells, I. B.
exposure to print, 12, 16, 23, 99–105, 108, 140, 154, 176, 177, 178. *See also* emergent literacy

family literacy-related rituals, 16, 138, 140, 142, 156, 157, 159, 170, 171
  reviewing family documents, letters, manumission papers, 101, 106
family perceptions of literacy needs, 154–179
Fisher, M. M.
  collection of African American songs, 9, 35, 97, 98, 99, 105, 139–140, 142, 155, 166–168
Foner, P. S., 18, 88
Forten, T., 127. *See also* community solidarity
Freedom's Journal, 109, 144, 149. *See also* newspapers; Russwurm, J. B.

Garnet, H. H., 22, 89, 120, 135, 136, 172
Garrison, W. L., 21. *See also Liberator*
Garrisonians, 120, 121. *See also* literary societies in America and Liberia
Garrison Literary Association, 116, 120, 147
Gates, H. L., 142, 146, 155, 156
Geertz, C., 15, 27
Genovesse, E., 1, 15, 90, 91, 93, 100, 156
Goodman, K. S., 4
Gross, B., 142, 149, 150

Hareven, T., 30. *See also* life course perspective

Harriet, The, 42–46
Hartgrove, W. B. 125–126
Hill, J.
  and adult literacy, 80–81
Hill, R., 18
hiring out, 45, 100, 178. *Compare with* overtime system
Hoffman, I., 14
Holiday, B. *See* conceptual and theoretical frameworks
holistic teaching practices. *See* Skipwith family

informal schools
  Douglass' informal adult reading instruction, 92–93
Ivy, 146

Jones, A., 133, 149

Leile, G., 136, 137
letter
  sounds, names, 59, 77, 171, 177
letters and letter writing, 16, 178
  as family documents, 101
  manumission letters as proof of legal status, 101
  as public addresses, 145
  as travel reports, 143–144
  and the Underground Railroad, 85–87
liberation theology, 9, 133, 134, 135, 136, 168
  and multiple purposes of African American churches, 133–138
Liberator, 21, 118, 146. *See also* Garrison, W. L.
Liberia, 2, 42–47, 60–75, 82, 83, 117, 166
life course perspective, 26, 29–30, 38
literacy instructional materials
  accessibility to, 109
  book talks, 120–122
  commonly mentioned in family and community document, 109
  community libraries, 124
  family medical books, 69, 160
  family reference books, 59–60, 109
  material culture, 107–133, 108
  Webster's blue-back spellers, 96, 108–109, 177
  nonfiction, 108–109
  public or private home inventories, 74–76, 89, 118
  purchase of, 100–102
  titles of, 69, 70, 108, 109
  values, 101, 108, 156
literary societies in America and Liberia, 3, 18, 21, 39, 87, 115–123, 127, 133, 144, 149, 150, 151, 174, 181

McGuffy Reader. *See* literacy instructional materials
Miller, R., 24
  insights on Cocke family, Skipwith family, and plantation culture, 47–49, 52–54
  letters of Cocke and Skipwith families, 47–60
  National Reformer, 118. *See also* newspapers

neighborhood lending libraries. *See* Phoenix Society
New England Speller. *See* literacy instructional materials
New Guide to Health. See literacy instructional materials
newspapers, African American, 16, 18, 21, 23, 39, 66, 68, 69, 70, 71, 74, 77, 108, 109, 117–136, 146, 147, 148, 151, 158, 167–168, 171, 176, 177, 179
  the African American press, 115, 146, 166
  family and community uses of:announcement of social and school events, 21; autobiographies, biographies, narrative excerpts, 21;
  census reports regarding number of schools needed, 21; fashion news, 21; letters to the editor and public addresses, 21; literary enjoyment

newspapers (*continued*)
(essays, poetry, and short stories), 21; obituaries, 21; political issues, 21
and traveling agents to cities and rural areas, 22–23, 143, 144, 168

oral language, reading, and writing, 2–7, 12, 14, 16, 17, 21, 24, 41, 98, 104–105, 156, 169, 176, 177
oral reading, 51, 78, 91, 122
overtime system, 100

Payne, D., 22, 110, 117, 134, 136
and the founding of A.M.E. schools in the North and South, 134
homeschooling for young mothers, 134
Pennington, J. W. C., 22, 85, 96, 134, 143
periodicals, African American,
bulletins (church and community organizations), 138
and development of African American national community: *New York Weekly and Family Paper*, 146, and *Our Women and Children Magazine*, 146; magazines, 69, 70, 118, 146; for children, 23, contributors, 146–148, *Ivy*, 146, and for women, 23
newsletters (church), 23
pamphlets, 22, 51, 52, 69, 151
Phoenix Society, 116, 118, 119, 122, 127, 150
physical force, fear, and literacy learning, 94, 95

Rachman, S. 51, 52
reading and writing in family settings, 75, 76, 101, 102, 108, 117, 136, 140, 141, 142, 147, 154, 168, 175, 176, 177, 178
Craney Island, 107
literacy awareness, play, practice, and modeling, 12, 13, 85
Martin, S. 22, 101, 109, 171
reading interests, 10, 11, 16, 23, 109, 118
research questions
statement of, 1
Royster, J., 88, 123, 130, 146, 148. *See also* Wells, I. B.
Russwurm, J. B., 43–44, 74

Sabbath and Sunday schools, 42, 48, 49, 50, 55, 56, 71, 80, 92–93, 118, 119, 122, 133, 135, 165. *See also* literary societies in America and Liberia
African church congregational and leadership, promotion of, 71, 133
attendance, 92
funding of, 122
promoters of, 71
Sunday schools as a movement, 80
Sabbath School Collection, 109. *See also* Rachman, S.
book donations, 71
Massachusetts Sabbath School Society, 71
mission of, 42, 71
Skipwith family
letters from Hopewell, 47–60
letters from Liberia, 61–67
standards
academic. *See* Payne, D.
moral, 113, 129, 172
spelling and grammar, 73–74
Still, W., 21, 85, 87
African American conductor of the Underground Railroad, 21
aid to families, 87
and his journal entries documenting the history of the Underground Railway, 21
his uses of signs and symbols, metaphoric language in messages and letters, 85
letters and reports, 21
migrations of families, 87
symbolic interactionism, 26–30, 38

Tappan, A., 88
Taylor, S., 75–76, 176

telegraph messages
and Underground Railroad, 20–21, 85, 86
usage among African Americans, 21, 85, 86, 158
Turner, N.
as a rebel and fear of, 34–45, 46, 95, 168–169
as a songwriter, 98, 168

Underground Railroad and literacy uses, 87, 157. *See also under* telegraph messages

Webber, T., 15, 17, 24, 35
and qualitative research approaches, 15, 17, 24, 35
Wells, I. B., 22, 88, 109, 123, 145–148, 157
West African traditional educational institutions
for men: Poro, 97
for women: Sande, 97
Wiley, B. I.
insights regarding nineteenth-century family and community ways of life in America and Liberia, 47, 61, 62, 67–68, 69, 71, 165
inferences drawn from specific primary sources cited from Wiley collection of African American correspondence 61, 62, 63, 64, 66, 67, 68, 69, 70–75
specific letters cited from Wiley collection, 62–67, 69, 70, 71, 72, 73, 74
Woodson, C. G., 46
counterargument to the U. B. Phillips school of thought, 32
and history education before the Civil War, 95, 96, 122, 124, 134, 135, 157, 158, 160, 167, 172, 173, 174
and history of the African American church, 110
specific primary sources cited in the collection *The Mind of the Negro as Reflected in Letters Written During the Crisis, 1800–1860, The*, 20, 45, 46, 73, 74, 77, 82, 86–87, 90, 118–119, 127–128, 132–133, 134, 135, 143, 146, 147, 149, 150
Wheatley, P., 10–14, 119

ABOUT THE AUTHOR

PHYLLIS M. BELT-BEYAN is Assistant Professor of Literacy Research and Education at Western Michigan University.